Gary Craig

ISAIAH
Plain & Simple

ISAIAH
Plain & Simple

*The Message of Isaiah in
the Book of Mormon*

HOYT W. BREWSTER JR.

DESERET BOOK COMPANY
SALT LAKE CITY, UTAH

Library of Congress Cataloging-in-Publication Data

Brewster, Hoyt W.
  Isaiah plain and simple : the message of Isaiah in the Book of
Mormon / Hoyt W. Brewster Jr.
    p.   cm.
  Includes bibliographical references and index.
  ISBN 1-57345-084-7
  1. Bible. O.T. Isaiah—Criticism, interpretation, etc. 2. Book
of Mormon. Nephi—Criticism, interpretation, etc. 3. Book of
Mormon. Book of Mosiah—Criticism, interpretation, etc. 4. Isaiah
(Biblical prophet) I. Title.
BS1515.2.B668   1995
289.3'22—dc20   95-37716
                                                                 CIP

Printed in the United States of America

10 9 8 7 6 5 4 3 2 1

*In memory of
President Joseph Fielding Smith,
a latter-day prophet-scriptorian
who instilled in me a love of
prophets and the scriptures*

TABLE OF CONTENTS

KEY TO ABBREVIATIONS

ANW   Bruce R. McConkie. *A New Witness for the Articles of Faith*. Salt Lake City: Deseret Book Co., 1982.

AGQ   Joseph Fielding Smith. *Answers to Gospel Questions*. 5 vols. Salt Lake City: Deseret Book Co., 1957–66.

BICQ   Hoyt W. Brewster Jr. *Behold, I Come Quickly: The Last Days and Beyond*. Salt Lake City: Deseret Book Co., 1994.

BMC   Sidney B. Sperry. *Book of Mormon Compendium*. Salt Lake City: Bookcraft, 1968.

CR   Conference Reports. Salt Lake City: The Church of Jesus Christ of Latter-day Saints. Various months and years.

DCBM   Joseph Fielding McConkie and Robert Millet (with Brent Top on vol. 4). *Doctrinal Commentary on the Book of Mormon*. 4 vols. Salt Lake City: Bookcraft, 1987–92.

DCE   Hoyt W. Brewster Jr. *Doctrine and Covenants Encyclopedia*. Salt Lake City: Bookcraft, 1988.

DOD   Neal A. Maxwell. *Deposition of a Disciple*. Salt Lake City: Deseret Book Co., 1976.

DOR   Bruce R. McConkie. *Doctrines of the Restoration*. Compiled by Mark L. McConkie. Salt Lake City: Bookcraft, 1989.

DS   Joseph Fielding Smith. *Doctrines of Salvation*. 3 vols. Compiled by Bruce R. McConkie. Salt Lake City: Bookcraft, 1954–56.

DWW   Wilford Woodruff. *Discourses of Wilford Woodruff*. Selected by G. Homer Durham. Salt Lake City: Bookcraft, 1946.

EAIA   Neal A. Maxwell. *Even As I Am*. Salt Lake City: Deseret Book Co., 1982.

GAWI   Monte S. Nyman. *Great Are the Words of Isaiah*. Salt Lake City: Bookcraft, 1980.

HC   Joseph Smith. *History of The Church of Jesus Christ of Latter-day Saints*. Edited by B. H. Roberts. 7 vols. 2d ed. rev. Salt Lake City: The Church of Jesus Christ of Latter-day Saints, 1932–51.

Hymns   *Hymns of The Church of Jesus Christ of Latter-day Saints*. Salt Lake City: The Church of Jesus Christ of Latter-day Saints, 1985.

IE   *Improvement Era*. Salt Lake City: The Church of Jesus
      Christ of Latter-day Saints. Various months.

IPSP Victor L. Ludlow. *Isaiah: Prophet, Seer, and Poet*. Salt
      Lake City: Deseret Book Co., 1982.

JD   *Journal of Discourses*. 26 vols. London: Latter-day Saints'
      Book Depot, 1854–86.

JST   *Holy Scriptures: Inspired Version*. Independence, Missouri:
      Herald Publishing House, 1944. Also known as *Joseph
      Smith Translation*.

LDSBD Latter-day Saint Bible Dictionary. In The Holy Bible. Salt
      Lake City: The Church of Jesus Christ of Latter-day
      Saints, 1979.

LDSKJ The Holy Bible (Latter-day Saint King James Version).
      Salt Lake City: The Church of Jesus Christ of Latter-day
      Saints, 1979.

Mill M Bruce R. McConkie. *The Millennial Messiah*. Salt Lake
       City: Deseret Book Co., 1982.

MM   Bruce R. McConkie. *The Mortal Messiah*. 4 vols. Salt Lake
      City: Deseret Book Co., 1979–81.

MOK   Hoyt W. Brewster Jr. *Martyrs of the Kingdom*. Salt Lake
      City: Bookcraft, 1990.

MWW   LeGrand Richards. *A Marvelous Work and a Wonder*. Salt
      Lake City: Deseret Book Co., 1950.

OPW   Orson Pratt. *Orson Pratt's Works*. Orem, Utah: Grandin
      Books, 1990.

PM   Bruce R. McConkie. *The Promised Messiah*. Salt Lake
      City: Deseret Book Co., 1978.

SOT   Joseph Fielding Smith. *The Signs of the Times*.
      Independence, Missouri: Press of Zions Printing and
      Publishing Co., 1947.

Talmage James E. Talmage. *Jesus the Christ*. 25th ed. Salt Lake
      City: Deseret Book Co., 1956.

TOVBC J. R. Dummelow, ed. *The One Volume Bible Commentary*.
      New York: Macmillan Publishing Co., 1936.

TPJS Joseph Smith. *Teachings of the Prophet Joseph Smith*.
      Selected by Joseph Fielding Smith. Salt Lake City:
      Deseret Book Co., 1938.

WRL   Mark E. Petersen. *Why the Religious Life*. Salt Lake City:
      Deseret Book Co., 1966.

Note: All quotations from materials © The Church of Jesus Christ
of Latter-day Saints are used by permission.

Introduction

I have long noticed a widespread disease among readers of the Book of Mormon, one quite damaging to one's spiritual health. This Mormon malady is the tendency to *skip, shun,* or, at the very most, *skim* the writings of Isaiah in the Book of Mormon.

This malady, or spiritual sickness, is not confined to any one particular person or group. All are potential victims: the active and less active in the Church; new converts and those of long-standing membership; the casual or occasional reader of the Book of Mormon as well as the serious student of scripture.

Even teachers of the gospel have been afflicted by the disease. Some, in turn, have infected their students or class members by carelessly saying, "Let's just *skip* or *skim* Isaiah and go on to something more interesting or understandable."

Have you ever suffered from this malady? Have you ever said to yourself, "I'll just *skip* or *skim* the Isaiah portion of the Book of Mormon"? I confess that I have. In fact, I am ashamed to admit I used to regularly skip over the writings of Isaiah as I read or studied the Book of Mormon.

Yes, there were those wonderful passages from Isaiah regularly quoted at Christmastime in which I took delight and found spiritual uplift. (See 7:14; 9:6.) Yet, for the most part, the hidden treasures in the prophet's writings remained unmined and undiscovered by me because of my negligence and poor attitude.

I relate these personal feelings and experiences because I am convinced there are many in The Church of Jesus Christ of Latter-day Saints, and in the Christian world in general, who have had similar experiences.

Isaiah, whose words the resurrected Lord referred to as "great" (3 Nephi 23:1), is one of the most maligned and misunderstood of the prophets. Yet his words must be of singular importance to the world and to the Latter-day Saints in particular. Why else would the Nephite prophets have included them in their sacred record, especially since they knew their writings would come forth in the last days? (See Mormon 8:34–35.)

Nephi was very particular about that which he recorded on the plates containing the history and record of his people. "I desire," said he, "the room that I may write of the things of God.

"For the fulness of mine intent is that I may persuade men to come unto the God of Abraham, and the God of Isaac, and the God of Jacob [who is Jesus Christ], and be saved.

"Wherefore, the things which are pleasing unto the world I do not write, but the things which are pleasing unto God and unto those who are not of the world." (1 Nephi 6:3–5.)

Thus, Nephi's inclusion of the writings of Isaiah in The Book of Mormon: Another Testament of Jesus Christ must have been for the purpose of persuading us to "come unto Christ." Just as both the Old and New Testaments bore witness of the mission and message of the Messiah, so too "Another Testament" has provided a third witness to His role as our divine Redeemer.

The inclusion of Isaiah in the Book of Mormon is purposeful! Further evidence of this is found in the fact that Jesus Christ Himself quoted the words of this Old Testament prophet during His brief postmortal ministry in the Americas.

The resurrected Redeemer not only quoted the words of Isaiah, but He commanded that they should be *searched* (3 Nephi 20:11), not just skimmed or, even worse, skipped. Jesus later reemphasized: "Ye ought to search these things. Yea, a *commandment* I give unto you that ye *search* these things *diligently;* for great are the words of Isaiah." (3 Nephi 23:1; italics added.)

Perhaps the emphasis on the word "search" is indicative that the treasured truths of Isaiah will not yield themselves to the casual reader.

Elder Boyd K. Packer observed: "The prophecies of the Old Testament prophet Isaiah . . . loom as a barrier, like a roadblock or a checkpoint beyond which the casual reader, one with idle curiosity, generally will not go. . . . Perhaps only after you read the Book of Mormon and return to the Bible will you notice that the Lord quotes Isaiah seven times in the New Testament; in addition, the Apostles quote Isaiah forty more times. One day you may revere these prophetic words in Isaiah in both books. The Lord had a purpose in preserving the prophesies of Isaiah in the Book of Mormon, notwith-standing they become a barrier to the casual reader." (*Ensign*, May 1986, p. 61.)

As in all things, if we are to get the greatest benefit from studying, searching, and pondering the words of Isaiah, we must pay a price. Reading to the tick of the clock, or the count of pages, will not do. (Of course, we still must have regular or scheduled study of the scriptures.)

To get the most out of searching the scriptures we need to allow time for prayer and pondering without worrying about interruptions or appointments to be met. Each of us needs to determine for himself or herself what will work best to accomplish this end.

I fervently hope that this volume, *Isaiah Plain and Simple: The Message of Isaiah in the Book of Mormon,* will assist you in the personal process of gaining greater scriptural understand-ing of the writings of this giant among the prophets—as well as a greater witness of Him of whom Isaiah testifies.

Isaiah is a six-letter word. To get the most out of his writ-ings, consider other six-letter words such as *search, ponder,* and *prayer.* These six-letter words must be integral to your study of the prophet's writings. Only then will the meaning of the prophet's words become clear.

The promise is sure: "For he that diligently seeketh shall find; and the mysteries of God shall be unfolded unto them, by the power of the Holy Ghost, as well in *these times* as in times of old." (1 Nephi 10:19; italics added.)

A word of caution: The intent of this volume is to "open the door" to understanding. It does not, nor could it, provide a complete understanding of each prophecy and poetic utterance. Such understanding, as noted above, can come only by paying a personal price. Yet if this volume has opened the door and the reader can peer in and see the *Light*, then I have accomplished my purpose in writing this book.

CHAPTER 1

Understanding Isaiah

THE SIGNIFICANCE OF ISAIAH'S WRITINGS

Obviously words spoken directly by the Savior Himself—either as the premortal and postmortal Jehovah or as the mortal Jesus—should carry great weight and importance. They certainly should command our attention. Then what about words which Jesus quotes from another? Should they not have a similar impact?

The writings in the book of Isaiah fit in both categories: Much of the book of Isaiah consists of direct quotations from Jehovah. Later, Jesus Christ quoted Isaiah's writings during both his mortal and postmortal ministries. (For example, see Matthew 13:13–15; Luke 4:17–21; 3 Nephi 16:16–20; 22:1–17.) Furthermore, as noted in the introduction to this volume, the Savior has *commanded* us to "search these things [the writings of Isaiah] diligently." (3 Nephi 23:1; see also 20:11.)

The ancient American prophet Nephi tells us that Isaiah's words are "of great worth" to those of the last days (the days in which we are now living); and he states he has written them "for [our] good." (2 Nephi 25:8.)

Further significance of the prophet Isaiah's writings was postulated by a servant of the Lord in the last days, one who, like the Old Testament prophet who went before him, has testified of the Messiah in voluminous writings. Elder Bruce R. McConkie boldly declared:

"If our eternal salvation depends upon our ability to understand the writings of Isaiah as fully and truly as Nephi

understood them—and who shall say such is not the case!—
how shall we fare in that great day when with Nephi we shall
stand before the pleasing bar of Him who said: 'Great are the
words of Isaiah'? . . . It just may be that my salvation (and
yours also!) does in fact depend upon our ability to understand the writings of Isaiah as fully and truly as Nephi understood them. For that matter, why should either Nephi or
Isaiah know anything that is withheld from us? Does not that
God who is no respecter of persons treat all his children alike?
Has he not given us his promise and recited to us the terms
and conditions of his law pursuant to which he will reveal to
us what he has revealed to them?" (*Ensign*, October 1973,
p. 78.)

WHO WAS ISAIAH?

Just who was this prophet whose prophecies and poetic
writings are so important to each of us? We know that he
served as a prophet in Jerusalem during the forty-year period
from 740 to 701 B.C. While his ministry was essentially to the
tribe of Judah, or the southern kingdom of Israel, his prophecies extended to the northern kingdom and to gentile nations
of his time, as well as to the last days.

We know his father's name was Amoz (Isaiah 1:1), that he
was married (Isaiah 8:3), and that he had at least two children,
both sons: Shear-jashub (Isaiah 7:3) and Maher-shalal-hash-
baz (Isaiah 8:3). Their names, as well as his own, were symbolic of the substance of his teachings. *Shear-jashub* means "a
remnant shall return," and *Maher-shalal-hash-baz* signifies
"the spoil speedeth, the prey hasteth." The name *Isaiah* means
"The Lord is salvation" or "salvation is of Jehovah."

While the book of Psalms is the book most frequently
quoted in the New Testament, Isaiah is the Old Testament
prophet who is most quoted by Jesus and His apostles.
Furthermore, Isaiah is quoted more frequently in the Book of
Mormon and the Doctrine and Covenants than any other
prophet.

He was "among the great and mighty ones who were
assembled in [the] vast congregation of the righteous" when

the disembodied Jesus visited the spirit world following His crucifixion on Calvary. (D&C 138:38, 42.) There is no question that Isaiah also stood among the "noble and great ones" in the premortal council when the plans for this earth were laid. He certainly was foreordained and "chosen before [he was] born." (Abraham 3:22–23.)

There is strong tradition that Isaiah suffered a martyr's death, being "sawn asunder." Some maintain the apostle Paul alluded to this fate in his writings. (See MOK, 16; TOVBC, 409; Hebrews 11:37.)

WHAT WAS ISAIAH'S MESSAGE?

"The writings of Isaiah deal with events of his day as well as events beyond his time, some of which have already come to pass and others are yet to be. The bulk of Isaiah's prophecies deal with the coming of the Redeemer, both in his first appearance ('For unto us a child is born,' 9:6) and as the Great King at the last day, as the God of Israel. A major theme is that God requires righteousness of his people, and until they obey him they will be smitten and scattered by their enemies. But in the end, Israel will be restored; the barren land will be made fruitful and able to support a large population; and the Lord, the Holy One of Israel, will dwell in the midst of his people, who will be called Zion." (LDSBD, "Isaiah," p. 707.)

As noted, Isaiah's writings focus on the Messiah, the Lord Jesus Christ. Monte Nyman discovered that "of the 425 *separate* verses of Isaiah which are quoted in the Book of Mormon, 391 say something about the attributes or mission of Jesus Christ." (GAWI, 7; italics added.)

In keeping with the law of witnesses (2 Corinthians 13:1), Nephi cited Isaiah's witness that he had seen the Redeemer and declared that he, too, as well as his brother Jacob, had been given that sacred privilege. "Behold, my soul delighteth in proving unto my people the truth of the coming of Christ," Nephi testified. (2 Nephi 11:2–4.)

Indeed, Nephi deliberately quoted the prophet Isaiah as a means of testifying of Christ. In describing his efforts to teach his brothers, he declared, "But that I might more fully persuade them to believe in the Lord their Redeemer I did read unto them that which was written by the prophet Isaiah." (1 Nephi 19:23.)

Thus, the major reason for us to read and understand the writings of Isaiah is to strengthen our belief in the Lord our Redeemer.

ISAIAH AND THE BOOK OF MORMON

Scholars have calculated that over 30 percent of the Old Testament writings of Isaiah are found in the Book of Mormon. A comparison of the King James version of Isaiah with that found in the Nephite record "shows that there are differences in more than half of the 433 verses of Isaiah quoted in the Book of Mormon, while about 200 verses have the same wording as [the King James Version]." (2 Nephi 12:2, footnote *a*.)

The differences between the two texts are reproduced in the chapters of this commentary; they are shown in two ways: (1) Any changed text, including capitalization, punctuation, and plural usage, is identified by <u>underlining</u>. (2) Changes in spelling of the same word, or in word order, are identified by *italics*.

The reader will note that many changes in the Book of Mormon rendition provide significant insights and a greater understanding of the biblical text. Monte Nyman explained why the Nephite record is so valuable in understanding Isaiah:

"One reason why the Book of Mormon is such an excellent resource to help us understand Isaiah is that it preserves a better text. This text of Isaiah was taken from the brass plates of Laban and copied onto the plates from which the Book of Mormon was translated; it is at least five hundred years older than the oldest manuscript of the Isaiah text available today. The discovery of the Dead Sea texts of Isaiah was very significant because it moved the date of earliest Isaiah manuscripts from A.D. 900 (the Masoretic text) to about 100 B.C., the date of the Dead Sea Scroll texts. The plates of brass from which Nephi copied the text of Isaiah would have been recorded by at least 600 B.C., when Lehi and his party left Jerusalem. This places the Book of Mormon text of Isaiah within 100 to 150 years of the time of the original writing, making it closer to the time of the original writing than any other Old or New Testament manuscript. Therefore, this text is probably more accurate than any other account of Isaiah, so retentions in the Book of Mormon text should be given prime consideration." (GAWI, 10.)

The importance of the Book of Mormon in gaining an understanding of Isaiah is further emphasized by Elder Bruce R. McConkie, who declared: "May I be so bold as to affirm that no one, absolutely no one, in this age and dispensation has or does or can understand the writings of Isaiah until he first learns and believes what God has revealed by the mouths of his Nephite witnesses as these truths are found in that volume of holy writ." (*Ensign,* October 1973, p. 81.)

WHY IS ISAIAH SO DIFFICULT TO UNDERSTAND?

If it is so important to search and understand the writings of Isaiah, then why is it so difficult for so many to understand his message?

One major reason why the people of our day have such difficulty with Isaiah is that over 60 percent of the book is written in poetic form. It is very difficult to effectively translate the meanings enmeshed in this type of literary style into another language.

Another major difficulty is the prophet's extensive use of symbolism. Words, geographical locations, historical events, people, and even members of the animal kingdom that were readily familiar to the people of Isaiah's day—but which are foreign to us—were used by Isaiah to stand as symbols for events both in his day and in the latter days. Additionally, many prophesied events have multiple fulfillments or applications.

The prophet Nephi recognized the challenge many would have in trying to understand Isaiah's writings even though they were very "plain" to him. He listed the following reasons why people would have such difficulty: (1) "They know not concerning the manner of prophesying among the Jews"; (2) They are not "filled with the spirit of prophecy"; and (3) They have not been "taught after the manner of the things of the Jews." (2 Nephi 25:1–5.)

Victor Ludlow suggested another reason why Isaiah is hard to understand: He is often "deliberately difficult." Dr. Ludlow explained: "Isaiah, when facing a difficult teaching situation, did not use the parable as a tool; instead, he veiled his message in clouds of symbolism, poetry, and complex terminology. In other words, instead of speaking at a simple level and letting his listeners build upon that foundation, Isaiah spoke at a high intellectual and spiritual level, thus challenging or even forcing his listeners to attain that level before they could begin to understand his words. Isaiah was not only difficult, he was deliberately difficult."

Dr. Ludlow then added this counsel: "We must study his words, wrestle with them, and ponder them at great length before his powerful, sublime teachings begin to emerge and inspire us. Because of this, it is easy to become discouraged and give up before we begin to understand his message. However, through serious and prayerful study, when we finally grasp the language and ideas of a particular chapter until they not only make sense, but enlighten and inspire as well, we realize that we have arrived at a profound level of understanding." (IPSP, 134–35.)

SUGGESTIONS FOR UNDERSTANDING ISAIAH

Gaining greater spiritual understanding is a step-by-step, line-upon-line process. Thus the following suggestions, and the commentary throughout this volume, are provided in an effort to help lay a foundation for understanding.

Elder Bruce R. McConkie, an apostle of the Lord, provided the following "Keys to Understanding Isaiah":

"1. Gain an overall knowledge of the plan of salvation and of God's dealings with his earthly children. . . .

"2. Learn the position and destiny of the house of Israel in the Lord's eternal scheme of things. . . .

"3. Know the chief doctrines about which Isaiah chose to write. [These include] . . . (a) restoration of the gospel in latter days through Joseph Smith, (b) latter-day gathering of Israel and her final triumph and glory, (c) coming forth of the Book of Mormon as a new witness for Christ and the total revolution it will eventually bring in the doctrinal understanding of men, (d) apostate conditions in the nations of the world in the latter days, (e) messianic prophecies relative to our Lord's first coming, (f) second coming of Christ and the millennial reign, and (g) historical data and prophetic utterances relative to his own day. . . .

"4. Use the Book of Mormon. . . .

"5. Use latter-day revelation. . . .

"6. Learn how the New Testament interprets Isaiah. . . .

"7. Study Isaiah in its Old Testament context. . . .

"8. Learn the manner of prophesying used among the Jews in Isaiah's day. . . .

"9. Have the spirit of prophecy. . . .

"10. Devote yourself to hard, conscientious study." (DOR, 301–6.)

The Latter-day Saint Bible Dictionary states: "The reader today has no greater written commentary and guide to understanding Isaiah than the Book of Mormon and the Doctrine and Covenants. As one understands these works better he will understand Isaiah better, and as one understands Isaiah better, he more fully comprehends the mission of the Savior, and the meaning of the covenant that was placed upon Abraham and his seed by which all the families of the earth would be blessed." (LDSBD, "Isaiah," p. 707.)

Understanding Isaiah through the Spirit of Prophecy

As noted by Nephi, the key ingredient to understanding the writings and prophecies of Isaiah, or any other prophet, is to receive the guidance of the Spirit. The apostle Peter cautioned, "No prophecy of the scripture is of any private interpretation.

"For the prophecy came not in old time by the will of

man: but holy men of God spake as they were moved by the Holy Ghost." (2 Peter 1:20–21.)

With this in mind, I readily recognize the limitations of this particular volume, as well as those of other commentaries. In the end, one must be guided by the Spirit, being "filled with the spirit of prophecy," in order to grasp the spiritual insights of the scriptures.

Modern-day revelation gives sound counsel on this matter: "For they that are wise . . . have taken the Holy Spirit for their guide . . . and have not been deceived." (D&C 45:57.)

As you proceed through this book, I hope you will seek and receive the guidance of the Holy Ghost, both to help you in the understandings you might glean from this present volume, and also to help you understand the writings of the great prophet Isaiah.

CHAPTER 2

Isaiah 2 and 2 Nephi 12

OVERVIEW

With this chapter, the earliest Isaiah chapter to be quoted, Nephi begins the longest uninterrupted recitation of Isaiah's writings in the Book of Mormon. Thirteen consecutive chapters of the Old Testament seer are quoted. Nevertheless, the Nephite version shows many modifications in the text. As noted earlier, these differences are shown by *italics* or underlining.

On the surface, some differences appear to be minimal; yet they are significant. For example, the time frame in which these prophecies will be fulfilled is identified (the last days) by the insertion of the following words: "when" (vs. 2); "soon cometh" (vs. 12); and "the day of the Lord shall come" (vs. 13).

The Nephite prophets copied Isaiah's writings from the plates of brass in their possession. Among other things, these plates contained "the prophecies of the holy prophets, from the beginning, even down to the commencement of the reign of [King] Zedekiah." (See 1 Nephi 5:11–14.) The addition of the phrase "And upon all the ships of the sea" in verse 16 of 2 Nephi 12 is a testimony to the fact that the Isaiah text in the Book of Mormon came from a source other than the King James Bible. The addition is consistent with the text in the early Greek version of the Old Testament, or the Septuagint. (See footnote 16*a* of 2 Nephi 12.) Other examples might be cited as well. (See GAWI, 33; IPSP, 90–91.)

Chapter 2 of Isaiah begins with a vision of some events that will precede and/or occur during the Millennium. It continues with a rebuke and a promise of judgment upon the rebellious. The possessions of the proud will be taken from them. Isaiah contrasts the ways of the wicked with those of the Lord. For example, the Lord's house, which is truly "a house of prayer, a house of fasting, a house of faith, a house of learning . . . a house of God" (D&C 109:8), is "established in the top of the mountains . . . exalted above the hills" (Isaiah 2:2). On the other hand, the wicked seek to hide in "the tops of ragged rocks" or the crevices of cliffs. Here they vainly hope that darkness will shield them from the piercing rebuke of the Lord.

COMMENTARY

Isaiah 2:1–4 and 2 Nephi 12:1–4

Isaiah is shown in vision the establishment of the house of the Lord and its power to draw people to it. The righteous of all nations will seek to enter its holy portals, there to be taught in the ways of the Lord.

The prophet sees two headquarters for the Lord's kingdom—Zion and Jerusalem—with "the law" going forth from one and "the word of the Lord" from the other. The millennial Messiah is seen as the Judge who will establish peace on the earth.

Isaiah 2	2 Nephi 12
1 The word that Isaiah the son of Amoz saw concerning Judah and Jerusalem.	1 The word that Isaiah, the son of Amoz, saw concerning Judah and Jerusalem:
2 And it shall come to pass in the last days, that the mountain of the Lord's house shall be established in the top of the mountains, and shall be exalted above the hills; and all nations shall flow unto it.	2 And it shall come to pass in the last days, when the mountain of the Lord's house shall be established in the top of the mountains, and shall be exalted above the hills, and all nations shall flow unto it.

3 And many people shall go and say, Come ye, and let us go up to the mountain of the Lord, to the house of the God of Jacob; and he will teach us of his ways, and we will walk in his paths: for out of Zion shall go forth the law, and the word of the Lord from Jerusalem.

4 And he shall judge among the nations, and shall rebuke many people: and they shall beat their swords into *plowshares,* and their spears into *pruninghooks:* nation shall not lift up sword against nation, neither shall they learn war any more.

3 And many people shall go and say, Come ye, and let us go up to the mountain of the Lord, to the house of the God of Jacob; and he will teach us of his ways, and we will walk in his paths; for out of Zion shall go forth the law, and the word of the Lord from Jerusalem.

4 And he shall judge among the nations, and shall rebuke many people: and they shall beat their swords into *plow-shares,* and their spears into *pruning-hooks—*nation shall not lift up sword against nation, neither shall they learn war any more.

2:1 (2 Nephi 12:1). *"Judah and Jerusalem."* Sidney Sperry states, "Despite the fact that Isaiah speaks only of Judah and Jerusalem, his words may be 'likened' or applied to all the tribes of Israel—indeed, as Nephi says, 'unto all men.' (2 Nephi 11:8.)" (BMC, 173.)

Monte Nyman has written: "Although Isaiah notes that he saw things concerning Judah and Jerusalem (2:1), his vision includes references to three different peoples and two different lands. . . . The three peoples include the inhabitants of Jerusalem in general, the inhabitants of Zion in general, and the specific group from Zion and Jerusalem who constitute the beautiful and glorious branch of the Lord. The two lands include the land of Jerusalem and the land of the Americas.

"Justification for Isaiah's including people not of Judah and not living in Jerusalem in a vision of Judah and Jerusalem is shown in the Savior's words regarding Isaiah: 'For surely he spake as touching all things concerning my people which are of the house of Israel; therefore it must needs be that he must speak also to the Gentiles' (3 Nephi 23:2). Just as it was necessary to speak to or about the Gentiles to show all things concerning the house of Israel, it was also necessary to speak to or about Zion to show the ultimate destiny of Judah." (GAWI, 23–24.)

2:2 (2 Nephi 12:2). *"The mountain of the Lord's house shall be established in the top of the mountains."* During the dedicatory prayer for the Salt Lake Temple, President Wilford Woodruff mentioned Isaiah's prophecy in conjunction with that temple. (DWW, 337.) Over eight decades later, a member of the Quorum of the Twelve Apostles, Elder LeGrand Richards, declared the Salt Lake Temple to be "that house of the God of Jacob" of whom the Old Testament prophets Isaiah and Micah spoke. (CR, October 1975, p. 77; see also Micah 4:1; BICQ, 115–16.)

While Isaiah, Micah, and Nephi may have seen the Salt Lake Temple in vision, there is a broader application to this prophecy. Elder Bruce R. McConkie wrote: "This has specific reference to the Salt Lake Temple and to the other temples built in the top of the Rocky Mountains, and it has a general reference to the temple yet to be built in the New Jerusalem in Jackson County, Missouri. Those in all nations, be it noted, shall flow to the houses of the Lord in the tops of the mountains, there to make the covenants out of which eternal life comes." (ANW, 539.)

An additional application comes from latter-day revelation, which admonishes "Judah [to] flee unto Jerusalem, unto the mountains of the Lord's house." (D&C 133:13.) As seen by Zechariah, a temple must be built in old Jerusalem before the Second Coming, a temple to be built by proper priesthood authority. (Zechariah 6:12–15; BICQ, 121–24.)

Isaiah's prophecy may also have further implications: "The word *mountain* as it appears in the scriptures . . . is a place on earth where God meets his servants to instruct them and direct their activity. . . . When an earthly place has been sanctified to the Lord where he may commune with his servants (Exodus 25:21–22; 29:42–46), then such a place may be called 'the mountain of the Lord.' . . . Thus, the mountain of the Lord is the Lord's administrative center where he is at work directing the affairs of his kingdom until the kingdom of heaven comes to earth. The entire earth will then be a 'mountain.'" (DCE, 372.)

2:3 (2 Nephi 12:3). *"Out of Zion shall go forth the law, and the word of the Lord from Jerusalem."* Two world capitals will be established during the Millennium: Zion (the New Jerusalem) and (the old but restored) Jerusalem. (See BICQ, 161–62; 209–10.) From these two centers of strength, the world will be governed politically and spiritually. The city of Zion will be established on the North American continent, specifically in what is now Independence, Jackson County, Missouri. (D&C 57:1–3; Ether 13:6; BICQ, 151–63.)

There have been other interpretations applied to the meaning of "out of Zion shall go forth the law." For example, the Prophet Joseph Smith identified "the whole of America [as] Zion." (TPJS, 362.) Keeping this in mind, consider the Lord's declaration that He "established the Constitution of this land." (D&C 101:80.) Part of the dedicatory prayer given by President George Albert Smith at the Idaho Falls Temple in 1945 stated: "We thank thee that thou hast revealed to us that those who gave us our constitutional form of government were men wise in thy sight and that thou didst raise them up for the very purpose of putting forth that sacred document. . . . We pray that kings and rulers and the peoples of all nations under heaven may be persuaded . . . to adopt similar governmental systems, thus to fulfill the ancient prophecy of Isaiah [and Micah] that ' . . . out of Zion shall go forth the law.'" (IE, Oct. 1945, p. 564.)

That there might be multiple interpretations of the prophecy is illustrated by statements of Elder Mark E. Petersen of the Quorum of the Twelve Apostles. He suggested that the counsel given at the general conferences of The Church of Jesus Christ of Latter-day Saints was a fulfillment of the prophecy that "out of Zion shall go forth the law." (WRL, pp. 200–201, 305–7.)

2:4 (2 Nephi 12:4). "*He shall judge among the nations.*" Not only will we "all stand before the [final] judgment seat of Christ" (Romans 14:10) to be judged of our works and deeds (D&C 19:3), but He will also serve as sovereign Judge and Arbitrator among the nations of the earth during the Millennium.

2:4 (2 Nephi 12:4). "*Beat their swords into plowshares*" This is an obvious reference to millennial conditions when peace will prevail and "violence shall no more be heard in thy land." (Isaiah 60:18; BICQ, 215–16.) Weapons of war will give way to tools of industry.

Isaiah 2:5–9 and 2 Nephi 12:5–9

Following an idealistic glimpse at the future, Isaiah returns to the reality of the present and chastens Israel, admonishing her to "walk in the light of the Lord." The Book of Mormon text makes it clear that Israel has "gone astray."

The prophet states that the people are forsaken of the Lord because of their pursuit of wickedness and the things of this world. Once again the Nephite text clarifies the biblical text. The addition of the word "not" two times in verse 9 provides the intended meaning of Isaiah's statement.

5 O house of Jacob, come ye, and let us walk in the light of the Lord.	5 O house of Jacob, come ye and let us walk in the light of the Lord; yea, come, for ye have all gone astray, every one to his wicked ways.
6 Therefore thou hast forsaken thy people the house of Jacob, because they be replenished from the east, and are soothsayers like the Philistines, and they please themselves in the children of strangers.	6 Therefore, O Lord, thou hast forsaken thy people, the house of Jacob, because they be replenished from the east, and hearken unto soothsayers like the Philistines, and they please themselves in the children of strangers.

7 Their land also is full of silver and gold, neither is there any end of their treasures; their land is also full of horses, neither is there any end of their chariots<u>:</u>

7 Their land also is full of silver and gold, neither is there any end of their treasures; their land is also full of horses, neither is there any end of their chariots<u>.</u>

8 Their land *also is* full of idols; they worship the work of their own hands, that which their own fingers have made<u>:</u>

8 Their land *is also* full of idols; they worship the work of their own hands, that which their own fingers have made<u>.</u>

9 And the mean man boweth down, and the great man humbleth himself<u>:</u> therefore forgive <u>them</u> not.

9 And the mean man boweth <u>not</u> down, and the great man humbleth himself <u>not,</u> therefore, forgive <u>him</u> not.

2:5 (2 Nephi 12:5). *"Walk in the light of the Lord."* Let your paths be illuminated by the revelations or promptings from the Lord. He is your only true source of Light, the "light and the life of the world," who declared, "He that followeth me shall not walk in darkness, but shall have the light of life." (John 8:12; D&C 45:7; DCE, 324.) The apostle Paul admonished the Saints to "walk as children of light." (Ephesians 5:8.)

2:6 (2 Nephi 12:6). *"Replenished from the east."* One of the reasons the Lord forsook the house of Israel was that she kept herself supplied or filled with alien or apostate teachings, beliefs contrary to the true and living gospel of the Holy One of Israel. The children of Jacob "mingled among the heathen, and learned their works." (Psalm 106:35.)

2:6 (2 Nephi 12:6). *"Soothsayers like the Philistines."* As opposed to prophets who told the truth about the future, soothsayers were those who *pretended* to predict and foretell the future. Israel had turned from true prophets to false soothsayers. Mention of the Philistines may have reference to the time when the Israelite king Ahaziah sought help from Baal-zebub, the false god of the Philistine town of Ekron. (2 Kings 1.)

2:6 (2 Nephi 12:6). *"They please themselves in the children of strangers."* The Hebrew word for *please* here means, literally, to strike or shake hands. In the context of Isaiah's rebuke, it probably speaks of how the children of Israel had selfishly gone about pleasing themselves, rather than seeking to honor their God. They turned their backs on the God of Israel to make covenants with nonbelievers and agreements not in keeping with their faith. One of these covenants may have been the strongly forbidden practice of marrying those not of their faith.

2:7 (2 Nephi 12:7). *"Their land also is full of . . . treasures; . . . their land is also full of horses [and] chariots."* Isaiah refers here to their reliance on wealth and military power, rather than trusting in and remembering their God.

2:9 (2 Nephi 12:9). *"The mean man boweth not down, and the great man humbleth himself not."* As noted above, the added text in the Book of Mormon helps makes sense of an otherwise puzzling statement. The pride of the people is such that neither the "mean" (ordinary) man nor the "great" man bows before the true and living God of Israel.

Isaiah 2:10–22 and 2 Nephi 12:10–22

The prophet next lifts his voice against the proud and haughty in the last days. He uses symbols of materialism in his day to illustrate his message. Earthly wealth will be valueless when the Lord comes. Those who have spent their days seeking such transitory treasures will find no security in their possessions. Isaiah concludes with a final plea for the people to cease relying on mortals. The obvious implication is that they must turn to God.

10 Enter into the rock, and hide thee in the dust, for fear of the Lord, and for the glory of his majesty.	10 O ye wicked ones, enter into the rock, and hide thee in the dust, for the fear of the Lord and the glory of his majesty shall smite thee.

11 <u>T</u>he lofty looks of man shall be humbled, and the haughtiness of men shall be bowed down, and the Lord alone shall be exalted in that day.

12 For the day of the Lord of <u>h</u>osts <u>shall be</u> upon every one <u>that is</u> proud and lofty, and upon every one <u>that</u> is lifted up<u>;</u> and he shall be brought low<u>:</u>

13 <u>And</u> upon all the cedars of Lebanon, <u>that</u> are high and lifted up<u>,</u> and upon all the oaks of Bashan<u>,</u>

14 And upon all the high mountains, and upon all the hills <u>that</u> are lifted up,

15 And upon every high tower, and upon every fenced wall<u>,</u>

16 <u>A</u>nd upon all the ships of Tarshish, and upon all pleasant pictures.

17 And the loftiness of man shall be bowed down, and the haughtiness of men shall be made low<u>:</u> and the Lord alone shall be exalted in that day.

11 <u>And it shall come to pass that the</u> lofty looks of <u>man</u> shall be humbled, and the haughtiness of men shall be bowed down, and the Lord alone shall be exalted in that day.

12 For the day of the Lord of <u>H</u>osts <u>soon cometh upon all nations, yea,</u> upon every one<u>; yea, upon the</u> proud and lofty, and upon every one <u>who</u> is lifted up<u>,</u> and he shall be brought low<u>.</u>

13 <u>Yea, and the day of the Lord shall come</u> upon all the cedars of Lebanon, <u>for they</u> are high and lifted up<u>;</u> and upon all the oaks of Bashan<u>;</u>

14 And upon all the high mountains, and upon all the hills<u>, and upon all the nations which</u> are lifted up, <u>and upon every people;</u>

15 And upon every high tower, and upon every fenced wall<u>;</u>

16 <u>And upon all the ships of the sea,</u> and upon all the ships of Tarshish, and upon all pleasant pictures.

17 And the loftiness of man shall be bowed down, and the haughtiness of men shall be made low<u>;</u> and the Lord alone shall be exalted in that day.

18 And the idols he shall utterly abolish.

19 And they shall go into the holes of the rocks, and into the caves of the earth, for fear of the Lord, and for the glory of his majesty, when he ariseth to shake terribly the earth.

20 In that day a man shall cast his idols of silver, and his idols of gold, which they made each one for himself to worship, to the moles and to the bats;

21 To go into the clefts of the rocks, and into the tops of the ragged rocks, for fear of the Lord, and for *the glory of his majesty*, when he ariseth to shake terribly the earth.

22 Cease ye from man, whose breath is in his nostrils: for wherein is he to be accounted of?

18 And the idols he shall utterly abolish.

19 And they shall go into the holes of the rocks, and into the caves of the earth, for the fear of the Lord shall come upon them and the glory of his majesty shall smite them, when he ariseth to shake terribly the earth.

20 In that day a man shall cast his idols of silver, and his idols of gold, which he hath made for himself to worship, to the moles and to the bats;

21 To go into the clefts of the rocks, and into the tops of the ragged rocks, for the fear of the Lord shall come upon them and *the majesty of his glory* shall smite them, when he ariseth to shake terribly the earth.

22 Cease ye from man, whose breath is in his nostrils; for wherein is he to be accounted of?

2:10 (2 Nephi 12:10). "*O ye wicked ones, enter into the rock, and hide thee in the dust.*" The shame of the sinful will be evident in their countenances as well as in their consciences, and they will seek to hide themselves from the presence and wrath of the Lord. The wicked will cry out "to the mountains, Fall on us; and to the hills, Cover us." (Luke 23:30.) John the Revelator saw this occurrence as one of the signs of the last days. (Revelation 6:15–16.) However, there is no rock large enough, or pit deep enough, to hide them from the Lord. (See Amos 9:3.)

So it is with so-called "secret sins"; they are not hidden

from God. One either properly repents of them in this life or faces an ultimate day where they will be revealed. The Lord has given fair warning: "And the rebellious shall be pierced with much sorrow; for their iniquities shall be spoken upon the housetops, and their secret acts shall be revealed." (D&C 1:3; see also 2 Nephi 30:17.)

2:11, 17 (2 Nephi 12:11, 17). *"The Lord alone shall be exalted in that day."* In the day when the Lord comes, all idols, false gods, and objects of mortal adoration and worship—including the rich, famous, and powerful—must fall and give way to the One. Only the Holy One of Israel will stand supreme as the object of worship. A messianic psalm declared: "Be still, and know that I am God: I will be exalted among the heathen, I will be exalted in the earth." (Psalm 46:10; see also Isaiah 52:6.)

2:12 (2 Nephi 12:12). *"The day of the Lord of Hosts."* This refers to the second coming of Him who is the God of Israel (1 Chronicles 17:24) and the One who wrought the atonement in behalf of all. His coming will be a *great* day for the righteous and a *dreadful* day for the "proud and lofty."

2:13 (2 Nephi 12:13). *"The cedars of Lebanon."* One of the ways in which the proud will "be brought low" (vs. 12) is the destruction of, or the taking away of, those material possessions they hold so dear. Among these are the "cedars of Lebanon," which provided beautiful, fragrant wood for buildings of status.

2:13 (2 Nephi 12:13). *"The oaks of Bashan."* Bashan was the area east of Jordan and the Sea of Galilee and north of Gilead. Its wooded areas provided highly prized but scarce hardwood. It too will be taken from the proud.

2:14–15 (2 Nephi 12:14–15). *"All the high mountains . . . all the hills . . . every high tower, and . . . every fenced wall."* Mention of these barriers or defenses may be an allusion to the fortifications of kings Uzziah and Jotham. (See 2 Chronicles 26:9–10; 27:3–4.) In the great and dreadful day of the Lord, such defenses will provide a false sense of security to the proud and lofty, for they will surely fall.

2:16 (2 Nephi 12:16). "*The ships of the sea, and . . . the ships of Tarshish.*" The added phrase from the Book of Mormon is also found in the ancient Greek (Septuagint) text. "All the ships of the sea," represent the commercial enterprises of the proud and lofty. Tarshish is believed to be a location in Spain. Her ships were renowned for their strength, size, and ability to successfully complete long voyages. These too will be stripped from the wicked when the Lord returns.

2:16 (2 Nephi 12:16). "*Pleasant pictures.*" Sidney Sperry suggests that this might portray "delightful imagery." (BMC, 178.) Drawing upon more modern translations of the Bible, Victor Ludlow identifies them as "the 'beautiful craft' [that] were apparently the pleasure crafts or ships in which the wealthy traveled throughout the Mediterranean." (IPSP, 91.) J. R. Dummelow states: "The word rendered 'pictures' means something figured or with imagery upon it." He goes on to explain that because of its relation to the mention of ships, it may have reference to "the sails, which were often embroidered with figures in ancient times." (TOVBC, 415.) In any event, the Lord will take away these symbols of pride or power.

2:19 (2 Nephi 12:19). "*They shall go into the holes of the rocks, and into the caves of the earth.*" See commentary on 2:10.

2:20 (2 Nephi 12:20). "*A man shall cast his idols . . . to the moles and to the bats.*" In the day of the Lord, idolaters shall cast away their impotent idols made of precious metals. Victor Ludlow provides this insight: "The imagery of verse 20 is striking: the people will throw their gold and silver idols to moles and bats, animals who are blind from living so long in darkness. The irony of this is that people who understood the material value of the precious metals, and should also have seen the spiritual impotence of the idols, will throw these precious items to animals who will not be able to see them at all." (IPSP, 92.)

2:21 (2 Nephi 12:21). "*Go into the clefts of the rocks.*" See the overview of this chapter.

2:21 (2 Nephi 12:21). "*When he ariseth to shake terribly the earth.*" One of the final events preceding the Second Coming will be a great earthquake. (Revelation 11:11–13.) "This great earthquake, of a magnitude never before recorded on the Richter scale, will be 'such as was not since men were upon the earth.' (Revelation 16:18.) 'The mountains shall be thrown down, and the steep places shall fall.' (Ezekiel 38:20.) 'Every island [shall flee] away' (Revelation 16:20) as the earth's land masses join together (see D&C 133:23; Isaiah 62:4). 'All nations shall be shaken.' (Haggai 2:6–7.)

"The Savior will make His appearance during this earthquake: 'And then shall the Lord set his foot upon this mount [of Olives], and it shall cleave in twain, and the earth shall tremble, and reel to and fro, and the heavens also shall shake.' (D&C 45:48.)" (BICQ, 102–3.)

2:22 (2 Nephi 12:22). "*Cease ye from man, . . . for wherein is he to be accounted of?*" "Cease depending on mortal man; he is of little power compared to God." (LDSKJ, Isaiah 2:22, footnote *b*.)

CHAPTER 3

Isaiah 3 and 2 Nephi 13

OVERVIEW

This chapter focuses on the punishments to be poured out on the wicked and rebellious of Judah and Jerusalem. In fact, only once is an optimistic note of hope found: verse 10 of the Nephite text proclaims, "Say unto the righteous that it is well with them."

Rebellious Judah will suffer physically, spiritually, politically, and socially. Every means of support upon which she relies will be threatened or taken away from her. There are undoubtedly multiple fulfillments of these prophecies, for Jerusalem and the people of Judah were frequently the target of oppressors and aggressors, as was the rest of the house of Israel.

The "daughters of Zion" are particularly criticized by the prophet for their reliance on the ways of the world. Latter-day leaders of the Lord's church have occasionally applied these verses to vain women of our days who get caught up with worldly fashions and ways.

The chapter closes with a description of the woes that will befall the people as a whole.

This chapter of Isaiah should be read in conjunction with the previous and following chapters in order to get the "big picture." While being filled with warnings to the "proud and lofty," Isaiah 2 contains a great deal of hope. Chapter 3, however, presents the down side; focusing on judgments to be poured out on the rebellious. Finally, Isaiah 4 provides the hope of a future redemption for Zion and Jerusalem.

COMMENTARY

Isaiah 3:1–7 (2 Nephi 13:1–7)

Isaiah speaks of a period of great social chaos and oppression. As noted in the overview, Judah will experience the deprivation of everything on which she depends. There will be a scarcity of food, warriors, and leaders in both the spiritual and political sense. The people will plead for capable leadership but to no avail.

Isaiah 3	2 Nephi 13
1 For, behold, the Lord, the Lord of <u>hosts</u>, doth take away from Jerusalem and from Judah the stay and the staff, the whole <u>stay</u> of bread, and the whole stay of water,	1 For behold, the Lord, the Lord of <u>H</u>osts, doth take away from Jerusalem, and from Judah, the stay and the staff, the whole <u>staff</u> of bread, and the whole stay of water—
2 The mighty man, and the man of war, the judge, and the prophet, and the prudent, and the ancient,	2 The mighty man, and the man of war, the judge, and the prophet, and the prudent, and the ancient;
3 The captain of fifty, and the *honourable* man, and the *counsellor,* and the cunning artificer, and the eloquent orator.	3 The captain of fifty, and the *honorable* man, and the *counselor,* and the cunning artificer, and the eloquent orator.
4 And I will give children to be their princes, and babes shall rule over them.	4 And I will give children <u>unto them</u> to be their princes, and babes shall rule over them.
5 And the people shall be oppressed, every one by another, and every one by his *neighbour*: the child shall behave himself proudly against the ancient, and the base against the *honourable*.	5 And the people shall be oppressed, every one by another, and every one by his *neighbor*; the child shall behave himself proudly against the ancient, and the base against the *honorable*.

23

6 When a man shall take hold of his brother of the house of his father, *saying,* Thou hast clothing, be thou our ruler, and let this ruin <u>be</u> under thy hand<u>:</u>

6 When a man shall take hold of his brother of the house of his father, <u>and shall</u> *say<u>:</u>* Thou hast clothing, be thou our ruler, and let <u>not</u> this ruin <u>come</u> under thy hand—

7 In that day shall he swear, saying<u>,</u> I will not be *an* healer; for in my house is neither bread nor clothing<u>:</u> make me not a ruler of the people.

7 In that day shall he swear, saying<u>:</u> I will not be *a* healer; for in my house <u>there</u> is neither bread nor clothing<u>;</u> make me not a ruler of the people.

3:1 (2 Nephi 13:1). "*The stay and the staff.*" One meaning of the word "stay" is "support." "Staff" also bears the connotation of being a "support." In Hebrew, "staff" is the feminine form of the masculine "stay." "By using both forms," noted Victor Ludlow, "Isaiah seems to suggest complete destruction—spiritual, social, and physical. Thus, the prophet's language and imagery carry many implications beyond the threat of physical famine. . . . Removing the staff or support from a nation is analogous to suddenly taking away the props or stakes of a tent—the tent collapses shapeless on the ground." (IPSP, 101.) In essence, Judah is threatened with a total collapse of the support products or people upon which she depends.

3:2–3 (2 Nephi 13:2–3). "*Mighty man . . . man of war . . . [etc.].*" When we look at the Hebrew words in this passage, we learn that among those of whom Israel will be deprived are leaders ("mighty man"), warriors and military chiefs ("man of war"), diviners ("prudent"), the elder who holds village office ("ancient"), men of repute ("honorable man"), skilled craftsmen or wise men of magic arts ("cunning artificer"), and the skillful enchanter ("eloquent orator").

3:4 (2 Nephi 13:4). "*Children to be their princes.*" Judah's lack of leadership will be evident with the need to place the young and inexperienced—those who lack maturity and understanding—in these vital positions. Another possibility is the placement of outsiders in ruling positions over the Jews—outsiders who lack an understanding (as children do) of the Jewish culture and religious heritage.

3:4 (2 Nephi 13:4). "*Babes shall rule over them.*" Monte Nyman has given this insight: "With regard to the 'babes' who would rule over them, it should be remembered that Jacob had blessed Judah with the political leadership of all the house of Israel until the birth of Christ (see Genesis 49:8, 10). This leadership, of course, should have been exercised through the priesthood, as shown by the Prophet Joseph Smith in commenting upon the dominion given to Adam (see TPJS, p. 157). For 'babes' (or 'children,' if the word does not refer to the Gentiles) to rule over Judah, they would rule without the priesthood." (GAWI, 34–35.) (Also see the commentary in the preceding paragraph.)

3:5 (2 Nephi 13:5). "*The child shall behave himself proudly against the ancient.*" Children shall act insolently against the elderly.

3:6 (2 Nephi 13:6). "*A man shall take hold of his brother . . . saying . . . be thou our ruler.*" Victor Ludlow explains: "These verses are important because they reemphasize both the social breakdown of the patriarchal order and the extreme physical poverty of the state. That the man mentioned here should 'lay hold of his brother in his father's house' indicates, first of all, that the father has disappeared and left the family in upheaval, for the son (by custom, the eldest) refuses to fulfill the duty that is his by lineage. The cloak [clothing], or *simlah,* which is the brother's so-called claim to power, is not a rich robe but is itself a sign of extreme poverty. In other words, the petitioner is saying, 'You have at least some sort of cloak and the provisions necessary for physical sustenance, food and clothing.' Without either physical or social 'stays,' it is no wonder that the brother declines a position for which he might otherwise be ambitious." (IPSP, 103–4.)

3:7 (2 Nephi 13:7). "*I will not be an healer.*" As noted in the previous paragraph, the brother turns down the proffered position. His reply: "I cannot bind up your wounds or solve your problems. I've got problems of my own." (See LDSKJ, Isaiah 3:7, footnote *a*.)

Isaiah 3:8–11 and 2 Nephi 13:8–11

The prophet foretells the fall of Jerusalem and Judah because of wickedness so great it actually shows in the countenance of the people. The Nephite text declares "their sin <u>to be even</u> as Sodom, <u>and</u> they <u>cannot</u> hide it." (13:9.) As noted in the commentary on Isaiah 2:10, no sin will be hidden from the Lord. Isaiah draws a contrast between the well-being of the righteous and the woe that will come upon the wicked.

8 For Jerusalem is ruined, and Judah is fallen<u>:</u> because their tongue and their doings <u>are</u> against the Lord, to provoke the eyes of his glory.	8 For Jerusalem is ruined, and Judah is fallen<u>,</u> because their tongue<u>s</u> and their doings <u>have been</u> against the Lord, to provoke the eyes of his glory.
9 The *shew* of their countenance doth witness against them<u>;</u> and <u>they</u> declare their sin as Sodom, they hide it <u>not</u>. *Woe* unto their soul<u>!</u> for they have rewarded evil unto themselves<u>.</u>	9 The *show* of their countenance doth witness against them<u>,</u> and <u>doth</u> declare their sin <u>to be even</u> as Sodom, <u>and</u> they <u>cannot</u> hide it. *Wo* unto their souls<u>,</u> for they have rewarded evil unto themselves<u>!</u>
10 Say <u>ye to</u> the righteous<u>,</u> that it <u>shall be</u> well with <u>him:</u> for they shall eat the fruit of their doings.	10 Say <u>unto</u> the righteous that it <u>is</u> well with <u>them;</u> for they shall eat the fruit of their doings.
11 *Woe* unto the wicked<u>! it shall be ill with him:</u> for the reward of <u>his</u> hands shall be <u>given him.</u>	11 *Wo* unto the wicked<u>, for they shall perish;</u> for the reward of <u>their</u> hands shall be <u>upon them!</u>

3:8 (2 Nephi 13:8). *"Their tongue and their doings are against the Lord."* The words of their mouths as well as their deeds are both evil.

3:8 (2 Nephi 13:8). *"To provoke the eyes of his glory."* To rebel against the *glory* of the Lord, which He stated is "to bring to pass the immortality and eternal life of man." (Moses 1:39.) While all mortals will receive a resurrected body, thus achieving immortality, only the faithful who have kept all their covenants will receive eternal life. The rebellious disqualify themselves from this latter blessing.

3:9 (2 Nephi 13:9). *"The shew of their countenance doth witness against them."* When Satan instructed Cain to make an unacceptable offering to the Lord, and it was rejected by Deity, "Cain was very wroth, and his countenance fell." His fallen countenance was very evident to the Lord and was, in fact, a witness against Cain's evil intentions; for "Cain loved Satan more than God." (Moses 5:18–22.)

None can hide their feelings, intentions, thoughts, or deeds from God. We either gather light to our countenance through righteousness or we diminish and darken our countenance through sin. Ultimately, our countenance will reflect the degree of eternal glory we will receive.

"To the wicked, who are filled with darkness, one may ask, 'Where is thy glory?' (Moses 1:12–14.) Yet the righteous 'shall shine forth in the kingdom of God' (Alma 40:25), and of them it will be said they are 'glorious beyond description [with a] countenance truly like lightning' (JS–H 1:32)." (BICQ, 232–33.)

3:9 (2 Nephi 13:9). *"Their sin* <u>*to be even*</u> *as Sodom."* The wretched residents of Sodom unsuccessfully sought to defile the holy men visiting Lot. (Genesis 19.) Even as the men of Sodom publicly announced their sins, so shall the countenance of the wicked "declare" (show) their sins. Perhaps another meaning to be considered in the context of sins "even as Sodom" is the public campaign by some in these latter days to legalize and make acceptable that which God has declared abominable. (See BICQ, 39–49.)

3:9, 11 (2 Nephi 13:9, 11). "*They have rewarded evil unto themselves.*" The words of the Lamanite prophet, Samuel, provide excellent commentary on how the wicked reward themselves: "If they are condemned they bring upon themselves their own condemnation. And now remember, remember, my brethren, that whosoever perisheth, perisheth unto himself; and whosoever doeth iniquity, doeth it unto himself; for behold, ye are free; ye are permitted to act for yourselves." (Helaman 14:29–30.)

Isaiah 3:12–15 and 2 Nephi 13:12–15

Isaiah laments the lack of proven and trained leadership among the people. In fact, the leaders also lack moral integrity and cause the people to err. This spiritually sick society has degenerated socially as well, for the poor and the aged are oppressed and neglected. As a result, the Lord will pass judgment upon the oppressors.

12 <u>As for</u> my people, children are their oppressors, and women rule over them<u>.</u> O my people, they <u>which</u> lead thee cause thee to err, and destroy the way of thy paths.	12 <u>And</u> my people, children are their oppressors, and women rule over them<u>,</u> O my people, they <u>who</u> lead thee cause thee to err and destroy the way of thy paths.
13 The Lord standeth up to plead, and standeth to judge the people.	13 The Lord standeth up to plead, and standeth to judge the people.
14 The Lord will enter into judgment with the ancients of his people<u>,</u> and the princes thereof<u>:</u> for ye have eaten up the vineyard<u>;</u> the spoil of the poor is in your houses.	14 The Lord will enter into judgment with the ancients of his people and the princes thereof<u>;</u> for ye have eaten up the vineyard <u>and</u> the spoil of the poor in your houses.
15 What mean ye <u>that ye</u> beat my people to pieces, and grind the faces of the poor<u>?</u> saith the Lord God of <u>h</u>osts.	15 What mean ye<u>?</u> <u>Y</u>e beat my people to pieces, and grind the faces of the poor<u>,</u> saith the Lord God of <u>H</u>osts.

3:12 (2 Nephi 13:12). *"Children are their oppressors, and women rule over them."* Sidney Sperry applied the following meaning to this phrase: "The leaders of the people act like children in maltreating those who come under their rule, and the corrupting influence of their prominent women is also felt. In other words, the leaders of the people are misleaders; they bring about apostasy with their false teachings and exploit the helpless poor." (BMC, 181.)

On the other hand, Victor Ludlow commented that Isaiah is repeating "his earlier warning of social upheaval, suggesting that the leaders will be as weak as or will actually be women, an insult in ancient Israelite culture. This implies a dissolution of the traditional patriarchal social structure that was the norm of the time." (IPSP, 106.)

3:13–14 (2 Nephi 13:13–14). *"The Lord . . . standeth to judge the people."* Because Judah's wicked leaders will not properly care for the poor and elderly, the Lord will "plead" (contend) and judge accordingly. He will pass judgment upon the "ancients" (elders, the primary administrators of justice) and the "princes" (royal appointees, rulers, or leaders). They are guilty of having "eaten up" (plundered, pillaged, consumed) the vineyards of the people and the Lord. They have taken the "spoil" (embezzled gain or plunder) of the poor into their own homes. They have beaten (crushed and mistreated) the people in general, and the poor in particular.

3:16–23 and 2 Nephi 13:16–23

These few verses are probably the most scathing criticism of the vanity of some women that have been written. Sidney Sperry provided the following excellent commentary on this section: "Just as the prophet Amos had shown the sad state of Israel by describing its women (Amos 4:1–4)—he called them 'cows'— so Isaiah now portrays or symbolizes the unfortunate state of the nation by describing the unseemly conduct of 'the daughters of Zion' in their gaudy and extravagant articles of apparel. . . . We do not know the exact nature of all these articles of apparel, but that fact need not disturb us; we still see the point that Isaiah is trying to make. The Prophet Joseph Smith probably did not change the renderings of these articles of women's clothing, as given in the King James Version, for that very reason.

"The 'daughters of Zion,' representing Israel, strut proudly in their fine clothes and jewels, but the Lord will smite them with disease and exhibit their shame (vss. 16, 17). 'In that day,' the day of the Lord's judgment, they will be stripped of all their finery and be left bareheaded and scantily clad (vss. 18–23.)" (BMC, 181–82.)

16 Moreover the Lord saith, Because the daughters of Zion are haughty, and walk with *stretched forth* necks and wanton eyes, walking and mincing as they go, and making a tinkling with their feet:

17 Therefore the Lord will smite with a scab the crown of the head of the daughters of Zion, and the Lord will discover their secret parts.

18 In that day the Lord will take away the bravery of their tinkling ornaments about their feet, and their cauls, and their round tires like the moon,

19 The chains, and the bracelets, and the mufflers,

20 The bonnets, and the ornaments of the legs, and the headbands, and the tablets, and the *earrings.*

21 The rings, and nose jewels,

16 Moreover, the Lord saith: Because the daughters of Zion are haughty, and walk with *stretched-forth* necks and wanton eyes, walking and mincing as they go, and making a tinkling with their feet—

17 Therefore the Lord will smite with a scab the crown of the head of the daughters of Zion, and the Lord will discover their secret parts.

18 In that day the Lord will take away the bravery of their tinkling ornaments, and cauls, and round tires like the moon;

19 The chains and the bracelets, and the mufflers;

20 The bonnets, and the ornaments of the legs, and the headbands, and the tablets, and the *ear-rings;*

21 The rings, and nose jewels;

22 The changeable suits of apparel, and the mantles, and the wimples, and the *crisping pins,*	22 The changeable suits of apparel, and the mantles, and the wimples, and the *crisping-pins,*
23 The glasses, and the fine linen, and <u>the</u> hoods, and the *vails.*	23 The glasses, and the fine linen, and hoods, and the *veils.*

3:16 (2 Nephi 13:16). "*Walk with stretched forth necks.*" Heads held high in haughtiness; prideful, not humble.

3:16 (2 Nephi 13:16). "*Wanton eyes.*" Seductive eyes that focus on carnality.

3:16 (2 Nephi 13:16). "*Walking and mincing as they go.*" Walking in an affected manner with short, rapid steps that draw attention to them.

3:16 (2 Nephi 13:16). "*Making a tinkling with their feet.*" Ankle ornaments called bangles were often worn by women in Eastern countries. Sometimes a bell was attached.

3:17 (2 Nephi 13:17). "*Smite with a scab the crown of the head.*" The scab is some sort of itchy rash which will afflict these proud and vain women and detract from the beauty they desire to project. (See Deuteronomy 28:27.)

3:17 (2 Nephi 13:17). "*Discover their secret parts.*" Some modern versions of the Bible render this as "make their foreheads bare" (as a result of the scabs and subsequent loss of hair). In Hebrew the phrase means to expose, meaning to put them to shame.

3:18 (2 Nephi 13:18). "*The bravery of their tinkling ornaments.*" The Lord will take away the glory or beauty of their anklets.

3:18 (2 Nephi 13:18). "*Cauls.*" Possibly hair nets or headbands.

3:18 (2 Nephi 13:18). *"Round tires like the moon."* Crescent-shaped ornaments.

3:19 (2 Nephi 13:19). *"Chains . . . and the mufflers."* The chains are pendants or earrings; the mufflers are veils.

3:20 (2 Nephi 13:20). *"Bonnets, . . . ornaments of the legs, . . . headbands, and the tablets."* Headdresses, ankle chains, sashes, and perfume boxes.

3:22 (2 Nephi 13:22). *"Changeable suits of apparel."* Festival robes or resplendent garments.

3:22 (2 Nephi 13:22). *"Wimples."* Cloaks or shawls.

3:22 (2 Nephi 13:22). *"Crisping pins."* Purses or satchels.

3:23 (2 Nephi 13:23). *"Glasses."* Two possible meanings are considered. Several commentaries suggest this means polished metal mirrors or looking glasses. However, the footnote in Isaiah states these are "transparent garments." (LDSKJ, Isaiah 3:23, footnote *a*.)

3:23 (2 Nephi 13:23). *"Hoods."* Women's turbans.

Isaiah 3:24–26 and 2 Nephi 13:24–26

These last three verses depict a time of ravaging war. Perhaps this is where the women will lose all their finery. The smell of death will be strong and the people will be taken captive. They will mourn their oppressed condition.

24 And it shall come to pass, that instead of sweet smell there shall be stink; and instead of a girdle a rent; and instead of well set hair baldness; and instead of a stomacher a girding of sackcloth; and burning instead of beauty.	24 And it shall come to pass, instead of sweet smell there shall be stink; and instead of a girdle, a rent; and instead of well set hair, baldness; and instead of a stomacher, a girding of sackcloth; burning instead of beauty.

25 Thy men shall fall by the sword, and thy mighty in the war.	25 Thy men shall fall by the sword and thy mighty in the war.
26 And her gates shall lament and mourn; and she <u>being</u> desolate shall sit upon the ground.	26 And her gates shall lament and mourn; and she <u>shall be</u> desolate, and shall sit upon the ground.

3:24 (2 Nephi 13:24). *"Instead of sweet smell there shall be stink."* The stench of dead bodies and rottenness will sicken the air that once was filled with the sweet smell of perfume and pleasing spices.

3:24 (2 Nephi 13:24). *"Instead of a girdle a rent."* Something that is "rent" is ripped or torn. The "rent" could refer to rags, clothing symbolic of captivity or extreme poverty. Some versions of the Bible use the word *rope* instead of *rent*. It may be that girdles will be replaced with ropes of captivity.

3:24 (2 Nephi 13:24). *"Instead of well set hair baldness."* A bald or shaved head was a symbol of captivity. (See Isaiah 15:2; Ezekiel 7:18. See also commentary on 3:17.)

3:24 (2 Nephi 13:24). *"Instead of a stomacher a girding of sackcloth."* Sackcloth will replace robes. Sackcloth was a coarse, dark cloth made of the hair of goats or camels. Mourners wore clothing made of sackcloth, and it became symbolic of sorrow.

3:24 (2 Nephi 13:24). *"Burning instead of beauty."* Branding, once again a mark of captivity and slavery.

3:26 (2 Nephi 13:26). *"Her gates shall lament and mourn."* As noted elsewhere in this volume, the gates of a city were the public thoroughfares. Here is where public and private business was transacted. Here also is where public displays of lamenting and mourning were exhibited. The site of Jerusalem's gates will be the scene of such a display. (See Lamentations 2:8–10. See also commentary on Isaiah 13:2.)

3:26 (2 Nephi 13:26). *"She being desolate shall sit upon the ground."* Jerusalem shall virtually be emptied, cleaned out ("desolate"). To sit upon the ground is a posture of mourning.

Isaiah 4 and 2 Nephi 14

OVERVIEW

In his inspired revision or translation of the Bible (JST), the Prophet Joseph Smith placed verse 1 of this chapter as the last verse of the previous chapter, where it more logically fits. Chapter 3 of Isaiah is filled with woe and destruction, whereas chapter 4 focuses on hope and holiness in the millennial day.

Isaiah portrays the beauty of the Lord's Zion. He emphasizes that the future inhabitants of both Zion (the New Jerusalem) and (the old) Jerusalem will be holy. Just as in ancient times, the Lord's canopy will cover His people. His presence will be evident in their homes as well as their places of worship.

COMMENTARY

Isaiah 4:1–6 and 2 Nephi 14:1–6

Isaiah 4	2 Nephi 14
1 And in that day seven women shall take hold of one man, saying, We will eat our own bread, and wear our own apparel: only let us be called by thy name, to take away our reproach.	1 And in that day, seven women shall take hold of one man, saying: We will eat our own bread, and wear our own apparel; only let us be called by thy name to take away our reproach.

2 In that day shall the branch of the Lord be beautiful and glorious,_and_ the fruit of the earth shall be excellent and comely for them that are escaped of Israel.

3 And it shall come to pass, that he that is left in Zion, and he that _remaineth_ in Jerusalem, shall be called holy, even every one that is written among the living in Jerusalem:

4 When the Lord shall have washed away the filth of the daughters of Zion, and shall have purged the blood of Jerusalem from the midst thereof by the spirit of judgment, and by the spirit of burning.

5 And the Lord will create upon every _dwelling place_ of mount Zion, and upon her assemblies, a cloud and smoke by day, and the shining of a flaming fire by night: for upon all the glory shall be a defence.

6 And there shall be a tabernacle for a shadow in the daytime from the heat, and for a place of refuge, and for a covert from storm and from rain.

2 In that day shall the branch of the Lord be beautiful and glorious; the fruit of the earth excellent and comely to them that are escaped of Israel.

3 And it shall come to pass, they that are left in Zion and _remain_ in Jerusalem shall be called holy, every one that is written among the living in Jerusalem—

4 When the Lord shall have washed away the filth of the daughters of Zion, and shall have purged the blood of Jerusalem from the midst thereof by the spirit of judgment and by the spirit of burning.

5 And the Lord will create upon every _dwelling-place_ of mount Zion, and upon her assemblies, a cloud and smoke by day and the shining of a flaming fire by night; for upon all the glory of Zion shall be a defence.

6 And there shall be a tabernacle for a shadow in the daytime from the heat, and for a place of refuge, and a covert from storm and from rain.

4:1 (2 Nephi 14:1). "_Seven women shall take hold of one man._" This scripture is not, as some have supposed, a rallying call for polygamy; but rather it is a description of very adverse conditions. So many men will have been killed in wars (see

Isaiah 3:25) that there will be a shortage of eligible marriage partners for single women. "Seven women" (symbolically meaning "many") will propose marriage to "one man." Contrary to law, which requires the husband to provide for the wife (Exodus 21:10), in these desperate times the women will pledge to provide the necessities of life for themselves.

4:1 (2 Nephi 14:1). "*Only let us be called by thy name, to take away our reproach.*" In Near Eastern culture it was considered a disgrace to remain unmarried. Furthermore, for a woman to be childless was considered a great curse. (See Genesis 30:22–24; Luke 1:24–25.) Thus, Isaiah sees desperate women who want to marry to remove the stigma of being unmarried and childless. As an interesting side note, Victor Ludlow suggested the possibility that many men of this future time period might be incapable of fathering children because of sterility caused by exposure to radiation. (IPSP, 109.)

4:2 (2 Nephi 14:2). "*The branch of the Lord [shall] be beautiful and glorious.*" The word "branch" in Hebrew was symbolic of the Messiah. The Branch is the Messiah, even Jesus Christ, He whose "glory def[ies] all description." (JS–H 1:17; see also Jeremiah 23:5–6.) In another sense, the "branch" could represent dispersed remnants of the house of Israel who have been redeemed and brought back to the glory of the Lord. (See Isaiah 60:21; 61:3; 2 Nephi 3:5; Jacob 2:25.)

4:2 (2 Nephi 14:2). "*The fruit of the earth shall be excellent and comely.*" This speaks of a time when the earth will be renewed (the paradisiacal glory in the Millennium) and will be "productive, prosperous, and beautiful." (LDSKJ, Isaiah 4:2, footnote *c*.) It has also been suggested that the "fruit" could represent either the spiritual food provided by the Redeemer or the blessings of the restored gospel.

4:2 (2 Nephi 14:2). "*Them that are escaped of Israel.*" These are the redeemed of Israel, who are relying upon Jesus Christ for sustenance rather than depending on their former captors. (Isaiah 10:20.)

4:3 (2 Nephi 14:3). "*They that are left in Zion and remain in Jerusalem.*" At His coming, the Lord will burn the wicked, leaving only the righteous to dwell on earth during His millennial reign. (JST Matthew 13:41–45.) The inhabitants of Zion and Jerusalem will all be holy.

4:3 (2 Nephi 14:3). "*Every one that is written among the living in Jerusalem.*" Those who are "saved by approval of the Messiah." (LDSKJ, Isaiah 4:3, footnote *d*.)

4:4 (2 Nephi 14:4). "*When the Lord shall have washed away the filth of the daughters of Zion.*" When the Lord has cleansed the earth and only the righteous, those who have properly repented, remain.

4:4 (2 Nephi 14:4). "*Purged the blood of Jerusalem from the midst thereof by the spirit of judgment, and by the spirit of burning.*" All who are unholy will be purged from the earth at the Second Coming. They will be judged, found wanting, and burned or destroyed. (Malachi 3:2; 4:1; JST Matthew 13:29; BICQ, 194–98.)

4:5 (2 Nephi 14:5). "*The Lord will create . . . a cloud and smoke by day, and the shining of a flaming fire by night.*" The Lord made His presence and protective covering to ancient Israel evident by very visible signs: "And the Lord went before them by day in a pillar of a cloud, to lead them the way; and by night in a pillar of fire, to give them light; to go by day and night." (Exodus 13:21.)

In addition, "the cloud of the Lord was upon the tabernacle [the portable temple in the wilderness] by day, and fire was on it by night." (Exodus 40:38.)

In this future millennial day, the symbolic cloud of smoke and pillar of fire—representing the presence of the Lord—will not be limited to resting on a temple. As promised, His presence will extend to "every dwelling place [home] of mount Zion and upon her assemblies [places of worship]," for all will be holy places.

4:6 (2 Nephi 14:6). *"There shall be a tabernacle for a shadow in the daytime from the heat."* In that glorious day when literally the whole earth will be Zion ("for this is Zion—THE PURE IN HEART" [D&C 97:21]), the Lord will shield the people from heat and storm. His protective pavilion will encompass the pure in heart in all places.

Chapter 5

Isaiah 5 and 2 Nephi 15

Overview

This chapter combines a parable, six woes, and future promises of hope. It is viewed as an extension of the previous three chapters and as a transition to Isaiah 6. The chapter can logically be divided into three sections: (1) verses 1–7 describe the parable of the Lord's vineyard; (2) verses 8–25 pronounce six woes upon the wicked; and (3) verses 26–30 prophesy of a future time when the Lord will lift up an ensign to the nations of the world and gather His people.

Commentary

Isaiah 5:1–7 and 2 Nephi 15:1–7

Isaiah commences this chapter with a song or poetic parable in which he portrays his "well-beloved" (the Lord) as having a vineyard (the house of Israel, including those of Judah). It has been unproductive, in spite of having been planted under the best of conditions and having received the best of care. The Lord laments, "What could have been done more to my vineyard that I have not done in it?"

He pronounces judgment upon the vineyard, tearing down its protective fences and leaving it open to predators.

The reader would do well to study this chapter in conjunction with Jacob 5 in the Book of Mormon, where a similar parable or allegory is presented.

Isaiah 5

1 <u>Now</u> will I sing to my *wellbeloved* a song of my beloved touching his vineyard. My *wellbeloved* hath a vineyard in a very fruitful hill<u>:</u>

2 And he fenced it, and gathered out the stones thereof, and planted it with the choicest vine, and built a tower in the midst of it, and also made a *winepress* therein<u>:</u> and he looked that it should bring forth grapes, and it brought forth wild grapes.

3 And now, O inhabitants of Jerusalem, and men of Judah, judge, I pray you, betwixt me and my vineyard.

4 What could have been done more to my vineyard<u>,</u> that I have not done in it? <u>w</u>herefore, when I looked that it should bring forth grapes<u>,</u> *brought it* forth wild grapes<u>?</u>

5 And now go to; I will tell you what I will do to my vineyard<u>:</u> I will take away the hedge thereof, and it shall be eaten up; and break down the wall thereof, and it shall be trodden down<u>:</u>

2 Nephi 15

1 <u>And then</u> will I sing to my *well-beloved* a song of my beloved<u>,</u> touching his vineyard. My *well-beloved* hath a vineyard in a very fruitful hill<u>.</u>

2 And he fenced it, and gathered out the stones thereof, and planted it with the choicest vine, and built a tower in the midst of it, and also made a *wine-press* therein<u>;</u> and he looked that it should bring forth grapes, and it brought forth wild grapes<u>.</u>

3 And now, O inhabitants of Jerusalem, and men of Judah, judge, I pray you, betwixt me and my vineyard.

4 What could have been done more to my vineyard that I have not done in it? <u>W</u>herefore, when I looked that it should bring forth grapes *it brought* forth wild grapes<u>.</u>

5 And now go to; I will tell you what I will do to my vineyard<u>—</u>I will take away the hedge thereof, and it shall be eaten up; and <u>I will</u> break down the wall thereof, and it shall be trodden down<u>;</u>

6 And I will lay it waste: it shall not be pruned, nor digged; but there shall come up briers and thorns: I will also command the clouds that they rain no rain upon it.

7 For the vineyard of the Lord of hosts is the house of Israel, and the men of Judah his pleasant plant: and he looked for judgment, but behold oppression; for righteousness, but behold a cry.

6 And I will lay it waste; it shall not be pruned nor digged; but there shall come up briers and thorns; I will also command the clouds that they rain no rain upon it.

7 For the vineyard of the Lord of Hosts is the house of Israel, and the men of Judah his pleasant plant; and he looked for judgment, and behold, oppression; for righteousness, but behold, a cry.

The tower is the church among the people. It could also be the temple.

5:2 (2 Nephi 15:2). *"Built a tower in the midst of it."* Watchtowers were built in the midst of vineyards to keep an eye out for predators or thieves. Monte Nyman suggests this tower "could have been the temple built by Solomon. This inference is drawn from the latter-day parable concerning another tower (temple) which was to be built upon a 'very choice piece of land' (Jackson County, Missouri) but has not yet been built (see D&C 101:43–62)." (GAWI, 42–43.)

'winepress' is where the Lord expects to recieve the results of righteous behavior such as ordinances in the temple or baptisms of new members. When men are so wicked that

5:2 (2 Nephi 15:2). *"Made a winepress therein."* Two vats used for making wine. In one, the grapes were pressed or *they cannot* trodden under foot to produce the juice, which was collected *bring forth* in the second. The construction of such a device in the midst *good fruit* of the vineyard is indicative of the high expectations the Lord *they are considered* of the vineyard had for a bountiful harvest. *as 'wild grapes'*

wicked men

5:2 (2 Nephi 15:2). *"It brought forth wild grapes."* Although the vineyard was planted with "the choicest vine," which should have produced the sweetest fruit, it produced wild or sour grapes. (See Jeremiah 2:21.) The wild grapes are symbolic of Israel's apostasy.

5:5 (2 Nephi 15:5). *"Take away the hedge . . . and break down the wall."* The hedge is the inner enclosure, and the wall is the

mankind is no longer protected thru righteous behavior. The family is destroyed, the Church is weakened. Personal integrity is gone, + nobody can be trusted.

stone fence or outer enclosure protecting the vineyard. The Lord is declaring that His protecting hand is being removed from the house of Israel. (See Psalm 80:12–13.) The consequences of the Lord's absence from apostate Israel are spelled out in verses 5 and 6.

5:7 (2 Nephi 15:7). *"He looked for judgment . . . for righteousness."* This verse is the justification for the Lord's actions against the vineyard. He had looked for justice ("judgment") among His people but saw only injustice and bloodshed ("oppression"); He hoped to see righteousness but beheld only riotousness and raucousness. (See LDSKJ, Isaiah 5:7, footnote *c*.) *Lord is dissappointed w/ men's wickedness,*

Isaiah 5:8–25 and 2 Nephi 15:8–25

Six woes are pronounced upon the people because of their sinfulness. A woe is "a condition of deep suffering from misfortune, affliction, or grief." (DCE, 644.) In this instance, it is the result of the people's following forbidden practices and suffering the consequences.

8 *Woe* unto them that join house to house, that lay field to field, till there be no place, that they may be placed alone in the midst of the earth!	8 *Wo* unto them that join house to house, till there can be no place, that they may be placed alone in the midst of the earth!
9 In mine ears said the Lord of hosts, Of a truth many houses shall be desolate, even great and fair, without inhabitant.	9 In mine ears, said the Lord of Hosts, of a truth many houses shall be desolate, and great and fair cities without inhabitant.
10 Yea, ten acres of vineyard shall yield one bath, and the seed of *an* homer shall yield an ephah.	10 Yea, ten acres of vineyard shall yield one bath, and the seed of *a* homer shall yield an ephah.

11 *Woe* unto them that rise up early in the morning, that they may follow strong drink; that continue until night, <u>till</u> wine inflame them!

12 And the harp, and the viol, the tabret, and pipe, and wine, are in their feasts: but they regard not the work of the Lord, neither consider the operation of his hands.

13 Therefore my people are gone into captivity, because they have no knowledge: and their *honourable* men are famished, and their multitude dried up with thirst.

14 Therefore hell hath enlarged herself, and opened her mouth without measure: and their glory, and their multitude, and their pomp, and he that rejoiceth, shall descend into it.

15 And the mean man shall be brought down, and the mighty man shall be humbled, and the eyes of the lofty shall be humbled:

16 But the Lord of <u>h</u>osts shall be exalted in judgment, and God that is holy shall be sanctified in righteousness.

17 Then shall the lambs feed after their manner, and the waste places of the fat ones shall strangers eat.

11 *Wo* unto them that rise up early in the morning, that they may follow strong drink, that continue until night, <u>and</u> wine inflame them!

12 And the harp, and the viol, the tabret, and pipe, and wine are in their feasts; but they regard not the work of the Lord, neither consider the operation of his hands.

13 Therefore, my people are gone into captivity, because they have no knowledge; and their *honorable* men are famished, and their multitude dried up with thirst.

14 Therefore, hell hath enlarged herself, and opened her mouth without measure; and their glory, and their multitude, and their pomp, and he that rejoiceth, shall descend into it.

15 And the mean man shall be brought down, and the mighty man shall be humbled, and the eyes of the lofty shall be humbled.

16 But the Lord of <u>H</u>osts shall be exalted in judgment, and God that is holy shall be sanctified in righteousness.

17 Then shall the lambs feed after their manner, and the waste places of the fat ones shall strangers eat.

18 *Woe* unto them that draw
iniquity with cords of vanity,
and sin as it were with a cart
rope:

19 That say, Let him make
speed, <u>and</u> hasten his work,
that we may see it: and let
the counsel of the Holy One
of Israel draw nigh and
come, that we may know it!

20 *Woe* unto them that call
evil good, and good evil;
that put darkness for light,
and light for darkness; that
put bitter for sweet, and
sweet for bitter!

21 *Woe* unto <u>them that are</u>
wise in their own eyes, and
prudent in their own sight!

22 *Woe* unto <u>them that are</u>
mighty to drink wine, and
men of strength to mingle
strong drink:

23 <u>Which</u> justify the wicked
for reward, and take away
the righteousness of the
righteous from him!

24 Therefore as the fire
devoureth the stubble, and
the flame consumeth the
chaff, <u>so</u> their root shall be <u>as</u>
rottenness, and their
blossom shall go up as dust:
because they have cast away
the law of the Lord of <u>h</u>osts,
and despised the word of the
Holy One of Israel.

18 *Wo* unto them that draw
iniquity with cords of vanity,
and sin as it were with a cart
rope;

19 That say: Let him make
speed, hasten his work, that
we may see it; and let the
counsel of the Holy One of
Israel draw nigh and come,
that we may know it.

20 *Wo* unto them that call
evil good, and good evil,
that put darkness for light,
and light for darkness, that
put bitter for sweet, and
sweet for bitter!

21 *Wo* unto <u>the</u> wise in their
own eyes and prudent in
their own sight!

22 *Wo* unto the mighty to
drink wine, and men of
strength to mingle strong
drink;

23 <u>Who</u> justify the wicked
for reward, and take away
the righteousness of the
righteous from him!

24 Therefore, as the fire
devoureth the stubble, and
the flame consumeth the
chaff, their root shall be
rottenness, and their
blossom<u>s</u> shall go up as dust;
because they have cast away
the law of the Lord of <u>H</u>osts,
and despised the word of the
Holy One of Israel.

25 Therefore is the anger of the Lord kindled against his people, and he hath stretched forth his hand against them, and hath smitten them: and the hills did tremble, and their *carcases* were torn in the midst of the streets. For all this his anger is not turned away, but his hand is stretched out still.

25 Therefore, is the anger of the Lord kindled against his people, and he hath stretched forth his hand against them, and hath smitten them; and the hills did tremble, and their *carcasses* were torn in the midst of the streets. For all this his anger is not turned away, but his hand is stretched out still.

immorality - People are houses' + they are all joined them immoralnets. Per diseases sex join them.

5:8 (2 Nephi 15:8). "*Woe unto them that join house to house.*" This woe is pronounced on the wealthy landowners who covet and buy up property, thus depriving the poor of their heritage. (See Micah 2:1–2.) The law of ancient Israel prescribed that land could not "be sold for ever." (Leviticus 25:23; see also 1 Kings 21.) It was to remain within families as a heritage for posterity. When economical circumstances necessitated the sale of land, it was to be returned to the original owners in the year of jubilee, which occurred every fifty years. (LDSBD, "Jubilee, Year of," p. 718.)

Another interpretation of this verse has been posited by Monte Nyman. He believes this expression is an indictment of the socialistic practice of a central government controlling the property. Such a system would prevent Zion from being established because it would eliminate the possibility of practicing the law of stewardship and consecration. (GAWI, 43–44.)

5:8 (2 Nephi 15:8). "*Till there be no place, that they may be placed.*" The wealthy landowners leave no place for the poor to dwell alone (in their own home), or without indenture to another. *Those who are immoral are not alone spiritually, they have connected themselves to other's thru immoral*

5:9 (2 Nephi 15:9). "*Many houses shall be desolate.*" The pronounced woe will take the homes from the wealthy landgrabbers. *The "houses" or bodies of men are desolate of the Holy Ghost due to immorality + sins*

5:10 (2 Nephi 15:10). "*Ten acres . . . one bath . . . a homer . . . an ephah.*" The lands of the wealthy will become extremely unproductive. *Ten acres* represents the amount of land that ten yoke of oxen can plow in a day, or the equivalent of five acres of land by our modern measurement. From this acreage, the yield will be only one bath (four to eight gallons of wine). One homer of seed (about six bushels) will yield only an ephah of produce (four to six gallons of dry measure).

[handwritten: Even many men cannot bring forth righteous fruits to the Lord due to their wickedness —]

5:11 (2 Nephi 15:11). "*Woe unto them that rise up early [to consume] strong drink.*" This second woe condemns drunkenness and riotous living. Wise Solomon said it well when he stated, "Who hath woe? who hath sorrow? . . . They that tarry long at the wine." (Proverbs 23:29–30.) This woe is not confined to drunks, but is an indictment of all who insatiably pursue raucous and riotous living. They pursue pleasure ("in their feasts") from "early in the morning . . . until night . . . but they regard not the work of the Lord." *[handwritten: People who do evil all the day long from start to end.]*

5:12 (2 Nephi 15:12). "*The harp, and the viol, the tabret, and pipe.*" The pleasure seekers will fill their feasts and places of entertainment with the music of the world. The instruments cited—"viol" (a lyre or lute—a hand-held stringed instrument), "tabret" (a small drum), "pipe" (flute)—are simply symbolic of the worldly merriment associated with the people's pursuit of pleasure.

5:13 (2 Nephi 15:13). "*My people are gone into captivity, because they have no knowledge.*" Because of their waywardness, the people have gone into spiritual bondage. They lack knowledge of God and His ways. The Lord declared, "It is impossible for a man to be saved in ignorance." (D&C 131:6.) In ignorance of what? The things of God! The apostle Paul wrote, "The things of God knoweth no man except he has the Spirit of God." (JST 1 Corinthians 2:11.) *[handwritten: men cannot hear the words of truth when spoken for they are drunk in sin.]*

5:13 (2 Nephi 15:13). "*Their honourable men are famished . . . their multitude dried up with thirst.*" The leaders

47

("honourable men") and the masses ("multitude") are without spiritual food or water. We recall the words of Jesus during His mortal ministry: "I am the bread of life: he that cometh to me shall never hunger; and he that believeth on me shall never thirst." (John 6:35; see also John 4:14.)

5:14 (2 Nephi 15:14). *"Therefore, hell hath enlarged herself."* Because of the spiritual famine, many will leave this life without the saving knowledge needed to keep them from the captivity of spirit prison. Therefore, the numbers in hell (the spirit prison) have swelled. *Also hell is expanding to men living on earth in sin.* thru

5:15 (2 Nephi 15:15). *"The mean man . . . and the mighty man."* Both the ordinary or common ("mean") man and the man of position or wealth ("mighty") shall be humbled. The Lord does not distinguish between the wealthy and the poor, only between the wicked and the righteous. The haughty shall be humbled. *All men are involved in this wickedness*

5:16 (2 Nephi 15:16). *"The Lord of Hosts shall be exalted . . . shall be sanctified."* The Lord *is* exalted in justice and He *is* sanctified in righteousness.

5:17 (2 Nephi 15:17). *"The waste places of the fat ones shall strangers eat."* Some commentaries suggest this verse should be placed next to verse 10. It is probably a reference to the desolate condition of the lands once inhabited by the wealthy. Rather than producing bountiful crops, their lands will provide forage for lambs and young goats or strangers. (The word "strangers" appears as "aliens" in early Hebrew texts while the Greek Septuagint uses "young goats.")

5:18 (2 Nephi 15:18). *"Woe unto them that draw iniquity with cords of vanity."* This woe is pronounced on those who are yoked to falsehoods and sin as an animal is to a cart. They are tethered to this heavy burden, pulling it wherever they go.

5:19 (2 Nephi 15:19). "*Let him make speed, and hasten his work, that we may see it.*" The woe is also pronounced upon the scoffers, who demand immediate fulfillment of prophecy. The apostle Peter saw such sign seekers in the last days, who shall say, "Where is the promise of his coming?" (2 Peter 3:1–4.) These disbelievers echo the words of others before their time who similarly mocked the faithful: "But there were some who began to say that the time was past for the words to be fulfilled. . . . And they began to rejoice . . . [and] make a great uproar throughout the land." (3 Nephi 1:5–7.)

5:20 (2 Nephi 15:20). "*Woe unto them that call evil good, and good evil.*" This woe is pronounced upon those who would pervert standards of morality and decency. They seek man's approval of that which God has condemned and disdain that which is good. They have been successful in getting legislation passed to make such perversion legal and acceptable by society. Immoral practices are called "alternate lifestyles" by those who practice them, and they label those who courageously speak against them as "radicals" or "narrow-minded bigots." A prophet of God, President Spencer W. Kimball, declared: "The fact that some governments and some churches and numerous corrupted individuals have tried to reduce such behavior from criminal offense to personal privilege does not change the nature nor the seriousness of the practice." (*Ensign,* November 1980, p. 97; see also BICQ, 38–51.)

Others upon whom this woe is pronounced are those who "lift up the heel against" the Lord's servants, "and cry they have sinned when they have not sinned." The Lord tells us that those who make such false accusations "do it because they are the servants of sin, and are the children of disobedience themselves." (D&C 121:16–17.)

5:21 (2 Nephi 15:21). "*Woe unto them that are wise in their own eyes, and prudent in their own sight!*" This woe is pronounced on those who reject the wisdom of God for their own learning. Jacob described and warned against such arrogance: "O the vainness, and the frailties, and the foolishness of men! When they are learned they think they are wise, and they hearken not unto the counsel of God, for they set it aside, supposing they know of themselves, wherefore, their wisdom is foolishness and it profiteth them not. And they shall perish." (2 Nephi 9:28; see also 2 Nephi 28:15.)

5:23 (2 Nephi 15:23). "*Who justify the wicked for reward.*" This refers to those who take bribes. Because this statement immediately follows a woe pronounced against drunkenness, one wonders if Isaiah saw those well-known figures in sports, entertainment, or other positions of notoriety who accept payment for endorsing harmful products such as alcohol.

5:23 (2 Nephi 15:23). "*Take away the righteousness of the righteous.*" At least two scholars suggest this refers to those who deprive the innocent of their legal rights. (BMC, 190; IPSP, 120.) It may also have reference to those who take away another's innocence or lead the righteous astray.

5:24 (2 Nephi 15:24). "*As the fire devoureth the stubble.*" The Lord Jesus Christ declared that at His coming, "all the proud and they that do wickedly shall be as stubble; and I will burn them up, for I am the Lord of Hosts; and I will not spare any that remain in Babylon." (D&C 64:24; see also BICQ, 194–98.)

5:25 (2 Nephi 15:25). "*The anger of the Lord.*" The Lord does not become angry in the sense that mortals understand the word. His anger is divine indignation that applies the laws of justice where necessary. (See DCE, 18.)

5:25 (2 Nephi 15:25). "*And the hills did tremble, and their carcases were torn in the midst of the streets.*" Any who have watched the devastation of war on a news program, or seen graphic pictures of mutilated bodies torn asunder by artillery shells, rockets, or falling bombs, have perhaps had a glimpse of what Isaiah saw. In any event, the prophet foresaw terrible scenes of destruction brought about because of the wickedness of the people.

5:25 (2 Nephi 15:25). "*His hand is stretched out still.*" Some interpret this phrase to mean that God is continuing to mete out punishment. However, another possible meaning is that He is ever reaching out to the repentant, inviting their return. (Also see commentary on Isaiah 9:12 and 10:4.)

Isaiah 5:26–30 and 2 Nephi 15:26–30

Isaiah now speaks words of encouragement. In the last days the Lord "will lift up an ensign to the nations from far." Those who gather to this ensign will come quickly and with power. They will do so amidst contrasting conditions of light and darkness or good and evil.

A secondary interpretation of these verses focuses on the Assyrian invasion of Israel in 722–721 B.C. Commentators who subscribe to this belief identify the speed with which the Assyrian soldiers invaded the land and the quick destruction they brought about. Nevertheless, the major focus of these verses appears to align itself more closely with events of the last days.

26 And he will lift up an ensign to the nations from far, and will hiss unto them from the end of the earth: and, behold, they shall come with speed swiftly:	26 And he will lift up an ensign to the nations from far, and will hiss unto them from the end of the earth; and behold, they shall come with speed swiftly; [Begin Isaiah 5:27.] *none shall be weary nor stumble among them.*
27 *None shall be weary nor stumble among them;* none shall slumber nor sleep; neither shall the girdle of their loins be loosed, nor the latchet of their shoes be broken:	27 None shall slumber nor sleep; neither shall the girdle of their loins be loosed, nor the latchet of their shoes be broken;

28 Whose arrows <u>are</u> sharp, and all their bows bent, their horses' hoofs shall be counted like flint, and their wheels like a whirlwind<u>:</u>

28 Whose arrows <u>shall be</u> sharp, and all their bows bent, and their horses' hoofs shall be counted like flint, and their wheels like a whirlwind, [Begin Isaiah 5:29.] *their roaring like a lion.*

29 *Their roaring <u>shall be</u> like a lion,* they shall roar like young lions; yea, they shall roar, and lay hold of the prey, and shall carry <u>it</u> away safe, and none shall deliver <u>it.</u>

29 <u>They</u> shall roar like young lions; yea, they shall roar, and lay hold of the prey, and shall carry away safe, and none shall deliver.

30 And in that day they shall roar against them like the roaring of the sea<u>:</u> and if <u>one</u> look unto the land, behold darkness and sorrow, and the light is darkened in the heavens thereof.

30 And in that day they shall roar against them like the roaring of the sea<u>;</u> and if <u>they</u> look unto the land, behold, darkness and sorrow, and the light is darkened in the heavens thereof.

5:26 (2 Nephi 15:26). "*An ensign to the nations.*" Elder Marion G. Romney declared: "This Church [The Church of Jesus Christ of Latter-day Saints] is the standard which Isaiah said the Lord would set up for the people in the latter days. . . . This Church is the ensign on the mountain spoken of by the Old Testament prophets." (CR, April 1961, p. 119.)

Victor Ludlow provides a variety of possible interpretations of "ensign," including the scriptural justification for each. He concludes by saying, "we see that an ensign in the last days can refer to Zion, the gospel, missionary work, the gathering, and the Book of Mormon. . . . In short, the term *ensign* encompasses the Lord's whole work, and all aspects of his Church serve as his 'standard' to the world." (IPSP, 122–23; see also D&C 115:5–6; commentary on Isaiah 49:22 and Isaiah 11:10, 12 in this volume.)

5:26 (2 Nephi 15:26). "*Hiss unto them from the end of the earth.*" To "hiss" is to whistle or summon. It is a signal to all quarters of the earth for the gathering. (In the context of 2 Nephi 29:2 it means to go forth.)

5:26–27 (2 Nephi 15:26–27). "*They shall come with speed swiftly . . . none shall slumber . . . nor [shall] the latchet of their shoes be broken.*" Whereas ancient travel often took many days or weeks, the future gathering will be so swift the travelers won't need to camp for the night, nor will they wear out their clothing and sandals during the trip.

5:28–29 (2 Nephi 15:28). "*Whose arrows are sharp, . . . their wheels like a whirlwind: Their roaring shall be like a lion.*" Elder LeGrand Richards has provided excellent commentary on these verses: "Since there were no such things as trains and airplanes in that day, Isaiah could hardly have mentioned them by name, but he seems to have described them in unmistakable words. How better could 'their horses' hoofs be counted like flint, and their wheel like a whirlwind' than in the modern train? How better could 'Their roaring . . . be like a lion' than in the roar of the airplane?" (MWW, 236.) To Isaiah, these future modes of transportation probably looked like great beasts which took their prey (passengers) to a safe destination.

At least one author suggests this may also depict missionaries traveling to the ends of the earth to gather converts who are safely enfolded within Zion's tent. (IPSP, 123.)

5:30 (2 Nephi 15:30). "*Behold darkness and sorrow, and the light is darkened in the heavens.*" Victor Ludlow stated: "The 'darkness and sorrow' might refer either to physical or spiritual conditions as destruction and apostasy rage upon the earth. The light 'darkened in the heavens' seems to suggest the gospel or the Messiah himself coming forth out of obscure darkness." (IPSP, 123–24.)

CHAPTER 6

Isaiah 6 and 2 Nephi 16

OVERVIEW

This chapter describes Isaiah's call to the ministry and the great vision that accompanied it. Logically, the chapter should probably be the first book in Isaiah's writings, for it not only includes his call but the charge that was given him. Possible reasons for its present placement are described by Victor Ludlow:

"There are many possible explanations as to why this sixth chapter of Isaiah is not placed at the head of his writings. Perhaps Isaiah wanted to introduce his message before he introduced himself; after delivering the important pronouncements found in the first five chapters, he wanted to provide a seal for his words by testifying concerning his prophetic authority. Or, it may even be that the vision and calling recorded in chapter 6 came to Isaiah after the visions of the first few chapters.

"Or, chapter 6 may be where it is to bridge the two major segments of his opening chapters. The first section of Isaiah, chapters 1–12, contains two major themes: the unrighteousness of the Israelites, and the promise of a new Zion in the last days. The first five chapters emphasize Israel's separation from the 'master of the vineyard,' while chapters 7–12 promise deliverance and the millennial day. Both themes are epitomized by Isaiah himself in chapter 6; he fears the Lord's judgment because of his own sins and yet is willing to serve the Lord because he knows that a latter-day remnant of Israel will believe and understand his prophecies." (IPSP, 126–27.)

Sidney Sperry stated that Nephi included this particular

54

chapter of Isaiah in the Book of Mormon because he probably "wanted his people to know about Isaiah's personal testimony that he had seen and talked to the pre-existent Christ." (BMC, 193; see also 2 Nephi 11:2–3.)

COMMENTARY

Isaiah 6:1–4 and 2 Nephi 16:1–4

As have prophets both before his time and since, Isaiah saw the Lord: He who was Jehovah of the Old Testament and who would become Jesus the Christ of the New Testament. The prophet saw the Lord's robe, throne, and some of the heavenly creatures crying holiness to His name.

Isaiah 6	2 Nephi 16
1 In the year that king Uzziah died I saw also the Lord sitting upon a throne, high and lifted up, and his train filled the temple.	1 In the year that king Uzziah died, I saw also the Lord sitting upon a throne, high and lifted up, and his train filled the temple.
2 Above it stood the seraphims: each one had six wings; with twain he covered his face, and with twain he covered his feet, and with twain he did fly.	2 Above it stood the seraphim; each one had six wings; with twain he covered his face, and with twain he covered his feet, and with twain he did fly.
3 And one cried unto another, and said, Holy, holy, holy, is the Lord of hosts: the whole earth is full of his glory.	3 And one cried unto another, and said: Holy, holy, holy, is the Lord of Hosts; the whole earth is full of his glory.
4 And the posts of the door moved at the voice of him that cried, and the house was filled with smoke.	4 And the posts of the door moved at the voice of him that cried, and the house was filled with smoke.

6:1 (2 Nephi 16:1). "*In the year that king Uzziah died.*" This king reigned over Judah for fifty years and died around 750 B.C.

6:1 (2 Nephi 16:1). "*His train filled the temple.*" In his vision of the Lord of Hosts, Isaiah describes the hem or skirts ("train") of Jehovah's garment as filling the temple in which He sat on a resplendent throne.

6:2–3 (2 Nephi 16:2–3). "*The seraphims.*" The Book of Mormon provides the correct rendering, "seraphim." Seraph is singular and seraphs or seraphim plural. Perhaps these unusual six-winged creatures seen by Isaiah have some association with the strange beasts John the Revelator saw near the throne of God. (Revelation 4:2–10; 5:11–14.) Joseph Smith explained that wings of the latter beasts "are a representation of power, to move, to act, etc." (D&C 77:2–4.) The Prophet further stated: "John heard the words of the beasts giving glory to God, and understood them. God who made the beasts could understand every language spoken by them." (TPJS, 291–92.)

In his dedicatory prayer of the Kirtland Temple, the Prophet pleaded that the Saints might have power to "mingle our voices with those bright, shining seraphs around thy throne, with acclamations of praise, singing Hosanna to God and the Lamb!" (D&C 109:79.) His description of "shining seraphs" is consistent with the Hebrew root of *seraph*, which is "burning." Thus, seraphs are burning (shining) or fiery beings. (See LDSBD, "Seraphim," p. 771.)

Joseph Smith described the heavenly messenger Moroni as having a "countenance truly like lightning." (JS–H 1:32.) Oliver Cowdery gave a similar description of the resurrected John the Baptist. (JS–H 1: note, p. 59.) It seems logical that the "seraphic hosts of heaven" (D&C 38:1) could be a combination of glorious, shining beings who represent saved beings from both the human and animal kingdoms. (See also DCE, 508–9.)

6:4 (2 Nephi 16:4). "*The posts of the door moved.*" The foundations of the threshold moved or trembled. "These could be the posts of the doorway leading into the Holy of Holies of the Jerusalem temple, or the heavenly doorway that leads into

God's presence. In either case, that there is a door or gateway into the divine presence is a concept that is also suggested in other scriptures. (John 10; 2 Ne. 9:41; Isa. 22:22.)" (IPSP, 130.)

6:4 (2 Nephi 16:4). *"The house was filled with smoke."* Symbolically, God's presence was seen and felt when He covered Mount Sinai with smoke. (Exodus 19:18.) The sacred slopes of Sinai thus became a temple to Moses. Perhaps experiencing something similar to Isaiah, John saw "the temple . . . filled with smoke from the glory of God." (Revelation 15:8.)

Isaiah 6:5–8 and 2 Nephi 16:5–8

Isaiah agonized over his own felt unworthiness, as well as that of the people to whom he was called to minister. The Lord knew his heart and mind and purged him of his sins, following which Isaiah boldly stepped forward to answer the call to serve.

5 Then said I, *Woe* is me! for I am undone; because I am a man of unclean lips, and I dwell in the midst of a people of unclean lips: for mine eyes have seen the King, the Lord of <u>h</u>osts.

6 Then flew one of the seraphim<u>s</u> unto me, having a live coal in his hand, which he had taken with the tongs from off the altar:

7 And he laid it upon my mouth, and said, Lo, this *hath* touched thy lips; and thine iniquity is taken away, and thy sin purged.

5 Then said I: *Wo* is <u>unto</u> me! for I am undone; because I am a man of unclean lips; and I dwell in the midst of a people of unclean lips; for mine eyes have seen the King, the Lord of <u>H</u>osts.

6 Then flew one of the seraphim unto me, having a live coal in his hand, which he had taken with the tongs from off the altar;

7 And he laid it upon my mouth, and said: Lo, this *has* touched thy lips; and thine iniquity is taken away, and thy sin purged.

8 Also I heard the voice of
the Lord, saying, Whom
shall I send, and who will go
for us? Then *said I,* Here am
I; send me.

8 Also I heard the voice of
the Lord, saying: Whom
shall I send, and who will go
for us? Then *I said:* Here am
I; send me.

6:5 (2 Nephi 16:5). "*Then said I, Woe is me! for I am undone;
because I am a man of unclean lips.*" Isaiah's call to the ministry kindled within him a desire to be totally worthy of his
call. He felt "undone" (cut off or lost) because he sensed the
personal shortcomings in his less than perfect life. His self-
evaluation is reminiscent of the process many go through
when called to serve: "Who am I that the Lord should give
me such a special assignment?" (See, for example, Enoch's
response in Moses 6:31.)

6:5 (2 Nephi 16:5). "*I dwell in the midst of a people of
unclean lips.*" In addition to being aware of his own faults, the
prophet was very much aware of the sins of the people among
whom he lived.

6:6–7 (2 Nephi 16:6–7). "*A live coal . . . from off the altar
. . . he laid . . . upon my mouth.*" The "live coal" was a symbol
of God's cleansing power. Through its touch, Isaiah's sins
were "purged" and he was sanctified to perform God's work.
The "live [hot] coal" could well be symbolic of being
"cleansed by the power of the Holy Ghost," which, or course,
was made possible through the Atonement. (Moroni 6:4.)
The altar Isaiah saw was probably the altar of incense inside
the temple. The Hebrew word for "live coal" is *ritzpah,* translated as a "glowing (incandescent) stone." (See IPSP, 131.)

6:8 (2 Nephi 16:8). "*I heard the voice of the Lord, saying,
Whom shall I send.*" While there are messianic overtones in
both the question of the Lord and in the prophet's response,
"Here am I," (compare Abraham 3:27), the direct application
is to Isaiah's willingness to serve. His initial, but brief, hesi-
tancy to serve was not based on his lack of faith in God's
power, but only because of his own feelings of unworthiness.

Once being assured he was cleansed and worthy to serve, he stepped to the forefront. Isaiah's response reminds one of Nephi's declaration regarding a difficult assignment given him. (See 1 Nephi 3:7.)

Isaiah 6:9–13 and 2 Nephi 16:9–13

The Lord gives Isaiah his charge to call the people to repentance, but ironically tells the prophet his efforts will be fruitless. The changed text in the Book of Mormon as well as other scriptural commentary provides understanding for otherwise difficult passages in verses 9 and 10.

Isaiah asks the Lord how long the hardhearted people will reject the message. The Lord's answer is not comforting. Yet, the final verse of the chapter gives hope that there will yet be a remnant of the people who will be redeemed.

9 And he said, Go, and tell this people, Hear ye indeed, but *understand* not; and see ye indeed, but perceive not.

9 And he said: Go and tell this people—Hear ye indeed, but they *understood* not; and see ye indeed, but they perceived not.

10 Make the heart of this people fat, and make their ears heavy, and shut their eyes; lest they see with their eyes, and hear with their ears, and understand with their heart, and convert, and be healed.

10 Make the heart of this people fat, and make their ears heavy, and shut their eyes—lest they see with their eyes, and hear with their ears, and understand with their heart, and be converted and be healed.

11 Then said I, Lord, how long? And he answered, Until the cities be wasted without inhabitant, and the houses without man, and the land be utterly desolate,

11 Then said I: Lord, how long? And he said: Until the cities be wasted without inhabitant, and the houses without man, and the land be utterly desolate;

12 And the Lord have removed men far away, and there be a great forsaking in the midst of the land.

12 And the Lord have removed men far away, for there shall be a great forsaking in the midst of the land.

13 But yet <u>in it</u> shall be a tenth, and <u>it</u> shall return, and shall be eaten<u>:</u> as a *teil tree,* and as an oak<u>,</u> whose substance is in them<u>,</u> when they cast their leaves<u>:</u> so the holy seed shall be the substance thereof.	13 But yet <u>there</u> shall be a tenth, and <u>they</u> shall return, and shall be eaten<u>,</u> as a *teil-tree* and as an oak whose substance is in them when they cast their leaves<u>;</u> so the holy seed shall be the substance thereof.

6:9 (2 Nephi 16:9). *"Tell this people—Hear ye indeed, but <u>they understood</u> not."* As noted above, the Nephite text makes clear that the Lord is not giving the people an impossible task by asking them to do something and then preventing them from doing it. It is the people who are at fault, obstinately refusing to respond to the divine requests. Another aspect of one's inability to understand the word of the Lord is lack of spiritual depth. Some simply do not have the spiritual maturity to recognize the light that is available. The Savior referenced this passage in Isaiah during His mortal ministry. (See JST Matthew 13:12–15; Luke 8:10.)

6:10 (2 Nephi 16:10). *"Make the heart of this people fat."* This statement describes the *consequence* of the people's rejection of Isaiah's message, not its *purpose.* The heart was regarded by the Hebrew people as the seat of understanding. The hearts of the wicked would be hardened or become insensitive to Isaiah's message. "Just as the hardening of one's physical heart's arteries can cause death to the body, so, in like manner, can the hardening of one's spiritual arteries lead to spiritual death." (DCE, 230.)

6:10 (2 Nephi 16:10). *"Make their ears heavy."* Ears that are heavy are ears that are deaf. The people don't "open their ears to hear" (see 3 Nephi 11:3–5) and consequently don't understand the message given. Again, this is a *consequence* of the people's rejection of the prophet's message.

6:10 (2 Nephi 16:10). *"<u>Be</u> convert<u>ed</u> and be healed."* Spiritual healing comes through repenting and turning to God. One cannot be cured of the sickness caused by sin without the intervention and mercy of the great Healer, Jesus Christ. Conversion requires change, turning away from the ways of the world and turning towards the will of God.

6:11 (2 Nephi 16:11). *"Then said I, Lord, how long? And he answered, Until the cities be wasted without inhabitant."* "The prophet wonders how long men will be so [rebellious and hardhearted], and the Lord answers: until mortal man is no more." (LDSKJ, Isaiah 6:11, footnote 11*a*.)

6:13 (2 Nephi 16:13). *"Yet in it shall be a tenth, and it shall return."* This may be symbolic of the Lord's portion—a tithe. Only those who *will be* (desire to be and live accordingly) the Lord's people will return or be gathered in with the redeemed of the Lord. The number of these returnees will be but a fraction ("a tenth") of the original group. (See Amos 5:3.)

6:13 (2 Nephi 16:13). *"And shall be eaten, as a teil tree and as an oak whose substance is in them when they cast their leaves."* Although the branches of Israel will have been broken off the main tree and scattered—casting off their dead and dried up leaves—the stump of the tree will yet produce edible fruit. According to the parable of the vineyard (see Jacob 5), scattered branches will be grafted into the original tree and its stump will produce good (edible) fruit. The potential to produce life ("substance") remains in the old tree. Teil tree, as used in this context, is "a rare English word for lime or linden tree. . . . Elsewhere the Heb[rew] word used is incorrectly translated [as] oak." (LDSBD, p. 780.)

6:13 (2 Nephi 16:13). *"The holy seed."* The consecrated remnant of Israel that will return and produce a new generation of believers. The Lord declared unto Israel, "thou art an holy people." (Deuteronomy 7:6.)

CHAPTER 7

Isaiah 7 and 2 Nephi 17

OVERVIEW

Perhaps the main message of this chapter is that we must trust in God and His promises of protection in spite of the threats of mortals. Isaiah sought unsuccessfully to teach this to Ahaz, king of Judah. At this time, the southern kingdom of Judah was threatened by an alliance of the northern kingdom of Israel with Syria. The kings of these two countries wanted Ahaz to join them in an alliance against the Assyrians, but the king of Judah decided to cast his lot with the Assyrians.

In verse 3, the Lord sends Isaiah to counsel Ahaz against entering any alliances; instead, he is to depend on the protection of the God of Israel. Isaiah prophesies that the threat from the northern kingdom and from Syria will come to naught and that these two countries will be the ones that will be destroyed.

The Lord offers to give the disbelieving Ahaz a sign of the verity of His words, but the king refuses to ask for confirmation of the prophecy. The Lord gives the king a sign anyway: a sign involving the future birth of the Messiah through the house of David.

Because of rejecting divine counsel, Judah suffers consequences that could have been avoided. The people are oppressed, scattered, and taken into slavery. The once-fertile lands are left barren of crops and become useful only for wandering animals.

COMMENTARY

Isaiah 7:1–9 and 2 Nephi 17:1–9

At this point in the book of Isaiah, the kingdom of Judah (the southern kingdom) is undergoing a great deal of turmoil. The capital city has been attacked, although unsuccessfully, by the kings of Israel (the northern kingdom) and Syria. The invading kings' desire is to place a puppet ruler over Judah, one who would be responsive to their desire to form a solid anti-Assyrian block. Seemingly concerned about the city's water supply, Ahaz is evidently inspecting it when he is approached by the prophet Isaiah, accompanied by his son, with a message from the Lord. Ahaz is told not to worry about the alliance of his enemies, for it will be broken ("It shall not stand") and their plans of invasion will not succeed ("neither shall it come to pass").

Isaiah 7	2 Nephi 17
1 And it came to pass in the days of Ahaz the son of Jotham, the son of Uzziah, king of Judah, that Rezin <u>the</u> king of Syria, and Pekah the son of Remaliah, king of Israel, went up toward Jerusalem to war against it, but could not prevail against it.	1 And it came to pass in the days of Ahaz the son of Jotham, the son of Uzziah, king of Judah, that Rezin, king of Syria, and Pekah the son of Remaliah, king of Israel, went up toward Jerusalem to war against it, but could not prevail against it.
2 And it was told the house of David, saying, Syria is confederate with Ephraim. And his heart was moved, and the heart of his people, as the trees of the wood are moved with the wind.	2 And it was told the house of David, saying<u>:</u> Syria is confederate with Ephraim. And his heart was moved, and the heart of his people, as the trees of the wood are moved with the wind.

3 Then said the Lord unto Isaiah, Go forth now to meet Ahaz, thou, and *Shear-jashub* thy son, at the end of the conduit of the upper pool in the highway of the fuller's field;

4 And say unto him, Take heed, and be quiet; fear not, neither be *fainthearted* for the two tails of these smoking firebrands, for the fierce anger of Rezin with Syria, and of the son of Remaliah.

5 Because Syria, Ephraim, and the son of Remaliah, have taken evil counsel against thee, saying,

6 Let us go up against Judah, and vex it, and let us make a breach therein for us, and set a king in the midst of it, even the son of Tabeal:

7 Thus saith the Lord God, It shall not stand, neither shall it come to pass.

8 For the head of Syria is Damascus, and the head of Damascus is Rezin; and within *threescore* and five years shall Ephraim be broken, that it be not a people.

9 And the head of Ephraim is Samaria, and the head of Samaria is Remaliah's son. If ye will not believe, surely ye shall not be established.

3 Then said the Lord unto Isaiah: Go forth now to meet Ahaz, thou and *Shearjashub* thy son, at the end of the conduit of the upper pool in the highway of the fuller's field;

4 And say unto him: Take heed, and be quiet; fear not, neither be *faint-hearted* for the two tails of these smoking firebrands, for the fierce anger of Rezin with Syria, and of the son of Remaliah.

5 Because Syria, Ephraim, and the son of Remaliah, have taken evil counsel against thee, saying:

6 Let us go up against Judah and vex it, and let us make a breach therein for us, and set a king in the midst of it, yea, the son of Tabeal.

7 Thus saith the Lord God: It shall not stand, neither shall it come to pass.

8 For the head of Syria is Damascus, and the head of Damascus, Rezin; and within *three score* and five years shall Ephraim be broken that it be not a people.

9 And the head of Ephraim is Samaria, and the head of Samaria is Remaliah's son. If ye will not believe surely ye shall not be established.

7:2 (2 Nephi 17:2). "*The house of David.*" The king and royal court of Judah.

7:2 (2 Nephi 17:2). "*Syria is confederate with Ephraim.*" Syria has entered into an alliance with Ephraim (the dominant tribe of the northern kingdom of Israel).

7:2 (2 Nephi 17:2). "*His heart was moved, and the heart of his people, as the trees of the wood are moved with the wind.*" The king's heart trembled with fear, as did the hearts of his people, upon hearing of the Ephraim-Syria confederacy. They shook as trees swaying in the wind.

7:3 (2 Nephi 17:3). "*Shear-jashub thy son.*" One of two known sons of Isaiah, his name means "the remnant shall return." The reason for the son's presence on this occasion has been suggested by Monte Nyman: "It may have been to remind Ahaz of the prophecy that Judah would not be utterly destroyed, or it may have been a reminder that the Lord had prophesied concerning Judah in order to prepare Ahaz for the prophecy which Isaiah was to deliver." (GAWI, 54.)

7:3 (2 Nephi 17:3). "*The conduit of the upper pool.*" The canal, aqueduct, or tunnel that carried the water supply into the city. (See 2 Kings 20:20.) Controlling this source of water appears to have been a major objective of the invading armies. (See 2 Kings 18:17; Isaiah 36:2.)

7:3 (2 Nephi 17:3). "*In the highway of the fuller's field.*" "By way of the launderers' field near the stream below the pool of Siloam." (LDSKJ, Isaiah 7:3, footnote *c*.) Fullers were those who cleansed and whitened garments in large tubs.

7:4 (2 Nephi 17:4). "*The two tails of these smoking firebrands.*" Judah's king is told not to fear his enemies—King Rezin of Syria and King Pekah ("the son of Remaliah") of Israel. A firebrand is a torch. When the fire is spent, smoke is all that is left. Isaiah tells Ahaz that his two enemies have little fire left in them.

7:5 (2 Nephi 17:5). "*Ephraim, and the son of Remaliah.*" Ephraim was the lead tribe of the northern kingdom and Pekah was the king. Isaiah appears to show his disdain for King Pekah by not mentioning his name, referring to him as "the son of Remaliah." That Pekah deserved this scorn is evident by this description of him: "And he did that which was evil in the sight of the Lord: he departed not from the sins of Jeroboam . . . , who made Israel to sin." (2 Kings 15:28.)

7:6 (2 Nephi 17:6). "*Let us make a breach therein for us, and set a king in the midst of it, even the son of Tabeal.*" The two enemy kings, Pekah and Rezin, desired to conquer Judah and divide it up. They proposed placing a puppet king ("the son of Tabeal") on Judah's throne. They obviously had confidence in their ability to control this proposed king.

7:8 (2 Nephi 17:8). "*The head of Syria is Damascus, and the head of Damascus is Rezin.*" Damascus is the capital city of Syria and King Rezin is head of the government.

7:8 (2 Nephi 17:8). "*Within threescore and five years shall Ephraim be broken, that it be not a people.*" Victor Ludlow explains: "In this prophecy, Isaiah promises that the Syro-Israelite alliance will fail and that Israel will be scattered within sixty-five years. The fulfillment came about in successive stages. First, Tiglath-Pileser III (Pul) attacked Syria and Israel in 732 B.C. and took many Israelites captive to Assyria, especially those from the northern tribes. Secondly, in 730–727, Pul annexed the Transjordan area and deported large numbers of the Israelite tribes from that area to the far reaches of the Assyrian Empire. Third, in 726, Hoshea refused to pay Assyrian tribute, and Pul's successor, Shalmaneser, retaliated by attacking Israel and besieging Samaria, which fell in 722 B.C. Thus, within a dozen years of Isaiah's prophecy, the alliance had completely failed, and three major groups of

Israelites had been deported. Finally, large groups of the Israelites fled from Assyria to the remote areas northward and became the lost Ten Tribes of Israel. Apparently, within about fifty years of their leaving Assyria, they were scattered so widely that many of them no longer existed as a cohesive group. Thereby Isaiah's prophecy to Ephraim was completely realized." (IPSP, 141–42.)

7:9 (2 Nephi 17:9). "*The head of Ephraim is Samaria, and the head of Samaria is Remaliah's son.*" Samaria is the capital of the northern kingdom ("Ephraim"), and King Pekah ("Remaliah's son") is the head of the government.

7:9 (2 Nephi 17:9). "*If ye will not believe, surely ye shall not be established.*" "If you lack faith, you will not be saved." (LDSKJ, Isaiah 7:9, footnote *b*.)

Isaiah 7:10–16 and 2 Nephi 17:10–16

Evidently King Ahaz had little faith in the promise of verse 9, for Isaiah followed with a challenge from the Lord. The king was invited to ask for a sign designed to build his faith in God's power to save. Ahaz rejected the invitation, not because he was fearful of "tempting" the Lord but because he had already put his trust in "the arm of flesh" of the Assyrians. He simply did not want to "try" the Lord or "prove" the power of God's word.

Isaiah gave the king a divine sign involving the future birth of the Messiah, who would come from the royal house of David. The prophet further prophesied that Judah would be rid of the two kings who were then tormenting her.

10 Moreover the Lord spake again unto Ahaz, saying,	10 Moreover, the Lord spake again unto Ahaz, saying:
11 Ask thee a sign of the Lord thy God; ask it either in the depth, or in the height above.	11 Ask thee a sign of the Lord thy God; ask it either in the depths, or in the heights above.

12 But Ahaz said, I will not ask, neither will I tempt the Lord.

12 But Ahaz said: I will not ask, neither will I tempt the Lord.

13 And he said, Hear ye now, O house of David; Is it a small thing for you to weary men, but will ye weary my God also?

13 And he said: Hear ye now, O house of David; is it a small thing for you to weary men, but will ye weary my God also?

14 Therefore the Lord himself shall give you a sign; Behold, a virgin shall conceive, and bear a son, and shall call his name Immanuel.

14 Therefore, the Lord himself shall give you a sign—Behold, a virgin shall conceive, and shall bear a son, and shall call his name Immanuel.

15 Butter and honey shall he eat, that he may know to refuse the evil, and choose the good.

15 Butter and honey shall he eat, that he may know to refuse the evil and to choose the good.

16 For before the child shall know to refuse the evil, and choose the good, the land that thou abhorrest shall be forsaken of both her kings.

16 For before the child shall know to refuse the evil and choose the good, the land that thou abhorrest shall be forsaken of both her kings.

7:11 (2 Nephi 17:11). *"Ask thee a sign."* Some ask, how does this request that Ahaz ask for a sign comport with the scriptural injunction that one should not seek for signs? (See Matthew 12:39; Isaiah 5:18–19.) Foremost, it was the Lord who offered to provide a sign. Additionally, there have been occasions when, for His purposes, the Lord has willingly provided such signs. (See Judges 6:36–40.) In latter-day revelation the Savior said: "Yea, signs come by faith, not by the will of men, nor as they please, but *by the will of God*." (D&C 63:10; italics added.)

7:11 (2 Nephi 17:11). *"Either in the depth, or in the height above."* Ahaz is told he can ask for his sign to be shown from the depths of Sheol, or the world of departed spirits, to the heights of the heavens above.

7:13 (2 Nephi 17:13). *"You [are willing to] . . . weary men, . . . will ye weary my God also?"* Isaiah declares that Ahaz and his royal court have exhausted the patience of men (particularly the prophet's patience) and asks if they must also weary God with their obstinateness and lack of faith.

7:14–16 (2 Nephi 17:14–16). *"A virgin shall conceive, and bear a son, and shall call his name Immanuel."* The New Testament identifies this as a prophecy of the conception and subsequent birth of Mary's divine Son—Jesus Christ—whose title of Immanuel means "God is with us." (Matthew 1:18–23.) The Book of Mormon adds additional testimony to the virgin birth of the Savior. (1 Nephi 11:14–21; Alma 7:9–10.) Latter-day leaders have added their testimony to this prophecy's being fulfilled in the divine birth of the Christ child.

Biblical scholars, however, question the application of this prophecy to the birth in Bethlehem. They indicate that the following two verses (15–16) make such an interpretation difficult to accept. Critics say the fulfillment of this prophecy had to be in the days of Isaiah. Latter-day Saint scholars have appropriately responded to the questions raised, adding strength to the messianic witness of the prophecy. Among these is the excellent explanation offered by Dr. Sidney B. Sperry:

"Now if Immanuel of verse 14 is the Messiah, the Savior, what is his connection with the 'child' of verses 15 and 16? Many Jewish commentators, not to mention some non-Jewish ones, think that the 'virgin' or 'young woman' of verse 14 may be a woman of the royal family, or any other young woman of Judah, and that her son, a boy whom she called Immanuel, does not refer to the Christ. Personally, I am inclined to accept Immanuel as a reference to the Savior, and especially in the light of [Isaiah 8:8], where Judah is referred to as Immanuel's land. The allusion to Immanuel suggests that the land of Judah (about which Ahaz was concerned) had a great destiny to fulfill, and hence that it was not about to be destroyed by Syria and Ephraim. Verses 15 and 16 of [Isaiah 7] simply make our Lord's infancy a symbolic representation of the short-lived nature of the threat to Judah." (BMC, 199; see also IPSP, 143–45; GAWI, 56–59.)

Monte Nyman adds this insightful comment: "The point was that, even if Ahaz rejected the counsel and advice of Jehovah through his prophet, and even if Ahaz led his people into captivity, the Lord Immanuel would still come as had been prophesied." (GAWI, 58.)

7:15, 22 (2 Nephi 17:15, 22). "*Butter and honey shall he eat.*" Butter (curd) and honey were symbolic of a desolated and depopulated land, other foods not being available. The land would be occupied by grazing animals, including those which are milk producing, and covered with swarms of bees. Butter and honey were food easily available to the poor.

7:16 (2 Nephi 17:16). "*Before the child shall know to refuse the evil and choose the good, the land that thou abhorrest shall be forsaken of both her kings.*" *Before* the child matures, knowing how to choose good from evil, Judah's two enemies—King Rezin of Syria and King Pekah of Ephraim—would be deposed. In other words, within just a few years (before a child can mature), the threatening neighbors to the north would be destroyed. For a fulfillment of this prophecy, see 2 Kings 15:29–30 and 16:9.

Isaiah 7:17–25 and 2 Nephi 17:17–25

With King Ahaz having rejected the word of the Lord, the prophet now proceeds to pronounce the penalties that would befall the king and the people of Judah. Instead of becoming a partner with the Assyrians, Ahaz and his people would become their prey. They would experience a devastation such as they had not seen since the days the northern tribes broke away from the united kingdom of the twelve tribes. Flies and bees would infest the land, and thorns and briers would take over the once-productive land. The people would be taken into captivity, and those who remain would have to forage for food.

17 The Lord shall bring upon thee, and upon thy people, and upon thy father's house, days that have not come, from the day that Ephraim departed from Judah; even the king of Assyria.

18 And it shall come to pass in that day, that the Lord shall hiss for the fly that is in the uttermost part of <u>the rivers of</u> Egypt, and for the bee that is in the land of Assyria.

19 And they shall come, and shall rest all of them in the desolate valleys, and in the holes of the rocks, and upon all thorns, and upon all bushes.

20 In the same day shall the Lord shave with a razor that is hired, <u>namely,</u> by them beyond the river, by the king of Assyria, the head, and the hair of the feet<u>:</u> and it shall also consume the beard.

21 And it shall come to pass in that day, <u>that</u> a man shall nourish a young cow, and two sheep;

22 And it shall come to pass, for the abundance of milk <u>that</u> they shall give he shall eat butter<u>:</u> for butter and honey shall every one eat that is left in the land.

17 The Lord shall bring upon thee, and upon thy people, and upon thy father's house, days that have not come from the day that Ephraim departed from Judah, the king of Assyria.

18 And it shall come to pass in that day that the Lord shall hiss for the fly that is in the uttermost part of Egypt, and for the bee that is in the land of Assyria.

19 And they shall come, and shall rest all of them in the desolate valleys, and in the holes of the rocks, and upon all thorns, and upon all bushes.

20 In the same day shall the Lord shave with a razor that is hired, by them beyond the river, by the king of Assyria, the head, and the hair of the feet; and it shall also consume the beard.

21 And it shall come to pass in that day, a man shall nourish a young cow and two sheep;

22 And it shall come to pass, for the abundance of milk they shall give he shall eat butter; for butter and honey shall every one eat that is left in the land.

23 And it shall come to pass in that day, <u>that</u> every place shall be, where there were a thousand vines at a thousand silverlings, <u>it</u> shall <u>even</u> be for briers and thorns.

23 And it shall come to pass in that day, every place shall be, where there were a thousand vines at a thousand silverlings, <u>which</u> shall be for briers and thorns.

24 With arrows and with bows shall men come thither; because all the land shall become briers and thorns.

24 With arrows and with bows shall men come thither, because all the land shall become briers and thorns.

25 And <u>on</u> all hills that shall be digged with the mattock, there shall not come thither the fear of briers and thorns: but it shall be for the sending forth of oxen, and <u>for</u> the treading of lesser cattle.

25 And all hills that shall be digged with the mattock, there shall not come thither the fear of briers and thorns; but it shall be for the sending forth of oxen, and the treading of lesser cattle.

7:17 (2 Nephi 17:17). "*Days that have not come, from the day that Ephraim departed from Judah.*" As noted above, this has reference to the days of Jeroboam when the Ten Tribes revolted from the united kingdom to form their own kingdom. (1 Kings 12.)

7:18–19 (2 Nephi 17:18–19). "*The Lord shall hiss for the fly . . . and for the bee. . . . And they shall come, and shall rest . . . upon all.*" There are at least two possible interpretations of this phrase. The fly and the bee might be representative of invading forces from the countries of Egypt and Assyria, who will come upon the people no matter where they are hiding. Another possible interpretation is that the devastation of the land of Judah will be so severe that swarms of flies and bees will be attracted (summoned or hissed for) to the desolate land from Egypt and Assyria.

7:20 (2 Nephi 17:20). "*Shave with a razor that is hired.*" "The land will be depopulated by a foreign invader." (LDSKJ, Isaiah 7:20, footnote *a*.) Shaving the beards and heads of captives was a common practice of invading armies. It was a sign of humiliation, particularly for Hebrew men. (See 2 Samuel 10:4–5.) It was also done to facilitate prisoner sanitation and to keep them separate from the rest of the population. (In their shaved condition they were easily identified, thus limiting escape possibilities.)

Monte Nyman suggests that "the Lord's 'shaving with a razor that is hired' symbolizes the comfort of having someone else perform a tedious or unpleasant task, such as . . . the Lord's using the king of Assyria to do the unpleasant task of punishing the wickedness of Judah." (GAWI, 59.)

7:21 (2 Nephi 17:21). "*A man shall nourish a young cow, and two sheep.*" "Only a few self-sustaining survivors shall remain" in the land. (LDSKJ, Isaiah 7:21, footnote *a*.)

7:22 (2 Nephi 17:22). "*For butter and honey shall every one eat that is left in the land.*" See commentary on verse 15.

7:23 (2 Nephi 17:23). "*Where there were a thousand vines at a thousand silverlings.*" This is a further indication of the land's desolation. Where once the fruit of productive vines had brought in pieces of silver ("silverlings"), there would now be only briers and thorns.

7:24 (2 Nephi 17:24). "*With arrows and bows shall men come thither.*" The once-agricultural land would now be a wilderness good only for hunters.

7:25 (2 Nephi 17:25). "*Digged with the mattock.*" Cultivated with the hoe.

7:25 (2 Nephi 17:25). "*Lesser cattle.*" Sheep or goats.

CHAPTER 8

Isaiah 8 and 2 Nephi 18

OVERVIEW

Having been unsuccessful in his efforts to persuade King Ahaz to put his trust in the Lord rather than in the Assyrians, Isaiah next turns his attention to the people of Judah. He repeats the assurance given in the previous chapter to their king that in a very short time Syria and the northern kingdom (Ephraim or Israel) will be destroyed. However, the faith of the people is as shortsighted as their royal ruler, and as a consequence Isaiah prophesies that the Assyrians will invade the southern kingdom of Judah.

Ultimately, Judah's enemies will be punished for their aggression. A remnant of Judah will survive, "for God is with us," declared Isaiah.

The prophet relates the Lord's personal counsel to him that he should not get caught up in the persuasions or fears of the people. Let God be your refuge and sanctuary, the prophet is told. Isaiah is informed that the wicked will stumble over the Lord's teachings. The apostle Peter would later teach this same concept: "Unto you therefore which believe he [the Lord Jesus Christ] is precious: but unto them which be disobedient . . . a stone of stumbling, and a rock of offence, even to them which stumble at the word, being disobedient." (1 Peter 2:7–8.)

Isaiah is told to record his testimony, and he testifies of his willingness to follow the Lord. He concludes the chapter with warnings against seeking spiritual help from the wrong sources. God is the only source of light. Those who seek elsewhere will find themselves immersed in darkness.

COMMENTARY

Isaiah 8:1–4 and 2 Nephi 18:1–4

Isaiah is told to write the name of his newborn son, Maher-shalal-hash-baz, on a large scroll or tablet. The child's name, which incidentally is the longest word in the Bible, means "to speed to the spoil, he hasteneth the prey" ("quick to the plunder, swift to the spoil"). The name was symbolic of the pending fall of Damascus (capital of Syria) and Samaria (capital of the northern kingdom) to the invading Assyrian armies.

Isaiah 8	2 Nephi 18
1 Moreover the Lord said unto me, Take thee a great roll, and write in it with a man's pen concerning Maher-shalal-hash-baz.	1 Moreover, the word of the Lord said unto me: Take thee a great roll, and write in it with a man's pen, concerning Maher-shalal-hash-baz.
2 And I took unto me faithful witnesses to record, Uriah the priest, and Zechariah the son of Jeberechiah.	2 And I took unto me faithful witnesses to record, Uriah the priest, and Zechariah the son of Jeberechiah.
3 And I went unto the prophetess; and she conceived, and bare a son. Then said the Lord to me, Call his name Maher-shalal-hash-baz.	3 And I went unto the prophetess; and she conceived and bare a son. Then said the Lord to me: Call his name, Maher-shalal-hash-baz.
4 For before the child shall have knowledge to cry, My father, and my mother, the riches of Damascus and the spoil of Samaria shall be taken away before the king of Assyria.	4 For behold, the child shall not have knowledge to cry, My father, and my mother, before the riches of Damascus and the spoil of Samaria shall be taken away before the king of Assyria.

8:1 (2 Nephi 18:1). *"Write in it with a man's pen."* In Hebrew this means an engraving tool of a man. In essence,

Isaiah is told to record his message with an ordinary or common writing tool.

8:2 (2 Nephi 18:2). "*I took unto me faithful witnesses to record.*" In keeping with the law of witnesses ("at the mouth of two witnesses . . . shall the matter be established" [Deuteronomy 19:15]), Isaiah has two witnesses on hand to record and testify of what was being said.

8:3 (2 Nephi 18:3). "*The prophetess.*" Isaiah's wife. It is reasonable to assume that Isaiah's wife had heard him speak often of the coming of the Messiah and that she too had a testimony of Christ. In this respect, it is of interest to note the words of President Wilford Woodruff: "Anybody is a prophet who has a testimony of Jesus Christ, for that is the spirit of prophecy." (JD 13:165.) The term "prophetess" is also used to identify other faithful women of the Bible such as Miriam (Exodus 15:20), Deborah (Judges 4:4–5), and Anna (Luke 2:36–38).

8:4 (2 Nephi 18:4). "*Before the child shall have knowledge to cry.*" Before Isaiah's son is old enough to speak, saying "my father, and my mother," the capitals of Syria and the northern kingdom will be overrun by the Assyrians.

Isaiah 8:5–10 and 2 Nephi 18:5–10

Because the people of Judah refused to accept the word of the Lord through His prophet, Isaiah prophesies they too will be victimized by the Assyrians. Instead of being soothed by the gentle "waters of Shiloah," which represented the tender care of Christ, they will be ravaged by the floodwaters of the invading Assyrians. Yet there is hope. In spite of the alliances formed against her, Judah will yet be the birthplace of the promised Messiah.

5 The Lord spake also unto me again, saying,	5 The Lord spake also unto me again, saying:

6 Forasmuch as this people refuseth the waters of Shiloah that go softly, and rejoice in Rezin and Remaliah's son;

7 Now therefore, behold, the Lord bringeth up upon them the waters of the river, strong and many, even the king of Assyria, and all his glory: and he shall come up over all his channels, and go over all his banks:

8 And he shall pass through Judah; he shall overflow and go over, he shall reach even to the neck; and the stretching out of his wings shall fill the breadth of thy land, O Immanuel.

9 Associate yourselves, O ye people, and ye shall be broken in pieces; and give ear, all ye of far countries: gird yourselves, and ye shall be broken in pieces; gird yourselves, and ye shall be broken in pieces.

10 Take counsel together, and it shall come to *nought;* speak the word, and it shall not stand: for God is with us.

6 Forasmuch as this people refuseth the waters of Shiloah that go softly, and rejoice in Rezin and Remaliah's son;

7 Now therefore, behold, the Lord bringeth up upon them the waters of the river, strong and many, even the king of Assyria and all his glory; and he shall come up over all his channels, and go over all his banks.

8 And he shall pass through Judah; he shall overflow and go over, he shall reach even to the neck; and the stretching out of his wings shall fill the breadth of thy land, O Immanuel.

9 Associate yourselves, O ye people, and ye shall be broken in pieces; and give ear all ye of far countries; gird yourselves, and ye shall be broken in pieces; gird yourselves, and ye shall be broken in pieces.

10 Take counsel together, and it shall come to *naught;* speak the word, and it shall not stand; for God is with us.

8:6 (2 Nephi 18:6). "*The waters of Shiloah.*" Isaiah uses the imagery of the soft-flowing waters of Jerusalem's only perennial spring to symbolize the soothing care of the Lord. It may be a parallel that the Lord's voice is generally described as "still" and "small," rather than as booming or loud. (See 1 Kings 19:12.)

8:6 (2 Nephi 18:6). "*Rejoice in Rezin and Remaliah's son.*" As noted in Isaiah 7, Rezin was the king of Syria and the son of Remaliah was Pekah, king of Ephraim or the northern kingdom of Israel. The word "rejoice" is somewhat puzzling. This may be a reference to possible rejoicing of the Judeans when Syria and Ephraim are attacked by the Assyrians. However, as noted in the commentary on the next two verses, Judah will also be overrun by the same invading forces.

8:7 (2 Nephi 18:7). "*The Lord bringeth up upon them the waters of the river.*" The Assyrians will come upon the northern kingdom ("them," verse 7) and the southern kingdom ("Judah," verse 8) like raging, torrential waters overflowing the banks of the riverbed.

8:8 (2 Nephi 18:8). "*He shall reach even to the neck; and the stretching out of his wings shall fill the breadth of thy land, O Immanuel.*" This word imagery is calculated to paint a picture of the widespread destruction the invading armies will have on the land. Instead of the gentle waters of Shiloah lapping at their feet, they will have the floodwaters of the Assyrians reaching to their necks and stretching out as wings to cover the entire land. By referring to the land as "Immanuel," meaning "God is with us," Isaiah reminds the people that the promised Immanuel (Isaiah 7:14) will yet be born in that land. Furthermore, it is an assurance that the people will not be entirely forsaken.

8:9–10 (2 Nephi 18:9–10). "*Associate yourselves, O ye people, and ye shall be broken in pieces.*" Verses 9 and 10 appear to be a warning that regardless of the alliances that are formed among those of "far countries," regardless of their conspiring ("counsel[ing] together"), their efforts will be unsuccessful ("come to nought"). They will be "broken to pieces" because Judah, the land of Immanuel ("God is with us"), will yet be spared.

Isaiah 8:11–18 and 2 Nephi 18:11–18

With great power the Lord tells Isaiah not to follow the ways of the people to whom he was to preach and prophesy.

He is not to fear the people but to trust in the Lord, who will be a place of safety for those who trust Him but a stumbling block to the disbelievers. The prophet is told to record his testimony—which we are now reading—and he affirms his willingness to follow the Lord.

11 For the Lord spake thus to me with a strong hand, and instructed me that I should not walk in the way of this people, saying,

11 For the Lord spake thus to me with a strong hand, and instructed me that I should not walk in the way of this people, saying:

12 Say ye not, A confederacy, to all <u>them</u> to whom this people shall say, A confederacy; neither fear ye their fear, nor be afraid.

12 Say ye not, A confederacy, to all to whom this people shall say, A confederacy; neither fear ye their fear, nor be afraid.

13 Sanctify the Lord of <u>h</u>osts himself; and let him be your fear, and let him be your dread.

13 Sanctify the Lord of <u>H</u>osts himself, and let him be your fear, and let him be your dread.

14 And he shall be for a sanctuary; but for a stone of stumbling and for a rock of *offence* to both the houses of Israel, for a gin and <u>for</u> a snare to the inhabitants of Jerusalem.

14 And he shall be for a sanctuary; but for a stone of stumbling, and for a rock of *offense* to both the houses of Israel, for a gin and a snare to the inhabitants of Jerusalem.

15 And many among them shall stumble, and fall, and be broken, and be snared, and be taken.

15 And many among them shall stumble and fall, and be broken, and be snared, and be taken.

16 Bind up the testimony, seal the law among my disciples.

16 Bind up the testimony, seal the law among my disciples.

17 And I will wait upon the Lord, that hideth his face from the house of Jacob, and I will look for him.

17 And I will wait upon the Lord, that hideth his face from the house of Jacob, and I will look for him.

18 Behold, I and the children whom the Lord hath given me are for signs and for wonders in Israel from the Lord of <u>h</u>osts, which dwelleth in <u>m</u>ount Zion.

18 Behold, I and the children whom the Lord hath given me are for signs and for wonders in Israel from the Lord of <u>H</u>osts, which dwelleth in <u>M</u>ount Zion.

8:11 (2 Nephi 18:11). *"The Lord spake thus to me with a strong hand."* Jehovah spoke to Isaiah with great power.

8:12 (2 Nephi 18:12). *"Say ye not, A confederacy, to all them to whom this people shall say, A confederacy."* "Judah should not rely on secret plots [confederacies] with others for safety." (LDSKJ, Isaiah 8:12, footnote *a*.) Monte Nyman suggests that this verse implies that "Isaiah was forbidden to preach unto Judah." (GAWI, 65.) Some newer translations of the Bible render this verse as: "Do not call conspiracy everything that these people call conspiracy."

8:13 (2 Nephi 18:13). *"Sanctify the Lord . . . and let him be your fear, and let him be your dread."* Regard the Lord as a holy being and act reverently and humbly before Him. Don't be afraid of that which others are afraid of; only be afraid of offending the Lord.

8:14 (2 Nephi 18:14). *"And he shall be for a sanctuary; but for a stone of stumbling and for a rock of offence."* God will be a "security for those who trust him, but dismay and suffering for unbelievers." (LDSKJ, Isaiah 8:14, footnote *a*.) Christ is the "stone of Israel." (D&C 50:44; DCE, 566.) The Book of Mormon prophet Jacob prophesied: "I perceive by the workings of the Spirit which is in me, that by the stumbling of the Jews they will reject the stone upon which they might build and have safe foundation." (Jacob 4:15.)

8:14 (2 Nephi 18:14). *"To both the houses of Israel."* Both the southern kingdom (Judah) and the northern kingdom (Israel or Ephraim).

8:14 (2 Nephi 18:14). *"For a gin and for a snare."* For a trap and for a snare.

8:16 (2 Nephi 18:16). *"Bind up the testimony, seal the law among my disciples."* This wording is also found in latter-day revelation, although in two instances the Lord speaks of "sealing the testimony" and "binding the law." (D&C 88:84; 109:46; 133:71–72.) The law represents teachings and the testimony represents the inspired utterances of God's messengers. One commentary indicates that the binding and sealing of the law is a symbolic process whereby one actually ties up a parchment roll, whereon the teachings of the prophets are recorded, as a witness against those to whom the message was delivered. (TOVBC, 420.) Another suggests that this may be figurative in the sense of a document being signed in the hearts of the disciples. (BMC, 204.)

8:17 (2 Nephi 18:17). *"The Lord, that hideth his face from the house of Jacob."* Because the house of Israel (children of Jacob) departed from the ways of the Lord, He turned away His face in displeasure. "In a little wrath [displeasure] I hid my face from thee for a moment," the Lord would later declare. But then the promise would follow: "But with everlasting kindness will I have mercy on thee, saith the Lord thy Redeemer." (Isaiah 54:8.)

8:18 (2 Nephi 18:18). *"I and the children . . . are for signs and for wonders in Israel from the Lord."* The very names of Isaiah and his children are given as signs of the veracity of the prophet's words. Isaiah's name means "Jehovah saves;" *Shear-jashub* means "a remnant shall return;" and *Maher-shalal-hash-baz* means "he hastens the prey." These names are constant reminders to Israel's twelve tribes of the Lord's threats of disaster and of His promises of restoration.

Isaiah 8:19–22 and 2 Nephi 18:19–22

In the concluding verses of the chapter, Isaiah rebukes those who follow the apostate practices of seeking for spiritual help from sorcerers and soothsayers. God is the only source of true spiritual light and understanding. The people can find His word in the scriptures and teachings of the prophets.

19 And when they shall say unto you, Seek unto them that have familiar spirits, and unto wizards that peep, and that mutter: should not a people seek unto their God? for the living to the dead?

19 And when they shall say unto you: Seek unto them that have familiar spirits, and unto wizards that peep and mutter—should not a people seek unto their God for the living to hear from the dead?

20 To the law and to the testimony: if they speak not according to this word, it is because there is no light in them.

20 To the law and to the testimony; and if they speak not according to this word, it is because there is no light in them.

21 And they shall pass through it, hardly bestead and hungry: and it shall come to pass, that when they shall be hungry, they shall fret themselves, and curse their king and their God, and look upward.

21 And they shall pass through it hardly bestead and hungry; and it shall come to pass that when they shall be hungry, they shall fret themselves, and curse their king and their God, and look upward.

22 And they shall look unto the earth; and behold trouble and darkness, dimness of anguish; and they shall be driven to darkness.

22 And they shall look unto the earth and behold trouble, and darkness, dimness of anguish, and shall be driven to darkness.

8:19 (2 Nephi 18:19). *"Them that have familiar spirits, and unto wizards that peep, and that mutter."* The children of Israel are expressly forbidden to associate with those who deal in black magic, such as those who consult with evil or "familiar spirits" and sorcerers ("wizards"). (See also Deuteronomy 18:10–12.) To "peep" is to chirp as a bird. According to J. R. Dummelow, chirping refers "to the thin and feeble voice of ghosts from Sheol [hell]." (TOVBC, 420.)

8:19 (2 Nephi 18:19). "*Should not a people seek unto their God for the living to hear from the dead?*" The Book of Mormon text significantly clarifies this verse. This clarification is not an invitation for one to seek contact with the dead. It seems this is Isaiah's way of saying we must avoid seances and other such nonsense. Fortune tellers, wizards, sorcerers, soothsayers, and others who claim to conjure up contact with the spirit world should be avoided like the plague. There is no doubt they can make contact with the evil spirits in Satan's world, and those who play with this fire will get spiritually burned. God is the God over the living and the dead, and He does not grant foolish requests.

8:20 (2 Nephi 18:20). "*To the law and to the testimony.*" In addition to seeking answers from God (vs. 20), the people should look to the "law" (teachings or Torah) and to the "testimony" (witness of the prophets in the scriptures).

8:20 (2 Nephi 18:20). "*If they speak not according to this word, it is because there is no light in them.*" If the false spiritualist media fail to speak according to revealed truth (God's word, scriptures, law) it is because they are filled with darkness.

8:21 (2 Nephi 18:21). "*And they shall pass through it hardly bestead and hungry.*" "Israel would be taken into captivity because they would not hearken." (LDSKJ, Isaiah 8:21, footnote *a*.) A modern translation of this verse renders it as follows: "Distressed and hungry, they will roam through the land; when they are famished, they will become enraged and, looking upward, they will curse their king and their God." (New International Version of the Bible.)

8:21 (2 Nephi 18:21). "*When they shall be hungry, they shall fret.*" When the captive children of Israel finally recognize their spiritual emptiness, they will be agitated at themselves for their loss and curse King Ahaz, whom they will blame for their predicament, as well as blaspheme God for His absence.

8:22 (2 Nephi 18:22). *"And they shall look unto the earth; and behold trouble and darkness, . . . dimness of anguish."* In despair, the conquered and captive Israelites will look around and see nothing but difficulties and dark affliction.

CHAPTER 9

Isaiah 9 and 2 Nephi 19

OVERVIEW

Bible commentators apply the early verses in this chapter to others besides Jesus Christ, but Latter-day Saints view them as very messianic. The Light of Christ will shine in the earth and in the world of departed spirits. He shall take His rightful place upon David's throne.

In verses 8 through 21, the prophet speaks of the past and future judgments that are to come upon Israel and Judah. "In all fairness it should be pointed out that it is difficult to tell whether these verses are completely a prediction of future events or a review of past events," wrote Sidney B. Sperry. "Some authorities think they refer only to Israel (the Northern Kingdom). Personally," continued Dr. Sperry, "I shall take a middle course among the various views that have been presented over the years. The main thing for us to remember is that the prophet is giving a warning of disaster to all Israel whether it be illustrated by past events or whether by the prediction of future events." (BMC, 208.)

COMMENTARY

Isaiah 9:1–7 and 2 Nephi 19:1–7

Verse 1 is a transition between chapters 8 and 9 of Isaiah. In fact, in Hebrew versions of Isaiah it is included as the last verse of the previous chapter. Thus the beginning word ("Nevertheless") is a word of hope.

The children of Israel are promised that the darkness will not last forever; a light will break forth. They will experience joy as they are released from the yoke of their burden of oppression. They are promised that a child will be born upon whose shoulders the government will rightfully rest forever.

Isaiah 9	2 Nephi 19
1 Nevertheless the dimness shall not be such as was in her vexation, when at the first he lightly afflicted the land of Zebulun and the land of Naphtali, and afterward did more grievously afflict her by the way of the sea, beyond Jordan, in Galilee of the nations.	1 Nevertheless, the dimness shall not be such as was in her vexation, when at first he lightly afflicted the land of Zebulun, and the land of Napthali, and afterwards did more grievously afflict by the way of the Red Sea beyond Jordan in Galilee of the nations.
2 The people that walked in darkness have seen a great light: they that dwell in the land of the shadow of death, upon them hath the light shined.	2 The people that walked in darkness have seen a great light; they that dwell in the land of the shadow of death, upon them hath the light shined.
3 Thou hast multiplied the nations, and not increased the joy: they joy before thee according to the joy in harvest, and as men rejoice when they divide the spoil.	3 Thou hast multiplied the nation, and increased the joy—they joy before thee according to the joy in harvest, and as men rejoice when they divide the spoil.
4 For thou hast broken the yoke of his burden, and the staff of his shoulder, the rod of his oppressor, as in the day of Midian.	4 For thou hast broken the yoke of his burden, and the staff of his shoulder, the rod of his oppressor.
5 For every battle of the warrior is with confused noise, and garments rolled in blood; but this shall be with burning and fuel of fire.	5 For every battle of the warrior is with confused noise, and garments rolled in blood; but this shall be with burning and fuel of fire.

6 For unto us a child is born, unto us a son is given: and the government shall be upon his shoulder: and his name shall be called Wonderful, *Counsellor,* The mighty God, The everlasting Father, The Prince of Peace.

6 For unto us a child is born, unto us a son is given; and the government shall be upon his shoulder; and his name shall be called, Wonderful, *Counselor,* The Mighty God, The everlasting Father, The Prince of Peace.

7 Of the increase of his government and peace there shall be no end, upon the throne of David, and upon his kingdom, to order it, and to establish it with judgment and with justice from henceforth even *for ever.* The zeal of the Lord of hosts will perform this.

7 Of the increase of government and peace there is no end, upon the throne of David, and upon his kingdom to order it, and to establish it with judgment and with justice from henceforth, even *forever.* The zeal of the Lord of Hosts will perform this.

9:1 (2 Nephi 19:1). "*The dimness shall not be such as was in her vexation, when at the first he lightly afflicted the land of Zebulun and the land of Naphtali.*" The future dimness (dark affliction or gloom) mentioned in Isaiah 8:22 will be more difficult than that brought upon the people when Tiglath-pileser and Sargon II of Assyria previously attacked the lands of the tribes of Israel. (LDSKJ, Isaiah 9:1, footnote *b.*) The tribes of Zebulun and Naphtali occupied the northernmost borders of the promised land of Canaan. These lands were the first captured by the invading Assyrians.

9:1 (2 Nephi 19:1). "*Afterward did more grievously afflict her by the way of the Red Sea.*" One commentator suggests that this phrase "probably has reference to a later captivity by Assyria." (GAWI, 67.) However, another states: "The latter time is a future period when God will 'be heavy' (from the Hebrew root, *kaved*) with the land. Translators differ as to the meaning of this term, saying variously that God will 'make glorious,' 'deal heavily' . . . , or 'grievously afflict' . . . the area.

Besides the unsurety of what the Lord's actions will be, the precise time of this manifestation is not presented, and, for unknown reasons, the land area to be affected in the latter time is larger than that which was anciently attacked by the Assyrians." (IPSP, 152.)

9:2 (2 Nephi 19:2). "*The people that walked in darkness have seen a great light.*" The darkness of captivity and apostasy will be dispersed by the great light of Christ. (LDSKJ, Isaiah 9:2, footnote *a;* see also John 8:12; Matthew 4:13–16.)

9:2 (2 Nephi 19:2). "*They that dwell in the land of the shadow of death.*" It seems logical to apply this verse to those who live in the world of departed spirits. During the three days in which His earthly body lay in the borrowed tomb of Joseph of Arimathaea, the spirit body of Christ brought light to those living in the spirit world, "declaring liberty to the captives who had been faithful" and opening the doors of darkness enclosing the rebellious. (D&C 138:18; see also verses 1–37.)

9:3 (2 Nephi 19:3). "*Thou hast multiplied the nation, and increased the joy.*" The Book of Mormon changes the meaning of this statement by deleting the word "not" before "increased the joy." The children of Israel, as promised to father Abraham (Abraham 2:9–10), will become numerous. Their joy will be great in the birth of the promised Christ child. Isaiah compares their joy to that received at the harvest festival, a time of national rejoicing, or when soldiers are victorious.

9:4 (2 Nephi 19:4). "*Thou hast broken the yoke of his burden.*" Christ, the promised Messiah, will release them from physical and spiritual captivity. (Isaiah 10:27.)

9:4 (2 Nephi 19:4). "*The staff of his shoulder.*" Reference to the cane by which Israel has been beaten by her taskmasters. Christ will remove yokes, staffs, and rods from the hands of oppressors.

9:4 (2 Nephi 19:4). "*As in the day of Midian.*" Just as the Lord had delivered the Midianites into the hands of Gideon, so shall He release Israel from future bondage through His power. (See Judges 7:7–25.) The omission of this phrase in the Book of Mormon is noticeable. Monte Nyman states: "This could have been an intentional omission by Nephi, as it did not apply to his people." (GAWI, 68.)

9:5 (2 Nephi 19:5). "*For every battle of the warrior is with confused noise, and garments rolled in blood; but this shall be with burning and fuel of fire.*" Sidney Sperry interprets these phrases to read, "For every boot of him that tramps in tumult of battle . . . And every mantle rolled in blood . . . shall be for burning, fuel for fire." (BMC, 207.) "This 'burning' is to be the cleansing of the earth by fire prior to the setting up of the Messianic kingdom." (LDSKJ, Isaiah 9:5, footnote *b;* see also Ezekiel 39:9; BICQ, 103–4.)

9:6 (2 Nephi 19:6). "*For unto us a child is born . . . and the government shall be upon his shoulder.*" As noted in the chapter overview, various interpretations have been applied to the identity of the promised child, but the author's position is that it primarily refers to Christ. One of the better summaries of the various interpretations of this verse was given by Victor Ludlow:

"If Isaiah is prophesying about Hezekiah [the young king of Judah who helped deliver the Israelites from the Assyrians], then verse 3 describes the Israelites' joy at their deliverance; verse 4 portrays how the Assyrians were defeated in spite of their greater numbers, just as the many Midianites were by Gideon and his 300 men (Judg. 7); verse 5 describes the Assyrian casualties; and verses 6 and 7 tell us about Hezekiah's titles and righteous, peaceful rule as king.

"If the verses describe a righteous people fighting against wickedness, then verse 3 describes their joy at success, verses 4 and 5 portray the defeat of the enemy, and verses 6 and 7 describe a new age of millennial peace that may be assisted or ushered in by a messianic figure.

"Finally, the identification of the ruler in verses 3–7 with Jesus Christ has a number of possibilities, as verse 3 talks about his many followers who rejoice at the spiritual blessings he has provided; verse 4 describes how he was able to overcome the temptations of Satan, break the yoke of sin, and maintain power over the legions of Satan's devils; verse 5 symbolizes his atonement and the cleansing powers of baptism and the Holy Ghost; verse 6 presents some of his titles and roles; and verse 7 describes his eternal position as the Lord and King of this earth." (IPSP, 154.)

9:7 (2 Nephi 19:7). "*Of the increase of his government and peace there shall be no end.*" The resurrected Christ declared to His disciples: "All power is given unto me in heaven and in earth." (Matthew 28:18.) "And of his kingdom there shall be no end." (Luke 1:33.) His work and glory will roll on throughout the eternities. (See Moses 1:39.)

9:7 (2 Nephi 19:7). "*The throne of David.*" King David's throne is to be established through Christ forever. (2 Samuel 7:12–13; see also Luke 1:32.)

Isaiah 9:8–12 and 2 Nephi 19:8–12

The Lord's decreed word is to all of the house of Jacob, to Israel or Ephraim on the north and to Judah on the south. However, Samaria, the capital of the northern kingdom, is particularly singled out for stern words from the Lord. In spite of past punishment for their arrogance and disobedience, the people have not repented. Therefore, more trouble is to come their way.

8 The Lord sent a word *into* Jacob, and it hath lighted upon Israel.	8 The Lord sent his word *unto* Jacob and it hath lighted upon Israel.
9 And all the people shall know, even Ephraim and the inhabitant of Samaria, that say in the pride and stoutness of heart,	9 And all the people shall know, even Ephraim and the inhabitants of Samaria, that say in the pride and stoutness of heart:

10 The bricks are fallen down, but we will build with hewn stones: the *sycomores* are cut down, but we will change them into cedars.	10 The bricks are fallen down, but we will build with hewn stones; the *sycamores* are cut down, but we will change them into cedars.
11 Therefore the Lord shall set up the adversaries of Rezin against him, and join his enemies together;	11 Therefore the Lord shall set up the adversaries of Rezin against him, and join his enemies together;
12 The Syrians before, and the Philistines behind; and they shall devour Israel with open mouth. For all this his anger is not turned away, but his hand is stretched out still.	12 The Syrians before and the Philistines behind; and they shall devour Israel with open mouth. For all this his anger is not turned away, but his hand is stretched out still.

9:10 (2 Nephi 19:10). *"The bricks are fallen down, but we will build with hewn stones."* This is indicative of the pride and arrogance of the people. They boast they will replace the destroyed bricks and wood with materials of higher quality.

9:11 (2 Nephi 19:11). *"The Lord shall set up the adversaries of Rezin against him."* The possible meaning of this phrase has been provided by J. R. Dummelow: "Perhaps we should read [as do some Hebrew manuscripts] 'the princes of Rezin' [the king of Syria]; the meaning would then be that the Syrian allies of Israel [Isaiah 7:1–2] will turn against it." (TOVBC, 421–22.)

9:12 (2 Nephi 19:12). *"The Syrians before, and the Philistines behind."* Israel, the northern kingdom, would be attacked on the east by the Syrians and on the west by the Philistines.

9:12, 17, 21 (2 Nephi 19:12, 17, 21). *"His anger is not turned away, but his hand is stretched out still."* While the Lord is displeased, dispensing justice on His rebellious people, He is still available to them if only they will turn to him. (Also see commentary on Isaiah 5:25 and 10:4.)

Isaiah 9:13–17 and 2 Nephi 19:13–17

In spite of the dire predictions that await them, and the predicament in which they find themselves, the people stubbornly refuse to repent and return to the Lord of Hosts. They are led by corrupt leaders who lead them astray. The scriptures remind us that "when the wicked rule the people mourn." (D&C 98:9; see also Proverbs 29:2.) Because of their apostasy, they will be destroyed or scattered.

13 For the people turneth not unto him that smiteth them, neither do they seek the Lord of <u>h</u>osts.	13 For the people turneth not unto him that smiteth them, neither do they seek the Lord of <u>H</u>osts.
14 Therefore *the Lord will* cut off from Israel head and tail, branch and rush, in one day.	14 Therefore *will the Lord* cut off from Israel head and tail, branch and rush in one day.
15 The ancient <u>and honourable</u>, he is the head; and the prophet that teacheth lies, he is the tail.	15 The ancient, he is the head; and the prophet that teacheth lies, he is the tail.
16 For the leaders of this people cause them to err; and they that are led of them are destroyed.	16 For the leaders of this people cause them to err; and they that are led of them are destroyed.
17 Therefore the Lord shall have no joy in their young men, neither shall have mercy on their fatherless and widows<u>:</u> for every one is *an* hypocrite and an evildoer, and every mouth speaketh folly. For all this his anger is not turned away, but his hand is stretched out still.	17 Therefore the Lord shall have no joy in their young men, neither shall have mercy on their fatherless and widows<u>;</u> for every one <u>of them</u> is *a* hypocrite and an evildoer, and every mouth speaketh folly. For all this his anger is not turned away, but his hand is stretched out still.

9:14–15 (2 Nephi 19:14–15). *"The Lord will cut off from Israel head and tail, branch and rush, in one day."* Because of her apostasy, the Lord will cut off the government, elder, or man of rank ("head . . . the ancient and honourable") and the false prophets ("tail"). The leaders ("branch") and the followers ("rush" or reed) will be cut off.

9:17 (2 Nephi 19:17). *"The Lord shall have no joy."* The Lord takes no pleasure in dispensing divine punishment upon the wicked. Furthermore, just as parents are saddened when their children rebel or make wrong choices, so too the Lord is deprived of joy when His children choose to be disobedient.

Isaiah 9:18–21 and 2 Nephi 19:18–21

In the last verses of this chapter, the prophet vividly describes the effects of disobedience and sin. We are reminded of the apostle Paul's statement, "The wages of sin is death." (Romans 6:23.)

However, the people won't have to wait until death to suffer the terrible consequences of their wickedness, for their mortal lives will be filled with much anguish. Famine, anarchy, and murder will prevail.

18 For wickedness burneth as the fire: it shall devour the briers and thorns, and shall kindle in the thickets of the forest, and they shall mount up like the lifting up of smoke.

19 Through the wrath of the Lord of hosts is the land darkened, and the people shall be as the fuel of the fire: no man shall spare his brother.

20 And he shall snatch on the right hand, and be hungry; and he shall eat on the left hand, and they shall not be satisfied: they shall eat every man the flesh of his own arm:

18 For wickedness burneth as the fire; it shall devour the briers and thorns, and shall kindle in the thickets of the forests, and they shall mount up like the lifting up of smoke.

19 Through the wrath of the Lord of Hosts is the land darkened, and the people shall be as the fuel of the fire; no man shall spare his brother.

20 And he shall snatch on the right hand and be hungry; and he shall eat on the left hand and they shall not be satisfied; they shall eat every man the flesh of his own arm—

21 Manasseh, Ephraim; and Ephraim, Manasseh: <u>and</u> they together shall be against Judah. For all this his anger is not turned away, but his hand is stretched out still.	21 Manasseh, Ephraim; and Ephraim, Manasseh; they together shall be against Judah. For all this his anger is not turned away, but his hand is stretched out still.

9:18 (2 Nephi 19:18). "*Wickedness burneth as the fire.*" Wickedness will spread like a roaring prairie fire driven by fierce winds. This is a powerful image, but there is a meaning to this verse that is even more significant. The Book of Mormon prophet-king Benjamin provided the following description: "Therefore if that man repenteth not, and remaineth and dieth an enemy to God, the demands of divine justice do awaken his immortal soul to a lively sense of his own guilt, which doth cause him to shrink from the presence of the Lord, and doth fill his breast with guilt, and pain, and anguish, *which is like an unquenchable fire, whose flame ascendeth up forever and ever.*" (Mosiah 2:38; italics added.)

There will also be a literal burning of the wicked at the Second Coming: "For, behold, the day cometh, that shall burn as an oven; and all the proud, yea, and all that do wickedly, shall be stubble." (Malachi 4:1; see also BICQ, 194–96.)

9:19 (2 Nephi 19:19). "*The people shall be as the fuel of the fire: no man shall spare his brother.*" Humans will become so coldhearted and bloodthirsty that the sanctity of life will no longer be a dearly held standard of society. People's lives will be dispatched with the same rapidity with which fire consumes fuel. This is truly a sign of "the love of men . . . wax[ing] cold." (JS–M 1:30; BICQ, 79–82, 90.)

9:20 (2 Nephi 19:20). "*They shall eat every man the flesh of his own arm.*" This prophecy probably has multiple fulfillments, one of which occurred during a later siege of Jerusalem when the people turned to cannibalism. (Jeremiah 19:9.) There may yet come a time when food will be so scarce that desperate survivors will eat the flesh of the dead.

9:21 (2 Nephi 19:21). "*Manasseh, Ephraim . . . they together shall be against Judah.*" Manasseh and Ephraim represent the tribes of the northern kingdom that have positioned themselves against the southern kingdom of Judah. This sibling infighting has saddened and displeased the Lord, yet He is anxious to reach out and unite them once again.

CHAPTER 10

Isaiah 10 and 2 Nephi 20

OVERVIEW

Isaiah continues with two common themes in this chapter: the destruction of the wicked and the ultimate return of a remnant of Israel to the fold of the Master Shepherd. The first four verses of the chapter are the final phrases of a prophetic poem that commences with verse 8 of the previous chapter; but the main focus of this chapter is on the Assyrian destruction of wayward Israel. This destruction is a commentary or a foreshadowing, as noted in the chapter heading, of the destruction of the wicked prior to the Second Coming.

Assyria was one of the great Eastern empires, and it exercised considerable conquering power over neighboring countries. It was situated in the Tigris valley to the north of Babylonia, with its capital city of Nineveh located on the east bank of the Tigris River. The Assyrians were noted for their cruelty, reigning with terror over their conquered victims.

In his excellent commentary, Victor L. Ludlow points out the introverted parallelism (chiasmus) which encompasses the entire chapter. This is a literary style in which a pattern of words or ideas is stated by the writer and then repeated, but in *reverse* order. As shown in the following outline, Isaiah presents eight initial themes or ideas in verses 1 through 21 and then repeats them in verses 22–34, but in reverse order:

"A. The wicked will bow down (vs. 1–4)

B. Assyria raised by the Lord (5)

C. The Assyrian king speaks against Jerusalem (6–11)

D. The Lord will punish proud Assyria (12–14)

E. An ax is used as a tool (15)

96

F. The Lord is a burning fire in the land (16–17)

G. Out of all the [multitudes]—only a remnant remains (18–19)

H. A remnant of Israel shall return to the Lord (20–21)

G'. Out of the "sands of the sea"—only a remnant returns (22)

F'. A divine consumption is in the land (23)

E'. A rod is used as an instrument (24–26)

D'. Assyria's yoke will be lifted (27)

C'. Assyrian army approaches Jerusalem (28–32)

B'. Assyria humbled by the Lord (33)

A'. The haughty will be cut down (34)"

(IPSP, 161.)

COMMENTARY

Isaiah 10:1–4 and 2 Nephi 20:1–4

The Lord's people are warned against neglecting (turning away from) and oppressing (taking away and robbing) the poor and needy. Judgment will come upon those who are guilty of such offenses. A penetrating question is then asked: In your own day of need, "to whom will ye flee (turn) for help?" Unless these neglectful and oppressive people repent, they cannot expect the help of the Lord in their hour of need.

Isaiah 10	2 Nephi 20
1 *Woe* unto them that decree unrighteous decrees, and that write grievousness which they have prescribed;	1 *Wo* unto them that decree unrighteous decrees, and that write grievousness which they have prescribed;
2 To turn <u>aside</u> the needy from judgment, and to take away the right from the poor of my people, that widows may be their prey, and that they may rob the fatherless!	2 To turn <u>away</u> the needy from judgment, and to take away the right from the poor of my people, that widows may be their prey, and that they may rob the fatherless!

3 And what will ye do in the day of visitation, and in the desolation which shall come from far? to whom will ye flee for help? and where will ye leave your glory?

4 Without me they shall bow down under the prisoners, and they shall fall under the slain. For all this his anger is not turned away, but his hand is stretched out still.

3 And what will ye do in the day of visitation, and in the desolation which shall come from far? to whom will ye flee for help? and where will ye leave your glory?

4 Without me they shall bow down under the prisoners, and they shall fall under the slain. For all this his anger is not turned away, but his hand is stretched out still.

10:4 (2 Nephi 20:4). *"But his hand is stretched out still."* While many commentaries interpret this to mean that God's wrath is unappeasable, Sidney Sperry suggests that this may mean: "But his hand is stretched out still if only you but change your ways." (BMC, 213.) (Also see commentary on Isaiah 5:25 and 9:12.)

Isaiah 10:5–12 and 2 Nephi 20:5–12

The Assyrian army is the rod whereby the Lord chastises errant Israel. It is hoped that the hypocritical nation of Israel (which claims to be God's chosen people but does not follow His chosen ways) will recognize this as a wake-up call to repent. Yet Assyria goes beyond its mission to chastise Israel. In "their indignation" (Book of Mormon), the Assyrians seek to destroy not only Israel, but other "nations not a few" (verse 7) as well. Not recognizing the hand of the Lord in its assigned role as a chastiser of the wicked, Assyria arrogantly boasts of its own strength and power. The Assyrians claim that their princes (army leaders or commanders) are "altogether kings," and they list the cities they've conquered (verse 9) as evidence of the nation's might.

5 O Assyrian, the rod of mine anger, and the staff in their hand is <u>mine</u> indignation.

5 O Assyrian, the rod of mine anger, and the staff in their hand is <u>their</u> indignation.

6 I will send him against *an* hypocritical nation, and against the people of my wrath will I give him a charge, to take the spoil, and to take the prey, and to tread them down like the mire of the streets.

7 Howbeit he meaneth not so, neither doth his heart think so; but *it is in his heart* to destroy and cut off nations not a few.

8 For he saith, Are not my princes altogether kings?

9 Is not Calno as Carchemish? is not Hamath as Arpad? is not Samaria as Damascus?

10 As my hand hath *found* the kingdoms of the idols, and whose graven images did excel them of Jerusalem and of Samaria;

11 Shall I not, as I have done unto Samaria and her idols, so do to Jerusalem and her idols?

12 Wherefore it shall come to pass, that when the Lord hath performed his whole work upon mount Zion and *on* Jerusalem, I will punish the fruit of the stout heart of the king of Assyria, and the glory of his high looks.

6 I will send him against *a* hypocritical nation, and against the people of my wrath will I give him a charge to take the spoil, and to take the prey, and to tread them down like the mire of the streets.

7 Howbeit he meaneth not so, neither doth his heart think so; but *in his heart it is* to destroy and cut off nations not a few.

8 For he saith: Are not my princes altogether kings?

9 Is not Calno as Carchemish? Is not Hamath as Arpad? Is not Samaria as Damascus?

10 As my hand hath *founded* the kingdoms of the idols, and whose graven images did excel them of Jerusalem and of Samaria;

11 Shall I not, as I have done unto Samaria and her idols, so do to Jerusalem and to her idols?

12 Wherefore it shall come to pass that when the Lord hath performed his whole work upon Mount Zion and *upon* Jerusalem. I will punish the fruit of the stout heart of the king of Assyria, and the glory of his high looks.

10:10–11 (2 Nephi 20:10–11). *"Idols."* Inasmuch as the false gods of Samaria and the other conquered nations did not save them from the invading Assyrians, can Jerusalem expect anything less? Although the God of Abraham, Isaac, and Jacob is the true and living God, the people of Jerusalem are in a godless (idolatrous) state at this time.

10:12 (2 Nephi 20:12). *"Mount Zion and . . . punish . . . the king of Assyria."* The Assyrians will attack Mount Zion, the hill upon which Solomon built his temple. (1 Kings 8:1.) (This attack occurred in 701 B.C., under the Assyrian king Sennacherib.) Yet the Lord will punish the king of Assyria for his "stout heart" and "high looks" (arrogance, pride, and boasting). This prophecy was fulfilled when a desolating sickness was sent into the Assyrian camps, causing many deaths, and the king was later slain by his own sons. (2 Kings 19:32–37; Isaiah 37:33–38.)

Isaiah 10:13–19 and 2 Nephi 20:13–19

The Lord's wrath (just retribution) was poured out upon the Assyrian king and his country because of their wickedness and boasting. The Assyrians did not recognize their refining role as the ax in the hands of the One who actually created and wielded this weapon. They claimed to have <u>moved</u> (enlarged) the <u>borders</u> of their nation and increased their treasures on their own initiative. In verse 15 Isaiah metaphorically asks, "Can man [the Assyrian king] prosper against God?"

13 For he saith, By the strength of my hand *I have done it, and by my wisdom;* for I am prudent: and I have <u>removed</u> the <u>bounds</u> of the people, and have robbed their treasures, and I have put down the inhabitants like a valiant man:	13 For he saith: By the strength of my hand *and by my wisdom I have done* these things; for I am prudent; and I have <u>moved</u> the <u>borders</u> of the people, and have robbed their treasures, and I have put down the inhabitants like a valiant man;

14 And my hand hath found as a nest the riches of the people: and as one gathereth eggs that are left, have I gathered all the earth; and there was none that moved the wing, or opened the mouth, or peeped.

15 Shall the *axe* boast itself against him that heweth therewith? or shall the saw magnify itself against him that shaketh it? as if the rod should shake itself against them that lift it up, or as if the staff should lift up itself, as if it were no wood.

16 Therefore shall the Lord, the Lord of hosts, send among his fat ones leanness; and under his glory he shall kindle a burning like the burning of a fire.

17 And the light of Israel shall be for a fire, and his Holy One for a flame: and it shall burn and devour his thorns and his briers in one day;

18 And shall consume the glory of his forest, and of his fruitful field, both soul and body: and they shall be as when a *standardbearer* fainteth.

19 And the rest of the trees of his forest shall be few, that a child may write them.

14 And my hand hath found as a nest the riches of the people; and as one gathereth eggs that are left have I gathered all the earth; and there was none that moved the wing, or opened the mouth, or peeped.

15 Shall the *ax* boast itself against him that heweth therewith? Shall the saw magnify itself against him that shaketh it? As if the rod should shake itself against them that lift it up, or as if the staff should lift up itself as if it were no wood!

16 Therefore shall the Lord, the Lord of Hosts, send among his fat ones, leanness; and under his glory he shall kindle a burning like the burning of a fire.

17 And the light of Israel shall be for a fire, and his Holy One for a flame, and shall burn and shall devour his thorns and his briers in one day;

18 And shall consume the glory of his forest, and of his fruitful field, both soul and body; and they shall be as when a *standard-bearer* fainteth.

19 And the rest of the trees of his forest shall be few, that a child may write them.

10:16 (2 Nephi 20:16). *"Under his glory he shall kindle a burning."* The prosperity (fatness) of Assyria shall be short-lived, for, as noted above, "leanness" (a desolating sickness) will emaciate her. Indeed, there shall be a "burning" (fever) of internal organs.

10:17 (2 Nephi 20:17). *"Fire . . . thorns and . . . briers."* Assyria is threatened with a fire or flame, which is the Lord Himself (the "light of Israel" and the "Holy One"). He shall "devour" (destroy) the "thorns and . . . briers" (rank and file of the Assyrian army). Sidney Sperry suggests that the "glory" mentioned in verse 16 may allude to the "upper echelons of [Assyria's] government and armies." (BMC, 217.)

10:18–19 (2 Nephi 20:18–19). *"Consume the glory of his forest."* The "forest" (people) of Assyria shall be destroyed so completely that a child will be able to count those ("trees") who remain. The Babylonians and Persians later fulfilled this prophesy, destroying completely the Assyrians as a nation and people.

Isaiah 10:20–23 and 2 Nephi 20:20–23

In these verses, Isaiah returns to a favorite theme—"a remnant will return," which is the meaning of the name of his son Shear-jashub. Although the country of Israel was overrun by her enemies and her people were scattered, yet a remnant would return. This return would not only be to the land of her ancestors, but also to her God—the great Jehovah. This prophecy extends to scattered Israel of the latter days as well. She will no longer "stay" (rely) on the "arm of flesh," but on the living God. (See D&C 1:19–20.)

Victor Ludlow provides the following commentary regarding the remnant that will gather: "Isaiah uses the term *remnant* to describe two distinct groups of Israelites: he talks about a remnant that remains in the land after the Assyrian destruction and promises the return of a future righteous remnant. The two groups are called the *historical remnant* and the *eschatological remnant* respectively. The historical remnant is the group present from a past event (such as the Assyrian invasions), while the eschatological remnant is the group that will emerge from a future action of God and have the qualifications of a latter-day, millennial society. Isaiah's urgent hope is that the historical remnant of the eighth century B.C. will return to the Lord and become the community from which the eschatological remnant will emerge." (IPSP, 164.)

20 And it shall come to pass in that day, that the remnant of Israel, and such as are escaped of the house of Jacob, shall no more again stay upon him that smote them; but shall stay upon the Lord, the Holy One of Israel, in truth.	20 And it shall come to pass in that day, that the remnant of Israel, and such as are escaped of the house of Jacob, shall no more again stay upon him that smote them, but shall stay upon the Lord, the Holy One of Israel, in truth.
21 The remnant shall return, even the remnant of Jacob, unto the mighty God.	21 The remnant shall return, yea, even the remnant of Jacob, unto the mighty God.
22 For though thy people Israel be as the sand of the sea, yet a remnant of them shall return: the consumption decreed shall overflow with righteousness.	22 For though thy people Israel be as the sand of the sea, yet a remnant of them shall return; the consumption decreed shall overflow with righteousness.
23 For the Lord God of hosts shall make a consumption, even determined, in the midst of all the land.	23 For the Lord God of Hosts shall make a consumption, even determined in all the land.

10:22 (2 Nephi 20:22). "*The consumption decreed shall overflow with righteousness.*" Shifting to a reference to the end of the world (destruction of the wicked) at the time of the Second Coming, the prophet declares that mercy is available to those who repent.

Isaiah 10:24–27 and 2 Nephi 20:24–27

With the promise fresh in his mind of the ultimate return of a remnant of Israel, Isaiah tells latter-day Israel (those who dwell in Zion, i.e., wherever the righteous are located) not to fear her enemies (symbolized by the conquering Assyrians and Egyptians of former days). Ultimately, the righteous must rely on the Lord's promise, "I will fight your battles." (D&C 105:14.) However, they must also remember that the righteous will not always be saved from pain and suffering, for the Lord has declared: "I will prove you in all things, whether you will abide in my covenant, even unto death, that you may be found worthy." (D&C 98:14.)

24 Therefore thus saith the Lord God of hosts, O my people that dwellest in Zion, be not afraid of the Assyrian: he shall smite thee with a rod, and shall lift up his staff against thee, after the manner of Egypt.

25 For yet a very little while, and the indignation shall cease, and mine anger in their destruction.

26 And the Lord of hosts shall stir up a scourge for him according to the slaughter of Midian at the rock of Oreb: and as his rod was upon the sea, so shall he lift it up after the manner of Egypt.

27 And it shall come to pass in that day, that his burden shall be taken away from off thy shoulder, and his yoke from off thy neck, and the yoke shall be destroyed because of the anointing.

24 Therefore, thus saith the Lord God of Hosts: O my people that dwellest in Zion, be not afraid of the Assyrian; he shall smite thee with a rod, and shall lift up his staff against thee, after the manner of Egypt.

25 For yet a very little while, and the indignation shall cease, and mine anger in their destruction.

26 And the Lord of Hosts shall stir up a scourge for him according to the slaughter of Midian at the rock of Oreb; and as his rod was upon the sea so shall he lift it up after the manner of Egypt.

27 And it shall come to pass in that day that his burden shall be taken away from off thy shoulder, and his yoke from off thy neck, and the yoke shall be destroyed because of the anointing.

10:26 (2 Nephi 20:26). *"The slaughter of Midian at the rock of Oreb."* Future enemies of the Lord's people will face the same fate meted out to the Midianites by Gideon and his three hundred warriors as recorded in Judges 7:19–25. One of the princes of these defeated enemies of Israel, a man named Oreb, was slain "upon the rock of Oreb."

20:27 (2 Nephi 20:27). *"His burden [and] yoke shall be destroyed."* The burden of oppression laid upon the shoulders of the Lord's people by those who oppose His work shall be removed because of the "anointing" (divine intervention of the Messiah, even Jesus Christ).

Isaiah 10:28–32 and 2 Nephi 20:28–32

In these verses Isaiah returns his attention to the future conquests of the invading Assyrians. The prophet lists a number of the cities that will fall before Assyria's armies as they march triumphantly towards Jerusalem. While the exact location of all these towns is unknown, they would certainly have been in the vicinity of Judah's capital city. The city of Nob was located near enough to Jerusalem that the invading king would be able from Nob to "shake his hand" (fist) against Jerusalem as his next intended victim. As previously noted, the invasion of Jerusalem did not succeed. (See Isaiah 36–37.)

Victor Ludlow suggests that "the invasion Isaiah foretells may also be eschatological and refer to the future attack upon Jerusalem by forces from the north. (See Zech. 14:2; Rev. 11:1–13; JST Matt. 24.) Another reason for looking at the end of chapter 10 from a latter-day context is that chapter 11 is definitely a prophecy to be fulfilled after 1823, for Moroni told Joseph Smith in September of that year 'that it was about to be fulfilled.' (JS–H 1:40.)" (IPSP, 165.)

28 He is come to Aiath, he is passed to Migron; at Michmash he hath laid up his carriages:	28 He is come to Aiath, he is passed to Migron; at Michmash he hath laid up his carriages.

29 They are gone over the passage: they have taken up their lodging at Geba; *Ramah* is afraid; Gibeah of Saul is fled.

30 Lift up <u>thy</u> voice, O daughter of Gallim: cause it to be heard unto Laish, O poor Anathoth.

31 Madmenah is removed; the inhabitants of Gebim gather themselves to flee.

32 As yet shall he remain at Nob that day: he shall shake his hand against the mount of the daughter of Zion, the hill of Jerusalem.

29 They are gone over the passage; they have taken up their lodging at Geba; *Ramath* is afraid; Gibeah of Saul is fled.

30 Lift up <u>the</u> voice, O daughter of Gallim; cause it to be heard unto Laish, O poor Anathoth.

31 Madmenah is removed; the inhabitants of Gebim gather themselves to flee.

32 As yet shall he remain at Nob that day; he shall shake his hand against the mount of the daughter of Zion, the hill of Jerusalem.

Isaiah 10:33–34 and 2 Nephi 20:33–34

The theme of these final verses is the destruction of Assyria. The metaphor of a forest being cut down is used to describe her eradication. Those of high and low stature shall all be hewn down, as boughs and trees are cut and toppled together.

33 Behold, the Lord, the Lord of <u>hosts</u>, shall lop the bough with terror: and the high ones of stature shall be hewn down, and the haughty shall be humbled.

34 And he shall cut down the thickets of the forest with iron, and Lebanon shall fall by a mighty one.

33 Behold, the Lord, the Lord of <u>Hosts</u> shall lop the bough with terror; and the high ones of stature shall be hewn down; and the haughty shall be humbled.

34 And he shall cut down the thickets of the forests with iron, and Lebanon shall fall by a mighty one.

CHAPTER 11

Isaiah 11 and 2 Nephi 21
(with Miscellaneous Other Citations)

OVERVIEW

This chapter of Isaiah's writings is particularly significant, as evidenced by the fact that it is referenced in all four of the Standard Works the Church accepts as scripture. In addition to the Old Testament and Book of Mormon accounts, portions of these writings are found in the New Testament (Revelation 2:16; 5:5; 19:15; and Romans 15:12) and the Doctrine & Covenants (19:15; 113:1–6; and 133:26–29); and in Joseph Smith's history as found in the Pearl of Great Price, he tells us that the entire chapter of Isaiah 11 was quoted to him by the Angel Moroni (JS–H 1:40). Additionally, on several occasions the Prophet provided commentary on verses in this chapter. (See TPJS, 14–15, 71, 93, 316.)

Isaiah's vision included a look at the latter days in which we live, as well as a view of millennial conditions. In fact, when Moroni appeared to young Joseph Smith on the night of 21 September 1823, he informed him that these particular writings of Isaiah were "about to be fulfilled." Isaiah obviously knew about the great work to be accomplished by the Lord through His servants in this last dispensation of time.

COMMENTARY

Isaiah 11:1–5 and 2 Nephi 21:1–5

The prophet-poet commences this chapter with metaphoric expressions through which he testifies of the coming forth of Jesus Christ and a specially called servant. Section

113 of the Doctrine and Covenants provides the Lord's commentary on this chapter.

Isaiah 11	2 Nephi 21
1 And there shall come forth a rod out of the stem of Jesse, and a Branch shall grow out of his roots:	1 And there shall come forth a rod out of the stem of Jesse, and a branch shall grow out of his roots.
2 And the spirit of the Lord shall rest upon him, the spirit of wisdom and understanding, the spirit of counsel and might, the spirit of knowledge and of the fear of the Lord;	2 And the Spirit of the Lord shall rest upon him, the spirit of wisdom and understanding, the spirit of counsel and might, the spirit of knowledge and of the fear of the Lord;
3 And shall make him of quick understanding in the fear of the Lord: and he shall not judge after the sight of his eyes, neither reprove after the hearing of his ears:	3 And shall make him of quick understanding in the fear of the Lord; and he shall not judge after the sight of his eyes, neither reprove after the hearing of his ears.
4 But with righteousness shall he judge the poor, and reprove with equity for the meek of the earth: and he shall smite the earth with the rod of his mouth, and with the breath of his lips shall he slay the wicked.	4 But with righteousness shall he judge the poor, and reprove with equity for the meek of the earth; and he shall smite the earth with the rod of his mouth, and with the breath of his lips shall he slay the wicked.
5 And righteousness shall be the girdle of his loins, and faithfulness the girdle of his reins.	5 And righteousness shall be the girdle of his loins, and faithfulness the girdle of his reins.

11:1–5 (2 Nephi 21:1–5). "*Stem of Jesse.*" Christ is the One spoken of in verse 1 as the stem. (D&C 113:1–2.) He is also the Branch, the messianic King David, who was prophesied to come forth in the last days. (See Jeremiah 23:5; ANW, 518.)

He was a descendant of Jesse, who was the father of King David. (Ruth 4:17; Matthew 1:5–6.) Verses 2 through 5 enumerate some of His attributes.

11:1 (2 Nephi 21:1). "*Rod out of the stem of Jesse.*" An 1838 revelation identified this as "a servant in the hands of Christ, who is partly a descendant of Jesse as well as of Ephraim, or of the house of Joseph, on whom there is laid much power." (D&C 113:3–4.) Certainly the priesthood power bestowed on Joseph Smith, the Prophet of the Restoration, qualifies him to be this servant. Consider also the Angel Moroni's proclamation, following a recitation of the eleventh chapter of Isaiah to young Joseph, that "it was about to be fulfilled." (JS–H 1:40.) Furthermore, the ancient seer Joseph, he who rose to such power in ancient Egypt, prophesied that one of his descendants—bearing the name of Joseph—would be raised up to do a great work for the Lord. (2 Nephi 3:6–15; JST Genesis 50:26–33.)

"With respect to Joseph's lineage, Brigham Young declared he was 'a pure Ephraimite' (JD 2:269). However, as Joseph Fielding Smith pointed out, 'No one can lay claim to a perfect descent from father to son through just one lineage' (AGQ 3:61). Therefore, though Joseph's lineage may be traceable directly back to Ephraim through a given line, of necessity there were intermarriages that took place, making it possible for his descent to have also come from Jesse through his forefather, Judah." (DCE, 479–80.)

One commentator suggests that the "rod" and "branch" may be a "great Jewish leader of the last days who will be called David. He further suggests that this individual "might not be a Christian or a member of Christ's true church, but he will respect the Lord and have concern for others." (IPSP, 169.) However, this interpretation is not consistent with the view generally held by Latter-day Saints, as described above.

11:3 (2 Nephi 21:3). "*Not judge after the sight of his eyes.*" The Savior will not judge by outward appearance nor by hearsay, "for the Lord seeth not as man seeth; for man looketh on the outward appearance, but the Lord looketh on the heart." (1 Samuel 16:7.)

11:4 (2 Nephi 21:4). *"The rod of his mouth . . . the breath of his lips."* "The rod, as an instrument, is frequently associated with discipline or justice. Thus, if the unrepentant are to be smitten with the rod of the Lord's mouth, they will be punished or disciplined by the decree of his mouth." (DCE, 477–78.) The words on His holy breath will condemn the wicked. Certainly the wicked who will be destroyed by fire at the Second Coming will feel the hot impact of these words. (See 1 Nephi 22:23; 2 Nephi 30:10.)

11:5 (2 Nephi 21:5). *"Righteousness shall be the girdle of his loins."* It is of interest to note that Nephi uses this same phrase elsewhere in the Book of Mormon. (2 Nephi 30:11.) The Savior's girdle of righteousness is a symbol of His strength.

Isaiah 11:6–9 and 2 Nephi 21:6–9

A glimpse of serene millennial conditions is next portrayed by the prophet. Peace will prevail and enmity will cease, not only between humans but in the animal kingdom as well. (D&C 101:26; see also BICQ, 215–16.) However, as to the question of whether vegetarianism will be the order of the day, Sidney B. Sperry gave the following opinion: "We all know that the Lord has placed a balance in nature. And to contend that man cannot eat meat or use the fowls of the air or fish in the streams and oceans for needed sustenance during the millennium is beyond what Isaiah meant to convey." (BMC, 224–25; see also D&C 49:18–19.)

6 The wolf also shall dwell with the lamb, and the leopard shall lie down with the kid; and the calf and the young lion and the fatling together; and a little child shall lead them.	6 The wolf also shall dwell with the lamb, and the leopard shall lie down with the kid, and the calf and the young lion and fatling together; and a little child shall lead them.

7 And the cow and the bear shall feed; their young ones shall lie down together: and the lion shall eat straw like the ox.

8 And the sucking child shall play on the hole of the asp, and the weaned child shall put his hand on the cockatrice' den.

9 They shall not hurt nor destroy in all my holy mountain: for the earth shall be full of the knowledge of the Lord, as the waters cover the sea.

7 And the cow and the bear shall feed; their young ones shall lie down together; and the lion shall eat straw like the ox.

8 And the sucking child shall play on the hole of the asp, and the weaned child shall put his hand on the cockatrice's den.

9 They shall not hurt nor destroy in all my holy mountain, for the earth shall be full of the knowledge of the Lord, as the waters cover the sea.

11:8 (2 Nephi 21:8). "*Asp [and] cockatrice.*" Infants and small children (as well as youth and adults), will not be harmed by asps (horned vipers or cobras) or by cockatrices (other venomous vipers).

11:9 (2 Nephi 21:9). "*My holy mountain.*" The entire earth, in its paradisiacal peace and splendor, will be as a temple—the abode of Deity, or house of the Lord.

11:9 (2 Nephi 21:9). "*The earth shall be full of the knowledge of the Lord.*" The Prophet Joseph Smith rendered this, "the earth will be filled with sacred knowledge." (TPJS, 93.) Surely the word of the Lord will fill the earth during this thousand-year period of peace. Men, women, and children will not only know of the Lord, but they will know Him!

Isaiah 11:10 and 2 Nephi 21:10

Commencing with verse 10, Isaiah leaves his description of millennial conditions and returns to the recovery of the remnant of Israel prior to the Second Coming.

10 And in that day there shall be a root of Jesse, which shall stand for an ensign of the people; to it shall the Gentiles seek: and his rest shall be glorious.

10 And in that day there shall be a root of Jesse, which shall stand for an ensign of the people; to it shall the Gentiles seek; and his rest shall be glorious.

11:10 (2 Nephi 21:10). *"Root of Jesse."* The Doctrine and Covenants identifies this individual as "a descendant of Jesse, as well as of Joseph, unto whom rightly belongs the priesthood, and the keys of the kingdom, for an ensign, and for the gathering of my people in the last days." (D&C 113:5–6.) The apostle Paul mistakenly identified the "root" as Christ. (Romans 15:12.) Dr. Sidney B. Sperry explained the reason for this mistake:

"Examination of Romans 15:12 demonstrates that Paul was closely following the Septuagint (LXX, Greek translation) text of Isaiah 11:10 rather than the Hebrew. As a matter of fact, the LXX version is only a paraphrase of the original Hebrew. We notice that the Greek version of Isaiah 11:1 translates the Hebrew text, 'stem of Jesse,' as the 'root of Jesse' and uses the same phrase in Isaiah 11:10. Of interest is the fact that the Greek word *riza* (root) is used in both verses to translate different Hebrew words. Paul would be quick to discern that the 'root of Jesse' of the LXX text of Isaiah 11:1–5 was the Christ. And when he observed that the phrase 'root of Jesse' was used again in verse 10, he would naturally assume that it, too, had reference to the Christ. Hence the reason for his quotation in Romans 15:12." (BMC, 227.)

Who, then, is the "root of Jesse?" It appears that the Prophet Joseph Smith is both the "rod" and the "root" that will come from Jesse. (See BMC, 223; DCBM 1:281; GAWI, 73–74.) He is the one upon whom the keys of the kingdom were bestowed, including the keys of the gathering of Israel. (See D&C 13:1; 27:12–13; 90:2–3; 110:11–16.) However, Victor Ludlow suggested that "Joseph Smith might not be the only 'root of Jesse' in these last days. Many presidents of the Church have been related to him by blood, and all have held the priesthood and the keys of the kingdom that he held. . . .

The 'root of Jesse' could also be that particular prophet who will hold the keys when Christ returns to preside personally over his kingdom. The term could even represent the office of the president of the Church. In any case, the 'root of Jesse' designates a great leader in the Church of Jesus Christ in this dispensation." (IPSP, 174.)

A most interesting commentary on Joseph Smith's divine calling was supplied by Victor Ludlow. Jewish tradition anticipates two "saviors" or "messiahs": "Messiah ben David" (a redeemer Messiah descended from David) and "Messiah ben Joseph" (a redeemer descended from Joseph). Regarding this second "Messiah," the *Encyclopedia Judaica* 11:1411 states: "A secondary messianic figure is the Messiah son of Joseph (or Ephraim), whose coming precedes that of the Messiah, son of David, and who will die in combat with the enemies of God and Israel." Dr. Ludlow then suggests, "Joseph Smith and his martyrdom could already be a fulfillment of this role." (IPSP, 177.)

11:10 (2 Nephi 21:10). "*Ensign of the people.*" The Prophet Joseph Smith, and his successors in the presidency of the Church he was directed to establish, are the "ensign *of* the people" to whom the Saints of the latter days will look for direction, as these prophets speak the word of the Lord. Truly, the phrase "follow the prophet" is a rallying cry for the righteous and their way of safety. (The "ensign *to* [or for] the nations" is discussed in the commentary in verse 12, as well as in Isaiah 49:22 and Isaiah 5:26.)

Isaiah 11:11–12 and 2 Nephi 21:11–12; 6:14; 25:17; 29:1; Jacob 6:2

Isaiah symbolically mentions seven countries plus the "islands of the sea" (continents) from whence the remnant of the Lord's people will be gathered for the second time. He used the names of nations with which the people of his day were most familiar, but the gathering of the last days will be worldwide in nature. The first gathering occurred after the

Babylonian captivity. Joseph Smith stated in January 1833 that the time for the second gathering had arrived. (HC 1:313.)

11 And it shall come to pass in that day, that the Lord shall set his hand again the second time to recover the remnant of his people, which shall be left, from Assyria, and from Egypt, and from Pathros, and from Cush, and from Elam, and from Shinar, and from Hamath, and from the islands of the sea.

11 And it shall come to pass in that day that the Lord shall set his hand again the second time to recover the remnant of his people which shall be left, from Assyria, and from Egypt, and from Pathros, and from Cush, and from Elam, and from Shinar, and from Hamath, and from the islands of the sea.

2 Nephi 6:14. And behold, according to the words of the prophet, the Messiah will set himself again the second time to recover them; wherefore, he will manifest himself unto them in power and great glory, unto the destruction of their enemies, when that day cometh when they shall believe in him; and none will he destroy that believe in him.

2 Nephi 25:17. And the Lord will set his hand again the second time to restore his people from their lost and fallen state. Wherefore, he will proceed to do a marvelous work and a wonder among the children of men.

2 Nephi 29:1. <u>But behold, there shall be many—at that day when I shall proceed to do a marvelous work among them, that I may remember my covenants which I have made unto the children of men, that I may</u> set <u>my</u> hand again the second time to recover <u>my</u> people, which <u>are of the house of Israel;</u>

Jacob 6:2. And <u>the</u> *day that* <u>he</u> shall set his hand again the second time to recover <u>his people, is the day, yea, even the last time, that the servants of the Lord shall go forth in his power, to nourish and prune his vineyard; and after that the end soon cometh.</u>

12 And he shall set up an ensign for the nations, and shall assemble the outcasts of Israel, and gather together the dispersed of Judah from the four corners of the earth.	12 And he shall set up an ensign for the nations, and shall assemble the outcasts of Israel, and gather together the dispersed of Judah from the four corners of the earth.

11:12 (2 Nephi 21:12). *"He shall set up an ensign for the nations."* The Church of Jesus Christ of Latter-day Saints is the ensign held up *for* the nations. It is the standard the Lord has raised for His people and one to which the gentiles of the nations of the earth should seek. (D&C 45:9; DCE, 157.) Elder Marion G. Romney declared: "This Church is the standard which Isaiah said the Lord would set up for the people in the latter days. . . . This Church is the ensign on the mountain spoken of by the Old Testament prophets." (CR, April 1961, p. 119.)

There is another possibility to consider regarding the

identity of this standard or ensign. Speaking particularly of the Book of Mormon, the Lord said to Nephi, "My words shall hiss forth unto the ends of the earth, for a standard unto my people, which are of the house of Israel." (2 Nephi 29:2.) The Prophet Joseph identified the Book of Mormon as "the keystone of our religion," making it inseparable with the truthfulness of the Church. Thus, whether we speak of the Church or the Book of Mormon, both are standards or ensigns to the nations of the earth. (See also commentary on Isaiah 49:22 and Isaiah 5:26.)

11:12 (2 Nephi 21:12). *"Outcasts of Israel, and . . . the dispersed of Judah."* After quoting this verse, Elder Orson Pratt said: "Here is a declaration that the two great kingdoms of Israel—its 'outcasts,' the ten tribes, scattered seven hundred and twenty years before Christ, and the 'dispersed of Judah,' dispersed among all nations, shall be gathered." (JD 14:66.) The Ten Tribes, or tribes of the northern kingdom of Israel, were taken into captivity by the Assyrians about 721 B.C. (See 2 Kings 17.) The return of these lost tribes, to receive their full blessings at the hands of Ephraim, is one of the basic beliefs of Latter-day Saints. (See D&C 133:26–34; BICQ, 135–42.) Judah, while having gathered to the nation of Israel in a political or cultural sense, has yet to be gathered to the fold of the True Shepherd in fulfillment of the Lord's admonition to "let them who be of Judah flee unto Jerusalem, unto the mountains of the Lord's house [His temples and His kingdom]." (D&C 133:13; BICQ, 125–34.)

11:12 (2 Nephi 21:12). *"Four corners of the earth."* Figuratively, the ends of the earth.

Isaiah 11:13–14 and 2 Nephi 21:13–14

When the remnants return, the long-standing adversarial relationship between Judah (the southern kingdom) and Ephraim (representing the northern kingdom) will end. They will be a united kingdom for the first time since Solomon's reign. Their feuding will be swallowed up in their common covenants with Christ. Combined Israel will then prevail over her enemies, symbolized by Edom, Moab, and Ammon.

13 The envy *also of Ephraim* shall depart, and the adversaries of Judah shall be cut off: Ephraim shall not envy Judah, and Judah shall not vex Ephraim.	13 The envy *of Ephraim also* shall depart, and the adversaries of Judah shall be cut off; Ephraim shall not envy Judah, and Judah shall not vex Ephraim.
14 But they shall fly upon the shoulders of the Philistines toward the west; they shall spoil them of the east together: they shall lay their hand upon Edom and Moab; and the children of Ammon shall obey them.	14 But they shall fly upon the shoulders of the Philistines towards the west; they shall spoil them of the east together; they shall lay their hand upon Edom and Moab; and the children of Ammon shall obey them.

11:14 (2 Nephi 21:14). "*Fly upon the shoulders of the Philistines.*" Sidney Sperry suggested that this phrase meant the gentiles, represented by the Philistines, would assist in the gathering of Israel. (BMC, 228.) However, another interpretation is that combined Israel would "attack the western slopes that [once] were Philistine territory." (LDSKJ, Isaiah 11:14, footnote *a*.) The Philistines were bitter enemies of Israel and originally occupied the lowland on the Mediterranean coast known then as Palestine and today as the Gaza Strip.

11:14 (2 Nephi 21:14). "*Edom and Moab; and the children of Ammon.*" Edom was the name of Esau's descendants and the territory they occupied in Mount Seir. The country lay southeast of Palestine, with Moab on the north and the Dead Sea on the northwest. The Edomites and Israelites shared a mutual hatred of one another. Moab was southeast of the Dead Sea, and its citizens were constantly at war with the Israelites. The Ammonites were descendants of Abraham's nephew, Lot. Their country was located east of Mount Gilead, north of Moab. They were a constant irritant to the Israelites.

The area occupied by the Edomites, Moabites, and Ammonites now comprises the country of modern Jordan. As noted above, Isaiah used the names of these countries to symbolize latter-day enemies of Israel.

Isaiah 11:15–16 and 2 Nephi 21:15–16

Even as God showed forth his power against ancient Egypt at the time of the Exodus, so shall He provide divine intervention during the gathering of the last days. He will perform modern miracles in order to accomplish His purposes.

15 And the Lord shall utterly destroy the tongue of the Egyptian sea; and with his mighty wind shall he shake his hand over the river, and shall smite it in the seven streams, and make men go over *dryshod*.

16 And there shall be *an* highway for the remnant of his people, which shall be left, from Assyria; like as it was to Israel in the day that he came up out of the land of Egypt.

15 And the Lord shall utterly destroy the tongue of the Egyptian sea; and with his mighty wind he shall shake his hand over the river, and shall smite it in the seven streams, and make men go over *dry shod*.

16 And there shall be *a* highway for the remnant of his people which shall be left, from Assyria, like as it was to Israel in the day that he came up out of the land of Egypt.

11:15 (2 Nephi 21:15). "*Utterly destroy the tongue of the Egyptian sea.*" There is uncertainty among LDS and other scriptural scholars as to the meaning of this prophecy. Sidney B. Sperry postulated that Isaiah was illustrating "the power of the Almighty by telling us that He will cut off or separate the tongue of the Egyptian sea, shake his hand over the Euphrates, smite it into many streams and cause men to go over it dryshod. Perhaps," said Dr. Sperry, "'Egyptian sea' and 'River' (vs. 15) are metonyms for places of exile and bondage. Such shall be overthrown when the time of redemption comes." (BMC, 229.)

The "tongue" according to Victor Ludlow "might be the western arm of the Red Sea (or Gulf of Suez, for which the modern Suez Canal was named) and the narrow body of water that extended north from the Red Sea into the desert. Another possibility," noted Dr. Ludlow, "is the delta (or tongue) of the Nile, which protruded into the Mediterranean Sea along Egypt's north coast. The most likely explanation, however, is the large inland sea created late each spring as the Nile overflows its banks and floods a large part of the valley, like a tongue sticking far inland. Isaiah 19:5–10 describes the destruction of the Nile River in greater detail. If the Nile River is the 'tongue of the Egyptian Sea,' then this prophecy might have been fulfilled since the building of the Aswan Dam and the destruction of the traditional way of life along the Nile." (IPSP, 176.)

Monte Nyman suggested that "this prophecy in verse 15 is one of those which will probably not be understood until it comes to pass, but when it does there will be no doubt as to its fulfillment." He cites 2 Nephi 25:7 as evidence of this conclusion. Said Nephi, "In the days that the prophecies of Isaiah shall be fulfilled men shall know of a surety, at the times when they shall come to pass." (GAWI, 76.)

11:16 (2 Nephi 21:16). *"There shall be an highway for the remnant."* One is reminded of the great prophecy regarding the return of the lost tribes—that "an highway shall be cast up in the midst of the great deep." (D&C 133:27.) The author has previously suggested that "this highway could be a literal road whereon the returning tribes will travel; it could [also] be symbolic of a highway of holiness (Isa. 35:8), which one scholar has identified as the strait and narrow path (Mill M, 327); or a combination of the two pathways." (DCE, 590.)

Whatever this highway will be, it will be a clear road or means of transportation whereby the Lord's people will find their way to His promised destination. Certainly the Lord's hand will be in the matter.

CHAPTER 12

Isaiah 12 and 2 Nephi 22

OVERVIEW

In a joyous outburst of thanksgiving and praise, because of the redemption of the remnant spoken of in the previous chapter, Isaiah records a hymn consisting of two short psalms. This song of praise will undoubtedly be sung in the future congregations of the redeemed of Israel.

COMMENTARY

Isaiah 12:1–3 and 2 Nephi 22:1–3

The redeemed remnant will be grateful for forgiveness. Because Israel will turn from sin to repentance, the Lord will turn from punishing her to comforting her. The Lord God Jehovah is not only a source of protecting strength to the once-beleaguered Israel, but He is also the source of her salvation in His role as the Redeeming One, or Savior.

Verse 3 has been referred to as "one of the loveliest in the Old Testament" (BMC, 231) and as "the most important verse in this set" (IPSP, 178). However, scholars are uncertain as to whether it belongs with the psalm in verses 1 and 2 or with the second psalm in verses 4 to 6.

Isaiah 12	2 Nephi 22
1 And in that day thou shalt say, O Lord, I will praise thee: though thou wast angry with me, thine anger is turned away, and thou *comfortedst* me.	1 And in that day thou shalt say: O Lord, I will praise thee; though thou wast angry with me thine anger is turned away, and thou *comfortedest* me.

2 Behold, God is my salvation; I will trust, and not be afraid: for the Lord JEHOVAH is my strength and my song; he also <u>is</u> become my salvation.

3 Therefore with joy shall ye draw water out of the wells of salvation.

2 Behold, God is my salvation; I will trust, and not be afraid; for the Lord JEHOVAH is my strength and my song; he also <u>has</u> become my salvation.

3 Therefore, with joy shall ye draw water out of the wells of salvation.

12:2 (2 Nephi 22:2). "*JEHOVAH.*" The covenant or proper name of the God of the Old Testament was so highly reverenced that it was rarely spoken. In fact, the original pronunciation of the name may be unknown to mortal man. When reading orally, the Israelites substituted the name *Adonai,* meaning literally, *my Lord.* Elder James E. Talmage tells us that "*Jehovah* is the Anglicized rendering of the Hebrew, *Yahveh* or *Jahveh,* signifying the *Self-existent One,* or *The Eternal.* This name is generally rendered in our English version of the Old Testament as LORD, printed in [small] capitals." (Talmage, p. 36; see also DCE, 276.) Of the four times the sacred name appears unchanged in the Old Testament, Isaiah uses it twice. (Isaiah 12:2; 26:4; see also Exodus 6:3; Psalm 83:18.)

Latter-day Saints affirm that this holy name is the premortal name of Jesus Christ and has been used in behalf of the Savior in sacred places during His postmortal ministry. The name can be found in the Book of Mormon, the Doctrine and Covenants, and the Pearl of Great Price. (2 Nephi 22:2; Moroni 10:34; D&C 109:34, 42, 56, 68; 110:3; 128:9; Abraham 1:16.)

12:3 (2 Nephi 22:3). "*Draw water out of the wells of salvation.*" This is an invitation for others to join with the redeemed remnant and experience the joy of the gospel. It is an invitation to repent and be baptized; or, as the apostle Paul would later proclaim, to put off old (sinful) ways and put on a new (cleansed) body whereby we would then "walk in newness of life." (See Romans 6.) The sure promise of Him who is the source of "living water" (John 4:10) is this: "I will give unto him that is athirst of the fountain of the water of life freely." (Revelation 21:6.)

Isaiah 12:4–6 and 2 Nephi 22:4–6

This second psalm focuses more on praising than on thanksgiving. Victor Ludlow points out that "in a praise psalm, attention is centered upon the person being extolled, but in a thanks psalm the viewpoint is focused on the person giving thanks and upon the blessing that he has received. The first psalm of chapter 12 is in the 'thanks' category; the second is more of a 'praise' type." (IPSP, 179.)

4 And in that day shall ye say, Praise the Lord, call upon his name, declare his doings among the people, make mention that his name is exalted.	4 And in that day shall ye say: Praise the Lord, call upon his name, declare his doings among the people, make mention that his name is exalted.
5 Sing unto the Lord; for he hath done excellent things: this is known in all the earth.	5 Sing unto the Lord; for he hath done excellent things; this is known in all the earth.
6 Cry out and shout, thou inhabitant of Zion: for great is the Holy One of Israel in the midst of thee.	6 Cry out and shout, thou inhabitant of Zion; for great is the Holy One of Israel in the midst of thee.

12:5 (2 Nephi 22:5). "*Sing unto the Lord.*" The admonition to "sing unto the Lord" is not one that is reserved for the redeemed remnant of the future. Sacred music invites the Spirit of the Lord into our midst and is a wonderful way in which to worship Deity. Modern revelation reminds us that the Lord's "soul delighteth in the song of the heart; yea, the song of the righteous is a prayer unto [Him]." (D&C 25:12.)

CHAPTER 13

Isaiah 13 and 2 Nephi 23

OVERVIEW

The authorship of this chapter is disputed by some of the uninspired worldly scholars, who rely on their academic learning but do not recognize the role of the Spirit in understanding scripture and prophetic utterances. Because Isaiah focuses on the destruction of Babylon, an event that occurred long after his time, and because these so-called scholars do not believe in prophecy, they assume that this chapter was written by someone after the event had come to pass. Such assumptions cause one to reflect on Jacob's astute observation:

"O that cunning plan of the evil one! O the vainness, and the frailties, and the foolishness of men! When they are learned they think they are wise, and they hearken not unto the counsel of God, for they set it aside, supposing they know of themselves, wherefore, their wisdom is foolishness and it profiteth them not. And they shall perish." (2 Nephi 9:28.)

Isaiah—ancient prophet, seer, and revelator of the Lord—not only foresaw the destruction of the mighty Babylon of his days, but also the ultimate destruction of spiritual Babylon (the world) in the last days. Surely the many who have trusted in the arm of flesh—who have worshiped the false idols of materialism, carnality, sophistry, status, and pride—will one day be faced with the truth that these gods of Baal cannot prevail against the true and living God! Then, perhaps, as was the case anciently, they will be led to declare: "The Lord [Jehovah], he is the God; the Lord, he is the God." (1 Kings 18:39.)

Certainly, in response, the Lord God Jehovah shall say:

"There is no God else beside me; a just God and a Saviour; there is none beside me. . . . [U]nto me every knee shall bow, every tongue shall swear." (Isaiah 45:21–23; see also Romans 14:11; Philippians 2:10; Mosiah 27:31; D&C 76:110; 88:104.)

COMMENTARY

Isaiah 13:1 and 2 Nephi 23:1

This opening verse speaks of the "burden" (message of doom) that is lifted up against Babylon. Isaiah's seeric powers allowed him to *see* in vision what was to take place.

Isaiah 13	2 Nephi 23
1 The burden of Babylon, which Isaiah the son of Amoz did see.	1 The burden of Babylon, which Isaiah the son of Amoz did see.

13:1 (2 Nephi 23:1). *"Babylon."* Babylon was the ancient capital city of Babylonia, a society noted for its wickedness and cruelty. In our day it is a representation of the wickedness of the world. In fact, the Lord Himself equated the "midst of wickedness" with "spiritual Babylon." (D&C 133:14.) The ancient city appeared to be impregnable to attack, with walls said to be 56 miles in circumference, 335 feet high, and 85 feet wide. Yet, as foreseen by Isaiah, this fortress of ancient Babylonia fell. The plea to come forth out of today's Babylon (D&C 133:5, 7, 14) is the clarion call to modern Israel to escape from the Babylonian bondage of wickedness to the freedom and light of the gospel of Jesus Christ (D&C 45:9; 50:24; 88:86.)

Isaiah 13:2–5 and 2 Nephi 23:2–5

In figurative language, Isaiah describes the mustering of those called to the service of the Lord (the "sanctified" and "mighty ones") to do battle against the wickedness of Babylon. These warriors of righteousness include not only mortal men (those "from a far country") but also destroying angels (those "from the end of heaven"), who are called to cut down the tares (destroy the wicked). (See Matthew 13:24–30; D&C 86:1–7.)

2 Lift ye up a banner upon the high mountain, exalt the voice unto them, shake the hand, that they may go into the gates of the nobles.

2 Lift ye up a banner upon the high mountain, exalt the voice unto them, shake the hand, that they may go into the gates of the nobles.

3 I have commanded my sanctified ones, I have also called my mighty ones for mine anger, even them that rejoice in my highness.

3 I have commanded my sanctified ones, I have also called my mighty ones, for mine anger is not upon them that rejoice in my highness.

4 The noise of a multitude in the mountains, like as of a great people; a tumultuous noise of the kingdoms of nations gathered together: the Lord of hosts mustereth the host of the battle.

4 The noise of the multitude in the mountains like as of a great people, a tumultuous noise of the kingdoms of nations gathered together, the Lord of Hosts mustereth the hosts of the battle.

5 They come from a far country, from the end of heaven, even the Lord, and the weapons of his indignation, to destroy the whole land.

5 They come from a far country, from the end of heaven, yea, the Lord, and the weapons of his indignation, to destroy the whole land.

13:2 (2 Nephi 23:2). *"A [my] banner."* The banner to be raised up is the battle flag or standard of the Lord. By inserting the word "my" before "banner," the Joseph Smith Translation makes it clear that this standard is the Lord's. (JST Isaiah 13:2.) This rallying standard unites the righteous of the world in the common cause of Christ. (See commentary for Isaiah 11:12 and 2 Nephi 21:12.)

13:2 (2 Nephi 23:2). *"Gates of the nobles."* The gates of Eastern cities were an important part of ancient city life. They were not only places of entrance and exit, but also served as places of private and public business transactions. The gates were often taken as representing the city itself. (See the commentary on Isaiah 3:26.) In the Isaiah context, the meaning is probably an invitation for those who are fleeing Babylon to enter the holy cities of Jerusalem and Zion (the new Jerusalem). (See D&C 133:12–14.)

13:3 (2 Nephi 23:3). *"Sanctified ones."* Footnote 3*a* (LDSKJ) identifies these as synonymous for "Saints." These are the consecrated ones who have made covenants with Christ through sacred and saving ordinances. They have "a determination to serve him to the end." (D&C 20:37.)

13:3 (2 Nephi 23:3). *"Mine anger is not upon them that rejoice in my highness."* The Book of Mormon clarification of this verse is most helpful in eliminating the ambiguity of the wording in the Bible. The Lord's "anger" (displeasure or wrath) is *not* directed toward those who "rejoice in [His] highness" (eminence or majesty). These are they who find joy in worshiping and serving Him.

Isaiah 13:6–9 and 2 Nephi 23:6–9

Great destruction will come upon the wicked in the days preceding the second coming of the Lord, as well as when He actually arrives. Fear shall grip the hearts of the wicked as, in the midst of sorrow, they face the reality that "wickedness never was happiness." (Alma 41:10.) Truly, for them this will be the "dreadful day of the Lord." (Malachi 4:5.)

6 Howl ye; for the day of the Lord is at hand; it shall come as a destruction from the Almighty.	6 Howl ye, for the day of the Lord is at hand; it shall come as a destruction from the Almighty.
7 Therefore shall all hands be faint, and every man's heart shall melt:	7 Therefore shall all hands be faint, every man's heart shall melt;

8 And they shall be afraid<u>:</u> pangs and sorrows shall take hold of them; <u>they shall be in pain as a woman that travaileth:</u> they shall be amazed one at another; their faces shall be as flames.	8 And they shall be afraid<u>;</u> pangs and sorrows shall take hold of them; they shall be amazed one at another; their faces shall be as flames.
9 Behold, the day of the Lord cometh, cruel both with wrath and fierce anger, to lay the land desolate<u>:</u> and he shall destroy the sinners thereof out of it.	9 Behold, the day of the Lord cometh, cruel both with wrath and fierce anger, to lay the land desolate<u>;</u> and he shall destroy the sinners thereof out of it.

13:6 (2 Nephi 23:6). *"Day of the Lord."* This phrase is used first by the prophets Isaiah and Amos. (Isaiah 2:12; Amos 5:18.) In general, this is that period of time just preceding the return of the resurrected Lord to this earth, as well as the time of His actual coming. In His postmortal ministry among the inhabitants of the ancient Americas, Jesus commanded that some of the writings of the Old Testament prophet Malachi be recited and recorded. Among these prophecies was the promise of "the coming of the great and dreadful day of the Lord." (Malachi 4:5–6; 3 Nephi 25:5–6.) It will truly be a *great* day to those who righteously await its onset; but, to the wicked, it shall be a *dreadful* day of exquisite sorrow. Some other appellations applied to this "day" are "day of visitation, and of judgment, and of indignation" (D&C 56:16); "day of wrath" (D&C 63:6); "day of vengeance" (D&C 133:51); and "day . . . that shall burn as an oven" (Malachi 4:1; D&C 133:64). (See also DCE, 222–23; BICQ, 194–99.)

Although the righteous will ultimately be saved in the kingdom of God, it should be pointed out that even some of them will fall prey to the war and pestilence that will precede the Second Coming. "It is a false idea," said the Prophet Joseph Smith, "that the Saints will escape all the judgments, whilst the wicked suffer; for all flesh is subject to suffer, and 'the righteous shall hardly escape;' still many of the Saints will escape, for the just shall live by faith; yet many of the righteous shall fall a prey to disease, to pestilence, etc., by reason of the weakness of the flesh and yet be saved in the Kingdom of God." (HC 4:11; see also BICQ, 91.)

13:7 (2 Nephi 23:7). "*Every man's heart shall melt.*" While this may have reference to despairing hearts, it is possible it could be descriptive of the abundance of *failing* hearts in the last days. (See Luke 21:26; D&C 45:26; Moses 7:66.)

13:8 (2 Nephi 23:8). "*Their faces shall be as flames.*" This could mean that the faces of sinners will burn with shame or be inflamed because of weeping. Or it may be possible that the amazement (astonishment) of the people in looking at one another could be expressive of their horror in viewing the ravages of a burning disease, or the result of chemical, biological, or nuclear warfare. Conceivably, such catastrophes could not only cause a face to "be as flames," but also the "flesh [to] fall from off [the] bones, and [the] eyes from [the] sockets." (D&C 29:18–19; see also BICQ, 92–93.)

Isaiah 13:10 and 2 Nephi 23:10

Samuel, the great Lamanite prophet of Book of Mormon times, prophesied that at the time of the crucifixion of the Savior "the sun shall be darkened . . . and also the moon and the stars . . . for the space of three days." (Helaman 14:20.) While the fulfillment of that prophecy was restricted to the ancient Americas, the prophecy of Isaiah regarding a future time when these heavenly bodies would refuse to give their light will be a worldwide event. (See Joel 2:10; Matthew 24:29.) Similar but somewhat divergent prophecies are found elsewhere in scripture. (Revelation 6:12–14; D&C 45:42; 88:87; 133:49.) These references include the moon turning to blood and the stars falling from the heavens. There may, in fact, be multiple fulfillments of these manifestations in the heavens. And it well may be that in spite of such signs and wonders the unbelieving and skeptical will "be less and less astonished at a sign or a wonder from heaven," just as occurred with some anciently. (3 Nephi 2:1–2.)

10 For the stars of heaven
and the constellations
thereof shall not give their
light: the sun shall be
darkened in his going forth,
and the moon shall not cause
her light to shine.

10 For the stars of heaven
and the constellations
thereof shall not give their
light; the sun shall be
darkened in his going forth,
and the moon shall not cause
her light to shine.

Isaiah 13:11–13 and 2 Nephi 23:11–13

The worldly will be punished for their evil ways. The destruction will be so widespread that, in comparison to the original population, there will be a scarcity of survivors.

11 And I will punish the
world for their evil, and the
wicked for their iniquity; and
I will cause the arrogancy of
the proud to cease, and will
lay low the haughtiness of
the terrible.

11 And I will punish the
world for evil, and the
wicked for their iniquity; I
will cause the arrogancy of
the proud to cease, and will
lay down the haughtiness of
the terrible.

12 I will make a man more
precious than fine gold; even
a man than the golden
wedge of Ophir.

12 I will make a man more
precious than fine gold; even
a man than the golden
wedge of Ophir.

13 Therefore I will shake the
heavens, and the earth shall
remove out of her place, in
the wrath of the Lord of
hosts, and in the day of his
fierce anger.

13 Therefore, I will shake
the heavens, and the earth
shall remove out of her
place, in the wrath of the
Lord of Hosts, and in the
day of his fierce anger.

13:12 (2 Nephi 23:12). *"The golden wedge of Ophir."* As a result of the terrible destruction, death will make mankind more rare than the golden wedge (gold) of Ophir (probably a port of southern Arabia, famed for its gold).

13:13 (2 Nephi 23:13). *"Shake the heavens."* One of the heavenly signs to be manifest in the last days will be a shaking (trembling) of the heavens. An elaboration of this prophecy was revealed to the Prophet Joseph Smith. The Lord declared: "And also cometh the testimony of the voice of thunderings, and the voice of lightnings, and the voice of tempests, and the voice of the waves of the sea heaving themselves beyond their bounds. And all things shall be in commotion; and surely, men's hearts shall fail them; for fear shall come upon all people." (D&C 88:90–91.)

In addition to the great rains and hailstorms which have been forecast for the last days, inspired servants of God have spoken of fire and brimstone being rained from the heavens. (See BICQ, 33–34.)

13:13 (2 Nephi 23:13). "*The earth shall remove out of her place.*" While it is true that Isaiah's seeric eyes could have seen the many earthquakes which will rock this planet in the last days, including the great one to occur at the time of the Second Coming, there may be a more significant explanation for what this Old Testament seer saw. One of the basic beliefs of Latter-day Saints is: "We believe . . . that the earth will be renewed and receive its paradisiacal glory." (A of F 1:10.) Before the fall of Adam and Eve, this earth was a terrestrial sphere in a Garden-of-Eden state of existence. This same condition will return and prevail throughout the thousand-year period of time known as the Millennium. This will include "bringing the mass of the earth back to the condition it was in before the continents and islands were separated, when the earth was 'divided.'" (See BICQ, 216–18.)

Isaiah 13:14–18 and 2 Nephi 23:14–18

Isaiah now returns his commentary to the destruction of the Babylon of his days. Her prophesied doom is sure. The citizens of Babylon will be hunted and killed, while the strangers or visitors within her walls will flee to their own lands for safety. None will be spared the savagery, including infants and children, nor will ransom payments or peace offerings be accepted by the invaders.

14 And it shall be as the chased roe, and as a sheep that no man taketh up: they shall every man turn to his own people, and flee every one into his own land.

15 Every one that is <u>found</u> shall be thrust through; and every one that is joined <u>unto them</u> shall fall by the sword.

16 Their children also shall be dashed to pieces before their eyes; their houses shall be spoiled, and their wives ravished.

17 Behold, I will stir up the Medes against them, which shall not regard silver; and <u>as for</u> gold, *they shall* <u>not</u> delight in it.

18 Their bows *also shall* dash the young men to pieces; and they shall have no pity on the fruit of the womb; their eye shall not spare children.

14 And it shall be as the chased roe, and as a sheep that no man taketh up; and they shall every man turn to his own people, and flee every one into his own land.

15 Every one that is <u>proud</u> shall be thrust through; <u>yea,</u> and every one that is joined <u>to the wicked</u> shall fall by the sword.

16 Their children also shall be dashed to pieces before their eyes; their houses shall be spoiled and their wives ravished.

17 Behold, I will stir up the Medes against them, which shall not regard silver and gold, <u>nor</u> *shall they* delight in it.

18 Their bows *shall also* dash the young men to pieces; and they shall have no pity on the fruit of the womb; their eye<u>s</u> shall not spare children.

13:14 (2 Nephi 23:14). "*The chased roe.*" The inhabitants of Babylon will be as hunted gazelles or deer.

13:14 (2 Nephi 23:14). "*Sheep that no man taketh up.*" The Babylonians will find none to gather them like sheep to the safety of a sheepfold. No protecting shepherd will rescue them from the invading predators.

13:15 (2 Nephi 23:15). "*Every one that is joined <u>to the wicked</u>.*" The Book of Mormon adds the significant insight that outsiders (visitors, strangers, or foreigners) who join in the wicked ways of the citizenry of Babylon will also be slain.

13:17 (2 Nephi 23:17). "*The Medes.*" They "came from Persia and easily conquered Babylon in 538 B.C. The walls were destroyed twenty years later, after which the city never again became the capital of an independent, strong Mesopotamian power. Two centuries later, after Alexander the Great and his Greek armies conquered the Persians, Babylon rapidly declined in commercial and cultural importance; Seleucia became the major city in the area. By the time of Christ, only a few astronomers and mathematicians continued to live in the ancient, sparsely populated city. After they left, Babylon became a deserted *tell* (mound), gradually covered by sand and brush until it became a hill used only by wild animals and as grazing land for nomadic flocks." (IPSP, 185.)

13:17 (2 Nephi 23:17). "*Shall not regard silver and gold.*" The invading Medes will not be deterred from their destruction by offers of precious metals or ransom money.

13:18 (2 Nephi 23:18). "*Bows shall also dash the young men to pieces.*" While this may have reference to the killing of the Babylonians with bows and arrows, it could also mean that the bows of the defenders of Babylon will be broken or made useless.

Isaiah 13:19–22 and 2 Nephi 23:19–22

In its time, Babylon "was the greatest city in all the world" said Elder LeGrand Richards. "Yet Isaiah announced that that city would be destroyed; he said that it would never be rebuilt, that it would never be inhabited from generation to generation, that it would become the abode of reptiles and wild animals and that the Arabs would no more pitch their tents there. That was a declaration that the greatest city in the world would not only be destroyed, but it would also never be rebuilt." (CR, April 1954, p. 54.)

19 And Babylon, the glory of kingdoms, the beauty of the Chaldees' excellency, shall be as when God overthrew Sodom and Gomorrah.

20 It shall never be inhabited, neither shall it be dwelt in from generation to generation: neither shall the Arabian pitch tent there; neither shall the shepherds make their fold there.

21 But wild beasts of the desert shall lie there; and their houses shall be full of doleful creatures; and owls shall dwell there, and satyrs shall dance there.

22 And the wild beasts of the islands shall cry in their desolate houses, and dragons in their pleasant palaces: and her time is near to come, and her days shall not be prolonged.

19 And Babylon, the glory of kingdoms, the beauty of the Chaldees' excellency, shall be as when God overthrew Sodom and Gomorrah.

20 It shall never be inhabited, neither shall it be dwelt in from generation to generation: neither shall the Arabian pitch tent there; neither shall the shepherds make their fold there.

21 But wild beasts of the desert shall lie there; and their houses shall be full of doleful creatures; and owls shall dwell there, and satyrs shall dance there.

22 And the wild beasts of the islands shall cry in their desolate houses, and dragons in their pleasant palaces; and her time is near to come, and her day shall not be prolonged. <u>For I will destroy her speedily; yea, for I will be merciful unto my people, but the wicked shall perish.</u>

13:21 (2 Nephi 23:21). "*Satyrs shall dance there.*" He-goats or demons of folklore.

13:22 (2 Nephi 23:22). "*Dragons.*" Jackals or wild dogs.

13:22 (2 Nephi 23:22). "*Her days shall not be prolonged.*" The Book of Mormon makes clear that Babylon and her wicked inhabitants will be destroyed with swift destruction.

CHAPTER 14

Isaiah 14 and 2 Nephi 24

OVERVIEW

In contrast to the terrible and total destruction decreed upon Babylon, as outlined in the previous chapter, this chapter opens with a declaration of hope to the once-downtrodden and scattered people of Israel. They shall be restored to their lands of promise and, more importantly, to their status as the covenant people of the Lord. Whereas the children of Israel, and perhaps more particularly those of Judah, had been despised and treated as second-class citizens or even slaves, they would now become the masters or the ruling class, so to speak.

In poetic fashion, the prophet Isaiah describes how the new position of power of these former servants will cause them to recite or sing a *taunt-song* (verses 4–21), which focuses on the now powerless position of their former persecutors. The king of Babylon is equated with Lucifer. Both held powerful positions at one time but both will ultimately be reduced to a state of nothingness. Judgment is also pronounced upon Assyria and Philistia. While much of this prophecy deals with ancient times, there are portentous portions that affect the last days, particularly those that relate to the demise and total dissolution of the devil's power on this earth.

COMMENTARY

Isaiah 14:1–3 and 2 Nephi 24:1–3

The people of Jacob (whose covenant name is Israel) will return to their own lands and even invite strangers to join them. In a reversal of roles, the former servants will now become the masters. Victor Ludlow suggests that "these verses can also find two fulfillments in the latter days. First, they may refer to The Church of Jesus Christ of Latter-day Saints, whose missionary work spreads to all nations and prepares for the peaceful conditions under which the Savior will establish his kingdom at the time of his second coming. Second, these verses may refer to the modern-day return of the Jews to the Holy Land and their building of the modern state of Israel. However, the full blessings of these verses will not be realized until the second coming of Christ, when the Jews will accept him as their Savior." (IPSP, 186; see also BICQ, 125–34.)

Isaiah 14	2 Nephi 24
1 For the Lord will have mercy on Jacob, and will yet choose Israel, and set them in their own land_: and the strangers shall be joined with them, and they shall cleave to the house of Jacob.	1 For the Lord will have mercy on Jacob, and will yet choose Israel, and set them in their own land_; and the strangers shall be joined with them, and they shall cleave to the house of Jacob.
2 And the people shall take them, and bring them to their place_: and the house of Israel shall possess them in the land of the Lord for servants and handmaids_: and they shall take them captives, whose *captives they were;* and they shall rule over their oppressors.	2 And the people shall take them and bring them to their place; yea, from far unto the ends of the earth; and they shall return to their lands of promise. And the house of Israel shall possess them, and the land of the Lord shall be for servants and handmaids; and they shall take them captives unto whom *they were captives;* and they shall rule over their oppressors.

3 And it shall come to pass in the day that the Lord shall give thee rest from thy sorrow, and from thy fear, and from the hard bondage wherein thou wast made to serve,	3 And it shall come to pass in that day that the Lord shall give thee rest, from thy sorrow, and from thy fear, and from the hard bondage wherein thou wast made to serve.

14:1 (2 Nephi 24:1). *"Strangers shall be joined with them."* What "strangers" will join with the house of Jacob or the covenant people of Israel? We are reminded of the apostle Paul's declaration to the converts to Christ of his day: "Now therefore ye are no more strangers and foreigners, but fellow-citizens with the saints, and of the household of God." (Ephesians 2:19.) Furthermore, we think of the promise regarding the posterity of the great patriarch Abraham, grandfather of Jacob: "And if ye be Christ's, then are ye Abraham's seed, and heirs according to the promise." (Galatians 3:29.) By accepting the gospel, "There is neither Jew nor Greek [Gentile] . . . for ye are all one in Christ Jesus." (Galatians 3:28.)

14:2 (2 Nephi 24:2). *"And the people shall take them, and bring them to their place."* Other nations shall help Israel gather to her promised lands. This promise has been partially fulfilled as the kings and queens of the earth (those in positions of political power) have materially helped the dispersed return to their homelands. (See Isaiah 49:22–24; 2 Nephi 6:6–7; 10:8–9; BICQ, 129–30.) However, the promise may also find fulfillment as heads of state open doors and break down barriers that have previously prevented the work of the Lord from moving forward.

Isaiah 14:4–8 and 2 Nephi 24:4–8

These verses begin the *taunt-song* aimed at the once-powerful king of Babylon. Even the trees rejoice in the demise of this once-powerful king. Although the historical context of these verses is couched in ancient Babylon, the application extends to the latter days as well. It could apply to the ultimate removal of any wicked leader, particularly Satan. He will be bound at the commencement of the Millennium, reducing him to the role of a powerless prisoner for one thousand years. (See D&C 88:110; BICQ, 198–99.)

4 That thou shalt take up this proverb against the king of Babylon, and say, How hath the oppressor ceased! the golden city ceased!	4 And it shall come to pass in that day, that thou shalt take up this proverb against the king of Babylon, and say: How hath the oppressor ceased, the golden city ceased!
5 The Lord hath broken the staff of the wicked, and the *sceptre* of the rulers.	5 The Lord hath broken the staff of the wicked, the *scepters* of the rulers.
6 He who smote the people in wrath with a continual stroke, he that ruled the nations in anger, is persecuted, and none hindereth.	6 He who smote the people in wrath with a continual stroke, he that ruled the nations in anger, is persecuted, and none hindereth.
7 The whole earth is at rest, and is quiet: they break forth into singing.	7 The whole earth is at rest, and is quiet; they break forth into singing.
8 Yea, the *fir trees* rejoice at thee, and the cedars of Lebanon, saying, Since thou art laid down, no feller is come up against us.	8 Yea, the *fir-trees* rejoice at thee, and also the cedars of Lebanon, saying: Since thou art laid down no feller is come up against us.

14:4 (2 Nephi 24:4). "*Take up this proverb against the king of Babylon.*" As used in these verses, the proverb is a *taunt-song*, which expresses great pleasure in the reversed role of the king of Babylon and his people. It is poetic satire.

14:4 (2 Nephi 24:4). "*The golden city ceased.*" This appears to be an obvious reference to the once-prized and proud city of Babylon, which will have ceased to exist. The footnote indicates that perhaps this has reference to the city's insolence or pride. Another possible interpretation is that the boisterous raging of her citizenry has ceased.

14:7 (2 Nephi 24:7). *"The whole earth is at rest, and is quiet."* The turmoil and commotion that have been so prevalent during the last days will cease. Not only will civil strife come to an end, but evidently "the voice of thunderings, and the voice of lightnings, and the voice of tempests, and the voice of waves of the sea heaving themselves beyond their bounds" (D&C 88:89–91), and "earthquakes . . . in divers places" (Matthew 24:7) shall cease.

14:8 (2 Nephi 24:8). *"No feller is come up against us."* The fir (cypress) and cedar trees figuratively rejoice because there is no more enemy to come and cut them down. It is a historical fact that the trees of Lebanon had been felled by the kings of Assyria. (See Habakkuk 2:17.) Conquering armies frequently ravaged the land as well as the people.

Isaiah 14:9–11 and 2 Nephi 24:9–11

As the king of Babylon enters the abode of the wicked in the spirit world, he is greeted by other once-powerful leaders ("chief ones") in mortality. They are amazed that he has become as weak and powerless as they are and they note that his once-influential voice is no longer listened to.

9 Hell from beneath is moved for thee to meet thee at thy coming: it stirreth up the dead for thee, even all the chief ones of the earth; it hath raised up from their thrones all the kings of the nations.

10 All they shall speak and say unto thee, Art thou also become weak as we? art thou become like unto us?

9 Hell from beneath is moved for thee to meet thee at thy coming; it stirreth up the dead for thee, even all the chief ones of the earth; it hath raised up from their thrones all the kings of the nations.

10 All they shall speak and say unto thee: Art thou also become weak as we? Art thou become like unto us?

138

11 Thy pomp is brought down to the grave, and the noise of thy viols: the worm is spread under thee, and the worms cover thee.	11 Thy pomp is brought down to the grave; the noise of thy viols is not heard; the worm is spread under thee, and the worms cover thee.

14:9 (2 Nephi 24:9). "*Hell.*" Sheol, or the abode of departed spirits. Particularly, this refers to the spirit prison where the wicked dwell. (See Alma 40:13–14; DCE, 238–39.)

14:9 (2 Nephi 24:9). "*Hell from beneath is moved for thee.*" The inhabitants (prisoners) of hell are stirred or excited about the arrival of this once-powerful person.

14:11 (2 Nephi 24:11). "*The worm is spread under thee, and the worms cover thee.*" The king, who was sought by the rich and powerful in life, is now reduced to fodder for worms and maggots.

Isaiah 14:12–14 and 2 Nephi 24:12–14

Isaiah now personifies the king of Babylon as Lucifer himself. He speaks of the devil's ill-fated attempt in the premortal world to usurp the position and power of God for his own evil ends, for which he and his followers were cast out. (See Moses 4:1–4; D&C 29:36–37; DCE, 134–35.)

12 How art thou fallen from heaven, O Lucifer, son of the morning! how art thou cut down to the ground, which *didst* weaken the nations!	12 How art thou fallen from heaven, O Lucifer, son of the morning! Art thou cut down to the ground, which *did* weaken the nations!
13 For thou hast said in thine heart, I will ascend into heaven, I will exalt my throne above the stars of God: I will sit also upon the mount of the congregation, in the sides of the north:	13 For thou hast said in thy heart: I will ascend into heaven, I will exalt my throne above the stars of God; I will sit also upon the mount of the congregation, in the sides of the north;

| 14 I will ascend above the heights of the clouds; I will be like the <u>m</u>ost High. | 14 I will ascend above the heights of the clouds; I will be like the <u>M</u>ost High. |

14:12 (2 Nephi 24:12). *"Lucifer, son of the morning."* Lucifer is the name whereby the devil was known in our pre-mortal existence. In Hebrew the title means morning star or son of dawn. It may have some implication to the timing of his birth as a spirit child in the premortal life or reference to his once-held position of prominence before his fateful fall. (See Elder Marion G. Romney, CR, April 1971, p. 23; DCE, 332.)

14:13 (2 Nephi 24:13). *"In the sides of the north."* Among the Babylonians and others, there was the belief that the abode of Deity was in the north. (See LDSKJ, Psalm 48:2, footnote *d;* Isaiah 14:13, footnote *e.*) Lucifer wished to ascend to this lofty place.

Isaiah 14:15–17 and 2 Nephi 24:15–17

Lucifer's lust for power and prominence landed him in the pit of hell rather than on the sought-after throne of God. The inhabitants of Sheol will be so surprised to see the now-powerless Lucifer that they will exclaim in disbelief, "Is this the man that made the earth to tremble?" Surely such a pitiful, powerless creature could not be the one who "did shake kingdoms" and wreaked such destruction on earth! (Such words could also be said of the king of Babylon, the once-powerful conqueror now reduced to the role of a serf.)

| 15 Yet thou shalt be brought down to hell, to the sides of the pit. | 15 Yet thou shalt be brought down to hell, to the sides of the pit. |
| 16 They that see thee shall narrowly look upon thee, and consider thee, *saying,* Is this the man that made the earth to tremble, that did shake kingdoms; | 16 They that see thee shall narrowly look upon thee, and <u>shall</u> consider thee, <u>and shall</u> *say:* Is this the man that made the earth to tremble, that did shake kingdoms<u>?</u> |

17 <u>That</u> made the world as a wilderness, and destroyed the cities thereof<u>; that</u> opened not the house of his prisoners?	17 <u>And</u> made the world as a wilderness, and destroyed the cities thereof<u>, and</u> opened not the house of his prisoners?

14:15 (2 Nephi 24:15). "*The sides of the pit.*" Figuratively, the remotest parts of hell. John the Revelator tells us that at the commencement of the Millennium the devil will be cast into a bottomless pit with a seal set upon him that will not be broken until the end of the thousand years, when he will be "loosed a little season." (Revelation 20:2–3; see also BICQ, 221–26.)

14:16 (2 Nephi 24:16). "*Narrowly look upon thee.*" They will squint at Lucifer and reflect upon him; or they will stare at him intently.

14:17 (2 Nephi 24:17). "*That opened not the house of his prisoners.*" Once one has been caught up (captured) in wickedness, it is very difficult to escape. Elder Neal A. Maxwell observed: "Lucifer is permissive on most things, but not on granting passports for citizens to leave his realm." (DOD, 12.)

Isaiah 14:18–20 and 2 Nephi 24:18–20

Isaiah now strikes at the heart of Lucifer's punishment. While those he has seduced into sin will lay their bodies down in graves—one day to be resurrected—the devil will have no need of a burial plot. His decision to rebel against the Almighty deprived him and those who followed him of *ever* receiving a mortal body. These demons are so desperate to take over a physical body that a legion of them even pleaded to be cast into the bodies of swine. (Mark 5:1–13.) Nor will the devil and his demoniacal followers ever have posterity. The only way Lucifer will ever be a "father" is as the "father of lies." (See Moses 4:4; BICQ, 52–53.)

18 All the kings of the nations, _even_ all of them, lie in glory, every one in his own house.

19 But thou art cast out of thy grave like an abominable branch, and _as_ the _raiment_ of those that are slain, thrust through with a sword, that go down to the stones of the pit; as a _carcase_ trodden under feet.

20 Thou shalt not be joined with them in burial, because thou hast destroyed thy land, and slain thy people_:_ the seed of _evildoers_ shall never be renowned.

18 All the kings of the nations, _yea,_ all of them, lie in glory, every one _of them_ in his own house.

19 But thou art cast out of thy grave like an abominable branch, and the _remnant_ of those that are slain, thrust through with a sword, that go down to the stones of the pit; as a _carcass_ trodden under feet.

20 Thou shalt not be joined with them in burial, because thou hast destroyed thy land and slain thy people; the seed of _evil-doers_ shall never be renowned.

14:18 (2 Nephi 24:18). "_Lie in glory._" There are at least two possible meanings of this phrase. First, kings (royalty, pharaohs, presidents, etc.) are generally buried with great pomp, ceremony, and splendor. Second, even wicked kings, once they have paid the price of penance and suffered the wrath of God (D&C 76:103–12), will be redeemed from the grave and resurrected to a degree of glory in the eternities. However, Lucifer and his minions will be cast into outer darkness, where there will be neither light nor glory. (See D&C 88:24; DCE, 301–2.)

14:18 (2 Nephi 24:18). "_Every one in his own house._" In his own family tomb. (See 1 Kings 2:34.)

14:19 (2 Nephi 24:19). "_Thou art cast out of thy grave like an abominable branch._" Again, there are two possible meanings here. Applied to Lucifer, the statement suggests he will have no more part in a grave than an unfruitful shoot or blighted branch will be part of the tree from which it was cut off. On the other hand, as applied to the king of Babylon, the implication is that his body would remain unburied (which anciently was considered to be a great curse).

14:19 (2 Nephi 24:19). "*The <u>remnant</u> of those that are slain.*" The Book of Mormon makes a significant substitution here. Isaiah is not speaking of clothing ("raiment"), but of people ("remnant"). The corpse of the dead king will lie among the remains of others who have been slain, all of them rotting like cast-off twigs and branches.

14:19 (2 Nephi 24:19). "*The stones of the pit.*" Ultimately, a common grave will be hastily dug, or stones will be flung together to form a burial plot on the battlefield. The mighty and the common will be heaped together as stones at the very bottom of this burial pit. As applied to Lucifer, the implication is that he will be thrown into the pit of outer darkness, from which there will never be an escape.

14:20 (2 Nephi 24:20). "*Thou shalt not be joined with them in burial.*" Neither the king of Babylon nor Lucifer will have the honor of a decent burial, an honor usually bestowed on the kings and mighty of the world.

14:20 (2 Nephi 24:20). "*The seed of evildoers shall never be renowned.*" The king of Babylon will have no offspring who will be honored, held in high esteem, or even mentioned by others. Lucifer, as noted above, will never have posterity.

Isaiah 14:21–23 and 2 Nephi 24:21–23

The posterity of the wicked king of Babylon will not be allowed to perpetuate his evil ways. Not only will his own children be slain, but his people will as well. In addition, his great city will be utterly destroyed. In reality, the deaths and destruction of his own people and lands are of his own doing.

21 Prepare slaughter for his children for the iniquity of their fathers; that they do not rise, nor possess the land, nor fill the face of the world with cities.

22 For I will rise up against them, saith the Lord of hosts, and cut off from Babylon the name, and remnant, and son, and nephew, saith the Lord.

23 I will also make it a possession for the bittern, and pools of water: and I will sweep it with the besom of destruction, saith the Lord of hosts.

21 Prepare slaughter for his children for the iniquities of their fathers, that they do not rise, nor possess the land, nor fill the face of the world with cities.

22 For I will rise up against them, saith the Lord of Hosts, and cut off from Babylon the name, and remnant, and son, and nephew, saith the Lord.

23 I will also make it a possession for the bittern, and pools of water; and I will sweep it with the besom of destruction, saith the Lord of Hosts

14:21 (2 Nephi 24:21). "*Prepare slaughter for his children.*" In essence, "Let not another evil generation arise and resume an evil regime." (LDSKJ, Isaiah 14:21, footnote *a*.) The decimation of the children of the wicked ruler is the natural consequence of his own crimes.

14:23 (2 Nephi 24:23). "*Make it a possession for the bittern, and pools of water.*" The lowly "bittern" (hedgehog) would typify the future life form of this once-proud land. When Cyrus conquered Babylon, he destroyed her irrigation works, turning the once lush and fruitful land into fetid pools of water (swamps or bogs).

14:23 (2 Nephi 24:23). "*Sweep it with the besom of destruction.*" The broom of destruction.

Isaiah 14:24–27 and 2 Nephi 24:24–27

Isaiah now shifts his focus from Babylon to Assyria. The Lord has foreseen the efforts of the Assyrians to overthrow Judah, but the invaders' efforts shall fail. Lest anyone doubt that His purposes will be accomplished, the Lord declares that whatever He has pronounced or seen in His omniscience shall come to pass.

24 The Lord of <u>h</u>osts hath sworn saying, Surely as I have thought, so shall it come to pass; and as I have purposed, so shall it stand:

24 The Lord of <u>H</u>osts hath sworn, saying: Surely as I have thought, so shall it come to pass; and as I have purposed, so shall it stand—

25 That I will <u>break</u> the Assyrian in my land, and upon my mountains tread him under foot: then shall his yoke depart from off them, and his burden depart from off their shoulders.

25 That I will <u>bring</u> the Assyrian in my land, and upon my mountains tread him under foot; then shall his yoke depart from off them, and his burden depart from off their shoulders.

26 This is the purpose that is purposed upon the whole earth: and this is the hand that is stretched out upon all the nations.

26 This is the purpose that is purposed upon the whole earth; and this is the hand that is stretched out upon all nations.

27 For the Lord of <u>h</u>osts hath purposed, and who shall disannul <u>it</u>? <u>and</u> his hand is stretched out, and who shall turn it back?

27 For the Lord of <u>H</u>osts hath purposed, and who shall disannul? <u>A</u>nd his hand is stretched out, and who shall turn it back?

14:24 (2 Nephi 24:24). "*Surely as I have thought, so shall it come to pass.*" As the Lord has "thought" (resolved) so shall it be. He does not change His mind. He is consistent and sure! One may, with full confidence, rely upon every word of the Lord, for "he never doth vary from that which he hath said." (Mosiah 2:22.) "His purposes fail not, neither are there any who can stay his hand." (D&C 76:3.)

14:25 (2 Nephi 24:25). "*I will <u>bring</u> the Assyrian in my land.*" The Book of Mormon substitutes the word "bring" for the biblical or Hebrew word "break." In either event, the invading Assyrian armies are foreseen by the Lord (brought into the land of Judah) but they will be broken or defeated. One renowned biblical commentary suggests that this was fulfilled in the defeat and destruction of the Assyrian King Sennacherib's army. (TOVBC, 426.) However, a Latter-day Saint scholar, with the advantage of additional revelation, states: "It is difficult to determine whether Isaiah is prophesying about the destruction of Sennacherib's Assyrian army in 701 B.C. or the defeat of the army of the nations led by King Gog in the last days. (Compare Isa. 36–37 with Ezek. 38–39.) In both cases, the Lord's punishment is felt by the wicked nations of the earth." (IPSP, 189.)

14:25 (2 Nephi 24:25). "*Upon my mountains tread him under foot.*" Upon the mountains of Judah, the enemy will be defeated or trodden under foot.

14:26 (2 Nephi 24:26). "*The purpose that is purposed upon the whole earth.*" The Lord purposes to ultimately defeat all the wicked upon the whole earth, thus lifting the burdens they have placed upon those they have oppressed.

14:26 (2 Nephi 24:26). "*The hand that is stretched out upon all the nations.*" The Lord ultimately controls the future of all nations. In an 1838 revelation He declared: "Do I not hold the destinies of all the armies of the nations of the earth?" (D&C 117:6.) Eventually all worldly nations will be overthrown and replaced by the kingdom of God, for "Christ will [return and] reign personally upon the earth." (A of F 1:10.)

14:27 (2 Nephi 24:27). "*Who shall disannul it?*" Nothing the Lord proclaims shall be disannulled (be completely annulled or come to naught) by any means; neither man, nature, nor the forces of the adversary shall stay His hand or make void His words. Said the Lord to the Prophet Joseph, "Behold, I, the Lord, declare unto you, and my words are sure and shall not fail." (D&C 64:31.)

Isaiah 14:28–31 and 2 Nephi 24:28–31

Another "burden" (prophecy of doom) is now pronounced. This time the victim is yet another enemy of Judah—Palestina, or Philistia. Sidney Sperry noted that "although the prophecy is more especially directed against Philistia, Judah is also involved. Unfortunately," he then adds, "a number of thorny, unresolved historical problems prevent the giving of a reasonably exact interpretation of some parts of the prophecy. But Isaiah seems to be telling Philistia not to rejoice over his predictions of the ruin and downfall of Judah, her traditional enemy. For whereas the kingdom of Judah will fall, there will come a glorious day when the people of Israel will rise above their troubles. . . . On the other hand, Philistia is to be ruined and to fall without having any prospects of recovery." (BMC, 244–45.)

28 In the year that king Ahaz died was this burden.	28 In the year that king Ahaz died was this burden.
29 Rejoice not thou, whole Palestina, because the rod of him that smote thee is broken: for out of the serpent's root shall come forth a cockatrice, and his fruit shall be a fiery flying serpent.	29 Rejoice not thou, whole Palestina, because the rod of him that smote thee is broken; for out of the serpent's root shall come forth a cockatrice, and his fruit shall be a fiery flying serpent.
30 And the *firstborn* of the poor shall feed, and the needy shall lie down in safety: and I will kill thy root with famine, and he shall slay thy remnant.	30 And the *first-born* of the poor shall feed, and the needy shall lie down in safety; and I will kill thy root with famine, and he shall slay thy remnant.
31 Howl, O gate; cry, O city; thou, whole Palestina, art dissolved: for there shall come from the north a smoke, and none shall be alone in his appointed times.	31 Howl, O gate; cry, O city; thou, whole Palestina, art dissolved; for there shall come from the north a smoke, and none shall be alone in his appointed times.

14:28 (2 Nephi 24:28). *"The year that king Ahaz died."* This identifies the time when the prophecy was given, which, according to the footnote reference in the LDS edition of the King James Bible, was about 720 B.C. Ahaz became king of Judah somewhere around 742–734 B.C. (See commentary on Isaiah 7 and 2 Nephi 17.)

14:29 (2 Nephi 24:29). *"Palestina."* The country of Philistia consisted essentially of five city-states, each governed by its own lord. The nation was home of the Philistines, detested enemies of Judah and the Israelites. This country was at the height of its power at the time of King Saul's death, but declined during the reign of King David. The Philistines were conquered by the Assyrians in 734 B.C., later they became part of the Persian Empire, and finally the land was annexed to Syria by the Romans. "Strangely enough the name of the territory of these detested enemies of the Jews has become one familiar title (Palestine) for the whole of the Holy Land." (LDSBD, "Philistines," 751.)

14:29 (2 Nephi 24:29). *"Rejoice not . . . because the rod . . . is broken."* The Philistines were warned not to be premature in exulting over the death of the oppressor who had wielded a rod (instrument of punishment) over them. The rejoicing may have been the result of Ahaz's death, but more likely was directed to other oppressors. J. R. Dummelow suggested that the broken rod applied more directly to the Assyrian king, Tiglath-pileser (747–734 B.C.), who had been an ally of Ahaz. (TOVBC, 426.) However, Victor Ludlow stated that this premature rejoicing was "either in the death of [Assyrian King] Shalmaneser V (727–722) or the freedom Philistia maintained after Sargon's conquest of Samaria and Israel (722–721)." (IPSP, 190.) In any event, the rejoicing would be short-lived because further oppression was prophesied.

14:29 (2 Nephi 24:29). *"Out of the serpent's root shall come forth a cockatrice, and his fruit shall be a fiery flying serpent."* Although Philistia shall see the death of one or more enemies as the means of deliverance from oppression, yet worse dangers (out of the serpent's root) are to come. Sidney Sperry points out the *serpent's root, cockatrice* (venomous viper), and *fiery flying serpent* are "all symbolic of evil to come upon her [Philistia]." (BMC, 245.) Each of these represents a more deadly threat than the previous one mentioned. J. R. Dummelow identified Sargon (Assyrian king from 722 to 705 B.C.) and Sennacherib (Assyrian king from 705 to 681 B.C.) as the cockatrice and fiery serpent, "each one proving more terrible and formidable to the nations of Western Asia than his predecessor." (TOVBC, 426.)

14:30 (2 Nephi 24:30). "*The first-born of the poor shall feed.*" The very poor, the low and helpless, shall yet find sustenance both of a physical and spiritual nature. Some scholars suggest this applies specifically to the children of scattered and despised Judah, while others have identified the defeated Philistines as the subject of this promise—they are also children of the Lord and He will not forget them. The identity of the redeemed poor does not matter. What is important is that their hungry bellies shall yet be filled with food and their starving spirits shall be fed with the bread of eternal truths.

14:30 (2 Nephi 24:30). "*I will kill thy root with famine, and he shall slay thy remnant.*" While Judah and Israel will ultimately survive their scatterings and oppression, Philistia will perish as a nation and as a people, never to recover. She is (vs. 31) "dissolved" or melted away.

14:31 (2 Nephi 24:31). "*There shall come from the north a smoke.*" An invading army (probably the Assyrians) shall come from the north.

14:31 (2 Nephi 24:31). "*None shall be alone in his appointed times.*" There will be no soldier missing from the ranks of the well-disciplined invading Assyrian armies. There will be no stragglers; each warrior will be found standing in his place of assembly, or at his appointed post.

Isaiah 14:32 and 2 Nephi 24:32

Isaiah concludes his chapter with a question and an answer.

32 What shall <u>one</u> then answer the messengers of the nation? That the Lord hath founded Zion, and the poor of his people shall trust in it.	32 What shall then answer the messengers of the nation<u>s</u>? That the Lord hath founded Zion, and the poor of his people shall trust in it.

14:32 (2 Nephi 24:32). "*What shall then answer the messengers of the nation?*" What reply should be given those who ask why God destroys (or allows to be destroyed) whole nations or people?

14:32 (2 Nephi 24:32). "*That the Lord hath founded Zion, and the poor of his people shall trust in it.*" This is the answer to the question raised in the first part of the verse. God will not tolerate wicked people or nations. His desire is to establish the *standard of Zion* in every heart, home, village, and nation throughout the world. Among other things, this standard calls for the "pure in heart" to "dwell in righteousness" and to see that there is "no poor among them." (See D&C 97:21; Moses 7:18.) In such a place there is no contention, envying, disharmony, or distrust, for the love of God will dwell in the hearts of each one. (See 4 Nephi 1:2–3, 12–13, 15–16.) This is the environment in which the poor or afflicted can seek refuge both physically and spiritually. They can trust in the standard of Zion!

CHAPTER 15

Isaiah 29 and 2 Nephi 25, 26, 27

OVERVIEW

After two chapters of personal but inspired commentary (2 Nephi 25 and 26), in which he has borne powerful witness to the divine nature and mission of Jesus Christ, Nephi returns to recording the writings of Isaiah. He quotes the Old Testament seer to show that Isaiah knew of the latter-day coming forth of the Book of Mormon: Another Testament of Jesus Christ.

Just as Isaiah's messianic prophecies in ancient times bore strong testimony to the coming of Jesus Christ, so a strong scriptural witness for Jesus Christ in the latter days would speak from the pages of another scriptural record which Isaiah saw through seeric vision.

The ancient seer saw those who would be raised up as latter-day witnesses to the truthfulness of this other scriptural record. Isaiah saw that it would come forth in a day of apostasy, as part of the great restoration of the gospel of Jesus Christ in its fulness. He even saw an anecdotal event that would involve the future translator of the sacred record, one of the witnesses to the book's divine authenticity, and several of the learned of the world.

It is ironic that the learned of the world today have little understanding of the significance or meaning of this inspired chapter of Isaiah's ancient prophecies. In the words of the apostle Paul, they are "ever learning, and never able to come to the knowledge of the truth." (2 Timothy 3:7.) The wisdom of the wise of the world is limited because they lack an understanding of, or acceptance of, latter-day prophets, revelation,

151

and scripture. Yet all of these are necessary to hold the key to unlocking the meaning of this great vision of the ancient seer, the prophet Isaiah.

COMMENTARY

Isaiah 29:1–2

These verses are not quoted by Nephi. However, as the Prophet Joseph Smith worked on his inspired translation of the Bible, he made a slight alteration in verse 2, adding the phrase "for thus hath the Lord said unto me" after the word "sorrow," and deleting the words "me as" between "unto" and "Ariel." (JST Isaiah 29:2.) Ariel (the city where David dwelt) was Jerusalem. It meant "altar of God" or "hearth of God." The hearth was the highest tier of the altar of Solomon's temple and was the place where sacrifices were consumed by fire. "Since the term is used to describe Jerusalem in her distressed condition (the word 'Zion' replaces this term in 2 Ne. 27:3), it implies that Judah will need to be humbled and that God's fire of judgment will refine her." (IPSP, 270–71.)

Isaiah 29	JST, Isaiah 29
1 Woe to Ariel, to Ariel, the city where David dwelt! add ye year to year; let them kill sacrifices.	1 Woe to Ariel, to Ariel, the city where David dwelt! add ye year to year; let them kill sacrifices.
2 Yet I will distress Ariel, and there shall be heaviness and sorrow: <u>and it</u> shall be unto <u>me as</u> Ariel.	2 Yet I will distress Ariel, and there shall be heaviness and sorrow; <u>for thus hath the Lord said unto me, It</u> shall be unto Ariel;

Isaiah 29:3–5 and 2 Nephi 26:15–18

These verses could refer to the nations of Judah and Israel being brought low, or destroyed. The ancient covenant people would then speak "low out of the dust" in the sense that they would speak out of the depths of their humbled condition.

A more probable interpretation of these verses would be

their application to the destruction of the ancient Nephite civilization. This is obviously the interpretation Nephi had in mind. This people, because of iniquity and unbelief, were to be "brought down low in the dust, even that they are not." Yet, even though destroyed as a people without posterity, their words "shall speak . . . out of the ground, and their speech shall be low out of the dust." The record of this ancient people—not only their secular history but more particularly their prophecies and sacred writings—shall be made available to future generations.

The last survivor of that ancient Nephite society was a prophet, scribe, and warrior named Moroni. He was charged with safeguarding those sacred writings. He discharged that duty by concluding the record and safely burying it in a protected place to which he was undoubtedly led. Over fourteen hundred years later, then a resurrected being, he was divinely directed to deliver the plates "out of the ground" to the young Prophet Joseph Smith. Joseph, in turn, was called to translate the sacred record into what is now known to millions throughout the earth as the Book of Mormon: Another Testament of Jesus Christ. (See JS–H 1:27–54, 59–60.)

Because Nephi is expounding on Isaiah, rather than simply quoting, his words cast a great deal of light on this passage.

Isaiah 29	2 Nephi 26
3 And I will camp against thee round about, and will *lay* siege against thee with a mount, and I will raise forts against thee.	15 After my seed and the seed of my brethren shall have dwindled in unbelief, and shall have been smitten by the Gentiles; yea, after the Lord God shall have camped against them round about, and shall have *laid* siege against them with a mount, and raised forts against them; and after they shall have been brought down low in the dust, even that they are not, yet the words of the righteous shall be written, and the

prayers of the faithful shall be heard, and all those who have dwindled in unbelief shall not be forgotten.

4 And thou shalt be brought down, and *shalt* speak out of the ground, and thy speech shall be low out of the dust, and thy voice shall be, as of one that hath a familiar spirit, out of the ground, and thy speech shall whisper out of the dust.

16 For those who shall be destroyed *shall* speak unto them out of the ground, and their speech shall be low out of the dust, and their voice shall be as one that hath a familiar spirit; for the Lord God will give unto him power, that he may whisper concerning them, even as it were out of the ground; and their speech shall whisper out of the dust.

17 For thus saith the Lord God: They shall write the things which shall be done among them, and they shall be written and sealed up in a book, and those who have dwindled in unbelief shall not have them, for they seek to destroy the things of God.

5 Moreover the multitude of thy strangers shall be like small dust, and the multitude of the terrible ones shall be as chaff that passeth away: yea, it shall be at an instant suddenly.

18 Wherefore, as those who have been destroyed have been destroyed speedily; and the multitude of their terrible ones shall be as chaff that passeth away—yea, thus saith the Lord God: It shall be at an instant, suddenly—

29:5 (2 Nephi 26:18). "*The multitude of their terrible ones shall be as chaff.*" The wicked shall be tossed to the wind as chaff that is separated from the good seed at harvest time. This could apply to the wicked in the latter days who oppose the Lord's standard of Zion, or it could have application to the past destruction of the wicked Nephite society: they who were "led about by Satan, even as chaff is driven before the wind." (Mormon 5:16–18.)

Isaiah 29:6–10 and 2 Nephi 27:2–5

These next few verses deal with judgments which are to come upon the wicked in the last days. Those who fight against Zion, who reject her ways and her prophets, will be disappointed; they will be as one who dreams and thinks he has eaten but wakes up empty, racked with hunger pangs.

Isaiah 29	2 Nephi 27
6 <u>Thou</u> *shalt* be visited of the Lord of <u>h</u>osts with thunder, and with earthquake, and great noise, with storm and tempest, and the flame of devouring fire.	2 <u>And when that day shall come they</u> *shall* be visited of the Lord of <u>H</u>osts, with thunder and with earthquake, and <u>with a</u> great noise, <u>and</u> with storm, and <u>with</u> tempest, and <u>with</u> the flame of devouring fire.
7–8 And <u>the multitude of</u> all the nations that fight against <u>Ariel, even all that fight against her and her munition</u>, and that distress her, shall be as a dream of a night vision. <u>It</u> shall *even be* as <u>when an</u> hungry man dreameth, and, behold, he eateth; but he awaketh, and his soul is empty: or <u>as when</u> a thirsty man dreameth, and, behold, he drinketh; but he awaketh, and, behold, he is faint, and his soul hath appetite: so shall the multitude of all the nations be, that fight against <u>m</u>ount Zion.	3 And all the nations that fight against <u>Zion</u>, and that distress her, shall be as a dream of a night vision; yea, it shall *be* <u>unto them</u>, *even* as <u>unto a</u> hungry man <u>which</u> dreameth, and behold he eateth but he awaketh and his soul is empty; or <u>like unto</u> a thirsty man <u>which</u> dreameth, and behold he drinketh but he awaketh and behold he is faint, and his soul hath appetite; yea, even so shall the multitude of all the nations be that fight against <u>M</u>ount Zion.

9 <u>Stay yourselves,</u> and wonder; *cry ye* out, and cry<u>:</u> <u>they are</u> drunken, but not with wine<u>; they</u> stagger, but not with strong drink.

4 <u>For behold, all ye that</u> <u>doeth iniquity,</u> stay yourselves and wonder<u>, for *ye*</u> shall *cry* out, and cry<u>; yea, ye</u> shall <u>be</u> drunken but not with wine<u>, ye shall</u> stagger but not with strong drink.

10 For the Lord hath poured out upon you the spirit of deep sleep<u>, and</u> *hath* closed your eyes<u>:</u> the prophets and your rulers, the seers hath he covered.

5 For <u>behold,</u> the Lord hath poured out upon you the spirit of deep sleep<u>. For</u> <u>behold, ye</u> *have* closed your eyes<u>, and ye have rejected</u> the prophets<u>;</u> and your rulers, <u>and</u> the seers hath he covered <u>because of your</u> <u>iniquity.</u>

29:6 (2 Nephi 27:2). *"Visited . . . with thunder . . . earthquake . . . great noise . . . storm and tempest."* The Lord has often used the elements to call people to repentance. He has specifically warned the inhabitants of the earth in the last days that He will speak to them through these voices of nature. (D&C 43:25; 88:89–91; 97:26; Mormon 8:29; BICQ, 25–37.)

29:7 (2 Nephi 27:3). *"Munition."* Fortification or place of safety.

29:8 (2 Nephi 27:3). *"His soul is empty . . . he is faint, and his soul hath appetite."* Not only will those who actively fight against Zion find their souls empty, but so also will those who simply stand idly by, allowing their spirits to atrophy. Those who reject *or* neglect the words of living bread that can stave off spiritual starvation, or the truths of living waters that can quench spiritual thirst, will find their souls empty and their spirits faint. No matter how often they eat bread at the tables of the learned, or drink the waters of the man-made religions of the world, they will not be satisfied.

Philosophies and theological teachings, no matter how well intended, that lack true spiritual nutrients (the fulness of the gospel and priesthood power) will not satisfy the soul's hunger for truth. We are reminded of the Savior's words to the woman at the well in Samaria: "Whosoever drinketh of the water that I shall give him shall never thirst; but the water that I shall give him shall be in him a well of water springing up into everlasting life." (John 4:14.)

Furthermore, we think of this divine promise: "And blessed are all they who do hunger and thirst after righteousness, for they shall be *filled with the Holy Ghost.*" (3 Nephi 12:6; italics added.)

The words of a prophet of old are worth pondering in this respect: "Cursed is he that putteth his trust in man, or maketh flesh his arm, or shall hearken unto the precepts of men, save their precepts shall be given by the power of the Holy Ghost." (2 Nephi 28:31.)

29:8 (2 Nephi 27:3). "*The multitude of all . . . that fight against Mount Zion.*" Joseph McConkie and Robert Millet offer the following insights: "As the phrase *mountain of the Lord's house* (2 Nephi 2:12) can properly be understood to apply to all temples, so the phrase *Mount Zion* can appropriately be used to refer to the gathering places of the Saints. . . .

"Those who would raze the temples of the true believers are left without defense and without refuge against the 'storm, and from wrath when it shall be poured out without mixture upon the whole earth' (D&C 115:6). They have poisoned the water in the well from which they too must drink." (DCBM 1:313–14.)

29:9 (2 Nephi 27:4). "*Stay yourselves.*" The Book of Mormon clarifies that this phrase is addressed to "all ye that doeth iniquity." A "stay" is a brace or support. The plea of the prophet is for those who are presently unanchored in the gospel to cease their pursuit of the ways of the world. "Brace yourselves against the winds of wickedness! Hold fast to the iron rod whereby you will be strengthened against sin!" (See 1 Nephi 8:30; "The Iron Rod," Hymns, no. 274.)

29:9 (2 Nephi 27:4). "*Drunken, but not with wine.*" They are "drunken with iniquity and all manner of abominations." (2 Nephi 27:1.) They are so intoxicated with wickedness in any of its forms, including a lust for power or position in the world, that they have lost their spiritual senses. They neither think nor walk straight.

29:10 (2 Nephi 27:5). "*The spirit of deep sleep.*" The apostle Paul refers to this as the "spirit of slumber." This is a deep sleep or spiritual stupor which prevents the spiritually unprepared from seeing and hearing things they are not prepared to receive, understand, or follow. (Romans 11:8.)

In this respect, we should consider the response of Jesus to those who questioned why He spoke in parables: "He answered and said unto them, Because it is given unto you to know the mysteries of the kingdom of heaven, but to them [the spiritually unprepared or asleep] it is not given.

"For whosoever receiveth, to him shall be given, and he shall have more abundance; but whosoever continueth not to receive, from him shall be taken away even that he hath.

"Therefore speak I to them in parables: because they seeing see not; and hearing they hear not, neither do they understand." (JST Matthew 13:10–13.)

29:10 (2 Nephi 27:5). "*The prophets and your rulers, the seers hath he covered <u>because of your iniquity</u>.*" Because of their spiritual blindness and iniquity, the Lord would remove the prophets and seers from among them. They would be left to grovel and stumble in spiritual darkness. The heavens and the voices of the prophets are silent to those whose ears will not hear. This is descriptive of the apostate condition that prevailed at the time young Joseph Smith sought for the truth. In response to his prayerful plea, and as foreordained in the premortal councils before this world was, the heavens were once again opened and the spiritual eyes and ears of the young Prophet Joseph were touched.

Isaiah 29:11–12 and 2 Nephi 27:6–24

The Book of Mormon adds major clarifying text to these two verses of Isaiah. The scholars of the world have no understanding of the Old Testament prophet's reference to the words of a sealed book that are delivered to both the learned and the unlearned. The added verses in the Book of Mormon reveal that the book will come from "them which have slumbered" (meaning the destroyed civilizations of the Nephites and the Jaredites). (2 Nephi 27:6.)

It will contain revelations that tell of events "from the beginning of the world to the ending thereof," but this information will be sealed up, yet to come forth in "the own due time of the Lord." (2 Nephi 27:7–11.)

The portion of the book which has not been sealed will be made available to the world, and "three witnesses shall behold it, by the power of God, . . . and they shall testify to the truth of the book." (2 Nephi 27:12.) In 1829, Oliver Cowdery, David Whitmer, and Martin Harris were called of God to be these witnesses. They bore testimony to the world of having seen the plates from which the Book of Mormon was translated, of seeing the heavenly messenger Moroni, and of hearing the voice of God bear record that the plates had been translated "by the gift and power of God."

The added text of Nephi also tells that, in addition to the translator of the record (Joseph Smith) and the Three Witnesses, "a few according to the will of God" will also be called "to bear testimony." (2 Nephi 27:13.) These few are known as the Eight Witnesses, who were divinely authorized to see and handle the plates under the direction of the Prophet Joseph. Those who bore testimony of their participation on this momentous occasion were Christian Whitmer; Jacob Whitmer; Peter Whitmer, Jr.; John Whitmer; Hiram Page; Joseph Smith, Sr.; Hyrum Smith; and Samuel H. Smith. Their testimony, as that of the Three Witnesses, can be found in the forepart of the Book of Mormon. (See also HC 1:58, note.)

In addition to the twelve formal witnesses listed above (including Joseph Smith), the truthfulness of the book will be testified "in the mouth of as many witnesses as seemeth [the Lord] good." (2 Nephi 27:14; see also 2 Nephi 11:3.) This prophecy has been fulfilled by the millions who have borne testimony of its truthfulness from the days it was first published until the present time; and millions, if not billions, will continue to add their testimony of it in the future.

The Nephite text also adds this warning: "And wo be unto him that rejecteth the word of God!" (2 Nephi 27:14.) Such rejection occurs not only when the book is spurned by unbelievers but also when Latter-day Saints—those who have accepted the book as the word of God—fail to take it seriously. Regarding such neglect, consider the warnings of two latter-day prophets.

President Joseph Fielding Smith, tenth prophet of the Lord in these latter days, stated: "No member of [The Church of Jesus Christ of Latter-day Saints] can stand approved in the presence of God who has not seriously and carefully read the Book of Mormon." (CR, October 1961, p. 18.)

President Ezra Taft Benson, the thirteenth man to wear the prophet's mantle in this dispensation, declared: "Every Latter-day Saint should make the study of this book a lifetime pursuit. Otherwise he is placing his soul in jeopardy and neglecting that which could give spiritual and intellectual unity to his whole life." (CR, April 1975, p. 97.)

6 And it shall come to pass that the Lord God shall bring forth unto you the words of a book, and they shall be the words of them which have slumbered.

7 And behold the book shall be sealed; and in the book shall be a revelation from God, from the beginning of the world to the ending thereof.

8 Wherefore, because of the things which are sealed up, the things which are sealed shall not be delivered in the day of the wickedness and abominations of the people. Wherefore the book shall be kept from them.

9 But the book shall be delivered unto a man, and he shall deliver the words of the book, which are the words of those who have slumbered in the dust, and he shall deliver these words unto another;

10 But the words which are sealed he shall not deliver, neither shall he deliver the book. For the book shall be sealed by the power of God, and the revelation which was sealed shall be kept in the book until the own due time of the Lord, that they may come forth; for behold, they reveal all things from the foundation of the world unto the end thereof.

11 And the day cometh that the words of the book which were sealed shall be read upon the house tops; and they shall be read by the power of Christ; and all things shall be revealed unto the children of men which ever have been among the children of men, and which ever will be even unto the end of the earth.

12 Wherefore, at that day when the book shall be delivered unto the man of whom I have spoken, the book shall be hid from the eyes of the world, that the eyes of none shall behold it save it be that three witnesses shall behold it, by the power of God, besides him to whom the book shall be delivered; and they shall testify to the truth of the book and the things therein.

13 And there is none other which shall view it, save it be a few according to the will of God, to bear testimony of his word unto the children of men; for the Lord God hath said that the words of the faithful should speak as if it were from the dead.

14 Wherefore, the Lord God will proceed to bring forth the words of the book; and in the mouth of as many witnesses as seemeth him good will he establish his word; and wo be unto him that rejecteth the word of God!

11 And the vision of all is become unto you as the words of a book that is sealed, which men deliver to one that is learned, saying, Read this, I pray thee:

15 But behold, it shall come to pass that the Lord God shall say unto him to whom he shall deliver the book: Take these words which are not sealed and deliver them to another, that he may show them unto the learned,

saying: Read this, I pray
thee. And the learned shall
say: Bring hither the book,
and I will read them.

16 And now, because of the
glory of the world and to get
gain will they say this, and
not for the glory of God.

. . . and he *saith*, I cannot;
for it is sealed:

17 And the man shall *say*: I
cannot bring the book, for it
is sealed.

18 Then shall the learned
say: I cannot read it.

12 And the book is delivered
to him that is not learned,
saying, Read this, I pray
thee: and he *saith*, I am not
learned.

19 Wherefore it shall come
to pass, that the Lord God
will deliver again the book
and the words thereof to him
that is not learned; and the
man that is not learned shall
say: I am not learned.

20 Then shall the Lord God
say unto him: The learned
shall not read them, for they
have rejected them, and I am
able to do mine own work;
wherefore thou shalt read
the words which I shall give
unto thee.

21 Touch not the things
which are sealed, for I will
bring them forth in mine
own due time; for I will
show unto the children of
men that I am able to do
mine own work.

22 Wherefore, when thou
hast read the words which I
have commanded thee, and

obtained the witnesses which
I have promised unto thee,
then shalt thou seal up the
book again, and hide it up
unto me, that I may preserve
the words which thou hast
not read, until I shall see fit
in mine own wisdom to
reveal all things unto the
children of men.

23 For behold, I am God;
and I am a God of miracles;
and I will show unto the
world that I am the same
yesterday, today, and forever;
and I work not among the
children of men save it be
according to their faith.

24 And again it shall come
to pass that the Lord shall
say unto him that shall read
the words that shall be
delivered him:

29:11 (2 Nephi 27:15–18). *"Deliver to one that is learned."*
This phrase deals with one of the classic stories of early Latter-
day Saint history. Joseph Smith is the man to whom God
delivered the plates from which the Book of Mormon was
translated. (2 Nephi 27:15.) The Prophet, in turn, delivered
some of the words (translation) "to another" (Martin Harris).
Martin showed the words (translation) and a copy of some of
the reformed Egyptian characters (see Mormon 9:32) copied
from the plates to a "learned" professor of classic languages
(Greek and Latin) at Columbia University by the name of
Charles Anthon.

Upon examination, Professor Anthon declared the characters to be authentic and the translation correct. Whether or
not he really had the skills to make such a scholarly assertion is
irrelevant to the incident. (He most likely did not possess such

skills but was seeking the praise of men.) What really matters is his utterance upon learning that he himself would not be allowed to see the original record, or plates, because "a portion was sealed." Anthon then declared: "I cannot read a sealed book," thus fulfilling the ancient prophecy pronounced originally by Isaiah and later recorded by Nephi. Martin Harris also visited a Dr. Samuel Mitchell, "who sanctioned what Professor Anthon had said respecting both the characters and the translation." (See JS–H 1:63–65.)

29:11 (2 Nephi 27:17–23). *"For it is sealed."* In describing the plates delivered to his care, the Prophet Joseph said: "The volume was something near six inches in thickness, *a part of which was sealed.*" (HC 4:537; italics added.) While others have suggested one-third to two-thirds of the plates were sealed, this is all that Joseph Smith said on the matter of public record.

What do we know about this sealed portion? We know that Book of Mormon prophets, like prophets in other times and places, were sometimes forbidden to record that which they had seen in vision or which had been revealed to them. (See 1 Nephi 14:28; Ether 13:13; DCE, 454.) On other occasions, prophets were allowed to record sacred information but were then commanded to seal it up. (Ether 3:27; 4:5.) The future translator of the Book of Mormon plates was specifically cautioned by the ancient seers not to touch the sealed portion of the plates. (Ether 5:1; 2 Nephi 27:21.)

Elder Bruce R. McConkie, one who held the apostolic office and was sustained as a prophet, seer, and revelator, provided the following explanation of the sealed portion:

"John the Revelator saw in the hands of the Great God a book sealed with seven seals. 'It contains,' as our revelation tells us, 'the revealed will, mysteries, and the works of God; the hidden things of his economy concerning this earth during the seven thousand years of its continuance, or its temporal existence,' each seal covering a period of one thousand years. As John saw, no one but the Lord Jesus—'the Lion of the tribe of Juda, the Root of David'—had power to loose these seven seals. (Rev. 5:5; D&C 77:6.)

"This same or like knowledge is contained in the sealed portion of the Book of Mormon. For aught we know the two sealed books are one and the same. Of this much we are quite certain: When, during the Millennium, the sealed portion of the Book of Mormon is translated, it will give an account of life in preexistence; of the creation of all things; of the Fall and the Atonement and the Second Coming; of temple ordinances in their fulness; of the ministry and mission of translated beings; of life in the spirit world, in both paradise and hell; of the kingdoms of glory to be inhabited by resurrected beings, and many such things (see, e.g., Ether 1:3–5).

"As of now, the world is not ready to receive these truths." (DOR, 276–77; see also D&C 10:9.)

When Joseph Smith had completed the translation of that portion of the plates he was allowed to read, he returned them to the care of the angel Moroni. (JS–H 1:60.) This appointed guardian will maintain his stewardship of the record until that future day when the God of miracles "shall see fit in [His] own wisdom to reveal all things unto the children of men." (2 Nephi 27:22.)

29:12 (2 Nephi 27:19–24). *"Him that is not learned."* The Lord chose Joseph Smith—most likely considered to be one of "the weak things of the world" (D&C 1:17–19), a man with virtually no formal learning—to be the translator of this ancient record. How did the unlearned young man accomplish this great task? Here is his own testimony: "Through the medium of the Urim and Thummim I translated the record by the gift and power of God." (HC 4:537.) While a special instrument had been prepared to assist Joseph in the process of translation, it should be remembered that the Urim and Thummim could be used only by chosen seers who possessed the gift and power of God.

Isaiah 29:13–14 and 2 Nephi 27:25–26; 25:17

The Nephite text in 2 Nephi 27 adds the introductory verse (24), which has the Lord speaking to Joseph Smith. He announces to this prophet of the restoration the coming forth of "a marvelous work and a wonder" in the latter days. It is of interest to note the similarity of these words recorded by Isaiah and Nephi anciently to those uttered by the Son of God in person to young Joseph Smith during what is known as the First Vision. (JS–H 1:17–19.)

13 Wherefore the Lord said, Forasmuch as this people draw near me with their mouth, and with their lips do *honour* me, but have removed their heart far from me, and their fear toward me is taught by the precept of men:	25 Forasmuch as this people draw near unto me with their mouth, and with their lips do *honor* me, but have removed their hearts far from me, and their fear towards me is taught by the precepts of men—
14 Therefore, behold, I will proceed to do a *marvellous* work among this people, even a *marvellous* work and a wonder: for the wisdom of their wise men shall perish, and the understanding of their prudent men shall be hid.	26 Therefore, I will proceed to do a *marvelous* work among this people, yea, a *marvelous* work and a wonder, for the wisdom of their wise and learned shall perish, and the understanding of their prudent shall be hid.
	2 Nephi 25:17. And the Lord will set his hand again the second time to restore his people from their lost and fallen state. Wherefore, he will proceed to do a *marvelous* work and a wonder among the children of men.

29:13 (2 Nephi 27:25). "*This people draw near me with their mouth.*" The essence of this phrase is hypocrisy: to profess one thing but to do another; to pretend to be something one is not, or to declare a belief in something that is not personally practiced. Some of the Lord's strongest rebukes have been directed at hypocrites whom He has labeled as "whited sepulchres" (whitewashed tombs), serpents, and vipers. (See Matthew 23:23–33.)

29:13 (2 Nephi 27:25). "*Fear toward me.*" Their regard or reverence for the Lord.

29:13 (2 Nephi 27:25). "*Precepts of men.*" These are principles of conduct espoused by men but devoid of the Spirit. Such precepts are not based on the "living water" of gospel truths but rather leave men either thirsting or spiritually poisoned from their ill effects. (John 4:10–14.) Precepts of men are false doctrines that cause men to err, to fail to recognize the truth, and to deny the power of God. (2 Nephi 28:14–15, 26; D&C 45:28–29; JS-H 1:19; DCE, 433–34.)

29:14 (2 Nephi 27:26). "*A marvelous work and a wonder.*" This phrase is well known as the title of the best-selling book on the restored gospel of Jesus Christ by the late apostle, Elder LeGrand Richards. Variations of the phrase are also found in the Doctrine and Covenants. (D&C 4:1; 6:1; 11:1; 12:1; 14:1; 18:44.) Its meaning was described by President Joseph Fielding Smith: "More than seven hundred years before the birth of Jesus Christ the Lord spoke through Isaiah of the coming forth of the Book of Mormon and the restoration of the Gospel. Isaiah, by prophecy, spoke of the restoration of the new and everlasting covenant, and the Lord performing a 'marvelous work and a wonder,' which should cause 'the wisdom of their wise men' to perish, and 'the understanding of their prudent men' to be hid. . . . This marvelous work is the restoration of the Church and the Gospel with all the power and authority, keys and blessings which pertain to this great work for the salvation of the children of men." (DCE, 346.)

29:14 (2 Nephi 27:26). "*The wisdom of their wise and learned shall perish.*" "The 'wisdom of the wise,' which shall be surpassed by the wisdom of the righteous (D&C 76:9), is the learning of the world. It is transitory and not of an eternal nature. It consists of the learning of those who 'hearken not unto the counsel of God, for they set it aside, supposing they know of themselves, wherefore, their wisdom is foolishness and it profiteth them not' (2 Ne. 9:28)." (DCE, 643.) The apostle Paul described such wisdom well when he said that those who pursue this course are "ever learning, and never able to come to the knowledge of the truth." (2 Timothy 3:7.)

29:14 (2 Nephi 27:26). "*The understanding of their prudent men shall be hid.*" "In the same manner in which *wise* can be applied both negatively and positively (1 Cor. 3:19; Proverbs 12:15), the term *prudent* can also be seen both ways. The Lord declared himself to be *prudent* (2 Ne. 20:13; Isa. 10:13); yet, he speaks harshly against those who are 'prudent in their own sight,' for the things of God shall be hid from them (2 Ne. 15:21; Isa. 5:21; D&C 76:9; 128:18). Webster states that one who is prudent is capable of directing or conducting oneself wisely and judiciously—cautious, circumspect, and discreet in conduct. The 'prudent' against whom the Lord speaks are those who feign prudence or who appear to be 'prudent in their own sight' but are blind and 'looking beyond the mark,' which is the 'stone of Israel,' even Jesus the Christ (Jacob 4:14–16; D&C 50:44)." (DCE, 447.)

Isaiah 29:15–16 and 2 Nephi 27:27

The Lord warns those who furtively, yet fruitlessly, try to hide their so-called secret acts from Him. God is omniscient and knows not only their secret acts, but also their secret thoughts and the desires of their hearts. (D&C 6:16.) Perhaps in mocking rhetoric, the Creator then asks, "Shall the work say of him that made it . . . He had no understanding?"

15–16 *Woe* unto them that seek deep to hide their counsel from the Lord, and their works are in the dark, and they say, Who seeth us? and who knoweth us? Surely your turning of things upside down shall be esteemed as the potter's clay: for shall the work say of him that made it, He made me not? or shall the thing framed say of him that framed it, He had no understanding?

27 And *wo* unto them that seek deep to hide their counsel from the Lord! And their works are in the dark; and they say: Who seeth us, and who knoweth us? And they also say: Surely, your turning of things upside down shall be esteemed as the potter's clay. But behold, I will show unto them, saith the Lord of Hosts, that I know all their works. For shall the work say of him that made it, he made me not? Or shall the thing framed say of him that framed it, he had no understanding?

Isaiah 29:17–21 and 2 Nephi 27:28–32

Isaiah foresees the time when the land of Lebanon will once again be fruitful. This will occur after the coming forth of the Book of Mormon, the words of which shall allow the spiritually deaf and blind to hear and see that which was previously hidden. The meek (humble and teachable) and the poor (in spirit) of the earth shall rejoice in the newly revealed word of the Lord.

17 *Is it* not yet a very little while, and Lebanon shall be turned into a fruitful field, and the fruitful field shall be esteemed as a forest?

28 But behold, saith the Lord of Hosts: I will show unto the children of men that *it is* yet a very little while and Lebanon shall be turned into a fruitful field; and the fruitful field shall be esteemed as a forest.

18 And in that day shall the deaf hear the words of the book, and the eyes of the blind shall see out of obscurity, and out of darkness.

29 And in that day shall the deaf hear the words of the book, and the eyes of the blind shall see out of obscurity and out of darkness.

19 The meek also shall increase their joy in the Lord, and the poor among men shall rejoice in the Holy One of Israel.

30 And the meek also shall increase, and their joy shall be in the Lord, and the poor among men shall rejoice in the Holy One of Israel.

20 For the terrible one is brought to *nought,* and the scorner is consumed, and all that watch for iniquity are cut off:

31 For assuredly as the Lord liveth they shall see that the terrible one is brought to *naught,* and the scorner is consumed, and all that watch for iniquity are cut off;

21 That make a man an offender for a word, and lay a snare for him that reproveth in the gate, and turn aside the just for a thing of *nought.*

32 And they that make a man an offender for a word, and lay a snare for him that reproveth in the gate, and turn aside the just for a thing of *naught.*

29:17 (2 Nephi 27:28). *"Lebanon shall be turned into a fruitful field."* Lebanon was the northernmost portion of Palestine. It was part of the land promised to the Israelites when they crossed into Canaan. (Deuteronomy 1:6–7; Joshua 1:1–4.) Isaiah's prophecy has been interpreted to include the entire land of Canaan. President Joseph Fielding Smith wrote of the "deplorable condition" of this land prior to its redemption in recent years, which redemption was in fulfillment of prophecy. (DS 3:260–61.)

Elder Orson Pratt noted that this changed condition would occur only following the publication of the book which Isaiah saw; "at which time Lebanon and all the land of Canaan is again to be blessed, while the fruitful field occupied by the nations of the Gentiles, 'will be esteemed as a forest:' the multitude of the nations of the Gentiles are to perish, and their lands which are now like a fruitful field, are to be left desolate of inhabitants and become as Lebanon has been for many generations past: while Lebanon shall again be occupied by Israel, and be turned into a fruitful field. These great events could not take place until the Lord should first bring forth a book out of the ground." (OPW, 276–77.)

29:20 (2 Nephi 27:31). *"The terrible one is brought to nought."* Isaiah appears to return to an earlier pronouncement against the wicked, whose works will ultimately fail ("brought to nought"). (See commentary on 29:5.) The "terrible one" could also refer to the devil himself, who will lose his power at the commencement of the Millennium and will ultimately be defeated during the "little season" at the end of this period of peace.

29:20 (2 Nephi 27:31). *"The scorner is consumed."* Those who mock sacred things and who make light of the words of the prophets are spiritually self-destructing. They are consumed in their wickedness and will forfeit the blessings that might have been theirs. They will be brought to the depths of personal suffering and sorrow. When they are brought to a realization, or, perhaps better said, an *admission* of what they have done, they may well cry out: "For our words will condemn us, yea, all our works will condemn us; we shall not be found spotless; and our thoughts will also condemn us; and in this awful state we shall not dare to look up to our God; and we would fain be glad if we could command the rocks and the mountains to fall upon us to hide us from his presence." (Alma 12:14.) Their torment will feel like a consuming, "unquenchable fire." (See Mosiah 2:37–38.)

29:20 (2 Nephi 27:31). *"All that watch for iniquity are cut off."* This includes those who look to "find fault one with another" (D&C 88:124), and those who actively seek to watch or participate in iniquity and abominations. The latter would include pornography in all its forms, including filthy jokes, sleazy magazines, and so-called adult entertainment. It would include those who cheat, steal, lie, embezzle, perjure, or prevaricate in any way. In essence, it is any who are not following the Lord's admonition to "stand ye in holy places, and be not moved." (D&C 87:8.)

In our dispensation the Lord declared, "They that have watched for iniquity shall be hewn down and cast into the fire." (D&C 45:50; see also DCE, 66.) They will be cut off from the presence of the Lord.

29:21 (2 Nephi 27:32). *"Make a man an offender for a word."* In one possible meaning, this phrase could apply to those who are offended because of their interpretation of another's words, even though no offense may have been intended. Another possibility is situations where one may make an offhand, perhaps even insensitive, remark that others turn into a great offense. The phrase could also apply to those who deliberately misconstrue or lie about another's words. All of these possibilities run counter to the repeated counsel in the scriptures to forgive, forget, and avoid faultfinding.

29:21 (2 Nephi 27:32). *"Lay a snare for him that reproveth . . . and turn aside the just for a thing of nought."* The wayward and wicked often seek to justify their actions by finding fault with the prophets or those who are called to set God's house in order. President Spencer W. Kimball astutely observed: "By one means or another, the swiftest method of rejection of the holy prophets has been to find a pretext, however false or absurd, to dismiss the man so that his message could also be dismissed." (CR, April 1978, p. 115.)

The word of the Lord to His falsely imprisoned prophet, Joseph Smith, adds insight to this matter: "Cursed are all those that shall lift up the heel against mine anointed, saith the Lord, and cry they have sinned when they have not sinned before me, saith the Lord, but have done that which was meet in mine eyes, and which I commanded them.

"But those who cry transgression do it because they are the servants of sin, and are the children of disobedience themselves." (D&C 121:16–17.)

Isaiah 29:22–24 and 2 Nephi 27:33–35

Isaiah ends this great chapter with a prophecy of hope for the posterity of Jacob. The Israelites will return to a loving and obedient relationship with their God. Those who have erred by believing in false doctrine will find the truth and be redeemed.

22 Therefore thus saith the Lord, who redeemed Abraham, concerning the house of Jacob, Jacob shall not now be ashamed, neither shall his face now wax pale.

23 But when he seeth his children, the work of *mine* hands, in the midst of him, they shall sanctify my name, and sanctify the Holy One of Jacob, and shall fear the God of Israel.

24 They also that erred in spirit shall come to understanding, and they that murmured shall learn doctrine.

33 Therefore, thus saith the Lord, who redeemed Abraham, concerning the house of Jacob: Jacob shall not now be ashamed, neither shall his face now wax pale.

34 But when he seeth his children, the work of *my* hands, in the midst of him, they shall sanctify my name, and sanctify the Holy One of Jacob, and shall fear the God of Israel.

35 They also that erred in spirit shall come to understanding, and they that murmured shall learn doctrine.

29:22 (2 Nephi 27:33). "*Jacob shall not now be ashamed, neither shall his face now wax pale.*" With the return of his descendants to their covenant place as firm believers in and followers of the Holy One of Jacob, or the God of Israel, father Jacob need no longer hang his head in shame or embarrassment. Nor need his face turn "pale," as it had previously done, because of their actions.

Furthermore, the children of Jacob themselves need no longer hang their heads in shame and sorrow as outcasts of society. Elder Orson Pratt noted: "The house of Jacob has been made ashamed, and his face has waxed pale, ever since he was driven away from Lebanon or Canaan, but the Lord has now brought forth out of the ground a book which shall, accompanied by His power, restore the tribes of Jacob from the four quarters of the globe, and establish them in the land of Palestine and Lebanon forever." (OPW, 278.)

29:23 (2 Nephi 27:34). "*They shall sanctify my name . . . and shall fear the God of Israel.*" Jacob will see his descendants sanctifying the Lord's name in the conduct of their personal lives, in their homes, in public, and in sacred houses of worship. They shall fear (stand in awe of) and worship the God of Israel, who is Jesus Christ.

29:24 (2 Nephi 27:35). "*They also that erred in spirit shall come to understanding.*" There are many who unintentionally err in spirit because they believe in and are following the philosophies of men disguised as the word of the Lord.

Perhaps Joseph Smith was thinking of those who have "erred in spirit" when he penned these words: "For there are many yet on the earth among all sects, parties, and denominations, who are blinded by the subtle craftiness of men, whereby they lie in wait to deceive, and who are only kept from the truth because they know not where to find it." (D&C 123:12.)

Jesus Christ declared, "I am the way, the truth, and the life: no man cometh unto the Father, but by me." (John 14:6.) There is only *one* way that leads to God, not multiple paths. As the apostle Paul preached, there is but "One Lord, one faith, one baptism." (Ephesians 4:5.)

The invitation of the Lord to all is to come unto Him, to cast off the burdens of sin, and to be perfected in Him. (Matthew 11:28; 3 Nephi 12:20; Moroni 10:32.) None are excluded, for "he inviteth them all to come unto him and partake of his goodness; and he denieth none that come unto him." (2 Nephi 26:33.) To come unto Christ means that one must disavow and turn away from all error, from anything that will prevent him or her from coming to a correct understanding of His doctrines, covenants, and saving ordinances.

CHAPTER 16

Isaiah 48 and 1 Nephi 20

OVERVIEW

Isaiah 48 and 49 are the first Isaiah chapters to be quoted in the Book of Mormon; they are quoted in context with other writings found in the plates of brass. These plates contained the writings and prophecies of Old Testament prophets up to the time of Jeremiah. Nephi began a great written sermon on the Messiah by reciting prophecies uttered by three presently unknown prophets of Old Testament times: Zenock, Neum, and Zenos. All three of these prophets foretold the coming of the Messiah in the flesh, even He who was known to the people of the Old Testament as "the God of Israel," "the God of Abraham, and of Isaac, and the God of Jacob," "the Holy One of Israel." (1 Nephi 19:7–14.)

Then, after his brief reference to these prophets and their prophecies, Nephi quoted two entire chapters from Isaiah.

It is obvious that Nephi esteemed highly the messages found in Isaiah's writings and felt them significant enough to duplicate, for he had declared: "I do not write anything upon plates save it be that I think it be sacred." (1 Nephi 19:6.) Certainly Nephi would not use the precious space on his metallic plates to write something he did not consider to be of great importance to future readers of his laboriously written record.

Nephi's stated purpose in quoting Isaiah 48 and 49 was "that I might more fully persuade [his brothers and those to whom this record would come] to believe in the Lord their Redeemer." He further declared, "Hear ye the words of the prophet [Isaiah], which were written unto all the house of Israel, and liken them unto yourselves." (1 Nephi 19:23–24.)

Thus, in reading and pondering these writings of Isaiah, our objective should be to strengthen our belief in the Universal Redeemer, even the Lord Jesus Christ, and to apply these sacred writings to our own personal circumstances.

COMMENTARY

Isaiah 48:1–2 and 1 Nephi 20:1–2

The prophet chastises the covenant people (who are known by the name of Jacob by birth, but whose covenant name is Israel) for their hypocrisy. They claim privilege based on lineage rather than on righteousness. They have made sacred covenants (in the waters of baptism) and pretend to follow the Lord of Hosts, claiming citizenship in God's community (His holy city or presence), yet their actions belie their words. The clear warning is that none but the righteous will ultimately enter God's presence.

Isaiah 48	1 Nephi 20
1 Hear <u>ye</u> this, O house of Jacob, <u>which</u> are called by the name of Israel, and are come forth out of the waters of Judah, <u>which</u> swear by the name of the Lord, and make mention of the God of Israel, <u>but</u> not in truth, nor in righteousness.	1 <u>Hearken and</u> hear this, O house of Jacob, <u>who</u> are called by the name of Israel, and are come forth out of the waters of Judah, <u>or out of the waters of baptism,</u> <u>who</u> swear by the name of the Lord, and make mention of the God of Israel, <u>yet they swear</u> not in truth nor in righteousness.
2 <u>For</u> they call themselves of the holy city, <u>and</u> stay themselves upon the God of Israel; The Lord of <u>h</u>osts is his name.	2 <u>Nevertheless,</u> they call themselves of the holy city, <u>but they do not</u> stay themselves upon the God of Israel, <u>who is the Lord of Hosts; yea,</u> the Lord of <u>H</u>osts is his name.

48:1 (1 Nephi 20:1). *"Or out of the waters of baptism."* This clarifying phrase was added in parentheses to the 1840 edition of the Book of Mormon, which was "Carefully Revised by the Translator" (Joseph Smith). It also appeared in the 1842 edition but was left out of subsequent editions until 1920, when it was added without the parentheses. Most likely it was not part of Isaiah's original text, but was added by a latter-day seer to clarify a phrase understood anciently but not today.

48:2 (1 Nephi 20:2). "*The Lord of Hosts is his name.*" Both the Book of Mormon and the Old Testament use this title over fifty times each. It refers to Jesus Christ or Jehovah and is used on occasions when a stern warning or reprimand is in order. It designates the Lord's role as the One who is "mighty in battle." (Psalm 24:8–10; DCE, 329.)

Isaiah 48:3–8 and 1 Nephi 20:3–8
The Lord reminds rebellious Israel that He alone has revealed future events to benefit or warn His people. Thus, in their stubborn and apostate condition, the people could not perversely give credit to false gods or idols for the events themselves or for a foreknowledge thereof.

3 I have declared the former things from the beginning; and they went forth out of my mouth, and I *shewed* them; I did them suddenly, and they came to pass.	3 Behold, I have declared the former things from the beginning; and they went forth out of my mouth, and I *showed* them. I did show them suddenly.
4 Because I knew that thou art obstinate, and thy neck is an iron sinew, and thy brow brass;	4 And I did it because I knew that thou art obstinate, and thy neck is an iron sinew, and thy brow brass;
5 I have even from the beginning declared it to thee; before it came to pass I *shewed* it thee: lest thou *shouldest* say, Mine idol hath done them, and my graven image, and my molten image, hath commanded them.	5 And I have even from the beginning declared to thee; before it came to pass I *showed* them thee; and I showed them for fear lest thou *shouldst* say—Mine idol hath done them, and my graven image, and my molten image hath commanded them.

6 Thou hast *heard, see* all this; and will *not ye* declare it? I have *shewed* thee new things from this time, even hidden things, and thou didst not know them.	6 Thou hast *seen and heard* all this; and will *ye not* declare <u>them</u>? <u>And that</u> I have *showed* thee new things from this time, even hidden things, and thou didst not know them.
7 They are created now, and not from the beginning; even before the day when thou heardest them not; lest thou *shouldest* say, Behold, I knew them.	7 They are created now, and not from the beginning, even before the day when thou heardest them not <u>they were declared unto thee,</u> lest thou *shouldst* say—Behold I knew them.
8 Yea, thou heardest not; yea, thou knewest not; yea, from that time <u>that</u> thine ear was not opened: for I knew that thou *wouldest* deal very treacherously, and wast called a transgressor from the womb.	8 Yea, <u>and</u> thou heardest not; yea, thou knewest not; yea, from that time thine ear was not opened; for I knew that thou *wouldst* deal very treacherously, and wast called a transgressor from the womb.

48:4 (1 Nephi 20:4). "*Thy neck is an iron sinew, and thy brow brass.*" In more modern terminology the obstinate or stubborn of Israel could be described as having necks that would not turn—they were *stiffnecked;* and their minds were not pliant to the promptings of the Spirit—they were *hardheaded.* A stiff neck does not turn in the direction of divine guidance. By contrast, the Lord promises to "feel after" those who "stiffen not their necks." (D&C 112:13.)

48:8 (1 Nephi 20:8). "*A transgressor from the womb.*" Unfortunately, the nation of Israel had been rebellious from her infancy.

Isaiah 48:9–11 and 1 Nephi 20:9–11

In spite of the people's obstinacy, the Lord promises Israel He will defer cutting them completely off. He will not give

His name or glory to another people, for Israel will be given opportunity to repent. The Lord's name will yet be held in reverence and will be praised by the repentant, to whom the door that opens unto God's good graces is always unlocked. But it must be appropriately opened by those who hope to return.

In the meantime, Israel (the "transgressor") will be refined with much adversity ("in the furnace of affliction").

9 For my name's sake will I defer mine anger, and for my praise will I refrain for thee, that I cut thee not off.

9 Nevertheless, for my name's sake will I defer mine anger, and for my praise will I refrain from thee, that I cut thee not off.

10 Behold, I have refined thee, but not with silver; I have chosen thee in the furnace of affliction.

10 For, behold, I have refined thee, I have chosen thee in the furnace of affliction.

11 For mine own sake, even for mine own sake, will I do it: for how should my name be polluted? and I will not give my glory unto another.

11 For mine own sake, yea, for mine own sake will I do this, for I will not suffer my name to be polluted, and I will not give my glory unto another.

48:11 (1 Nephi 20:11). "*I will not suffer my name to be polluted.*" This phrase from the Book of Mormon adds great clarity to Isaiah's text as found in the King James Bible. While such a statement might naturally turn our attention to the commandment that we should "not take the name of the Lord thy God in vain" (Exodus 20:7), it is of interest to note the words of the Lord's covenant with the great patriarch Abraham: "I will take thee, to put upon thee *my name,* even the *Priesthood* of thy father." (Abraham 1:18; italics added.)

Israel was chosen to be a "kingdom of priests, and an holy nation" (Exodus 19:6), and God would not allow His priesthood to be polluted. The apostle Peter reminded Israel in his day that they were a "royal priesthood, an holy nation." (1 Peter 2:9.) And, in our day, the Lord has warned that the rights of the priesthood can be controlled only "upon the principles of righteousness." (D&C 121:36.) Those who receive the priesthood are given a stewardship of trust, which, if violated, will be withdrawn, for the Lord will not suffer His name to be polluted.

Isaiah 48:12–13 and 1 Nephi 20:12–13

The Lord declares He is the First and the Last, the great Creator of the heavens and earth; verily, He is the God of the Old Testament—Jehovah—as well as the Savior of the New Testament—Jesus Christ! By His right, or covenant, hand He has created all things. He reminds His chosen (called) people that His creations obey Him.

12 Hearken unto me, O Jacob and Israel, my called; I am he; I am the first, I *also am* the last.	12 Hearken unto me, O Jacob, and Israel my called, for I am he; I am the first, and I *am also* the last.
13 Mine hand *also hath* laid the foundation of the earth, and my right hand hath spanned the heavens: when I call unto them, they stand up together.	13 Mine hand *hath also* laid the foundation of the earth, and my right hand hath spanned the heavens. I call unto them and they stand up together.

Isaiah 48:14–15 and 1 Nephi 20:14–15

The Israelites are commanded to assemble and hear the testimony of the true and living God regarding a servant whom the Lord has loved and called to His work ("pleasure"). Who is this servant? This question brings a variety of answers from Latter-day Saint scholars.

Sidney Sperry suggests the servant is Cyrus, king of Persia, through whom the Lord will accomplish His work. (BMC, 130.) This is consistent with the footnote reference in the LDS edition of the Bible. Monte Nyman believes the referent of "him" is Israel (GAWI, 171), while Victor Ludlow believes the description best fits the Lord Jesus Christ Himself (IPSP, 405). In the latter instance, Jesus could be delivering a prophecy about Himself as a Spokesman for the Father. In any event, the work to be done by this servant, whoever he may be, has the divine approbation of Deity.

14 All ye, assemble yourselves, and hear; <u>which</u> among them hath declared these things? The Lord hath loved him<u>:</u> he will do his pleasure on Babylon, and his arm shall <u>be on</u> the Chaldeans.

14 All ye, assemble yourselves, and hear; <u>who</u> among them hath declared these things <u>unto them</u>? The Lord hath loved him<u>; yea, and he will fulfil his word which he hath declared by them; and</u> he will do his pleasure on Babylon, and his arm shall <u>come upon</u> the Chaldeans.

15 I<u>, even</u> I<u>,</u> have spoken; yea, I have called him<u>:</u> I have brought him, and he shall make his way prosperous.

15 <u>Also, saith the Lord;</u> I <u>the Lord, yea,</u> I have spoken; yea, I have called him <u>to declare,</u> I have brought him, and he shall make his way prosperous.

48:14 (1 Nephi 20:14). *"Babylon."* This capital city of ancient Babylonia was noted for its wickedness, corruption, and cruelty. Although the ancient city was destroyed, its name continues to be used as a symbol of wickedness. A revelation given in 1831 declares: "Go ye out from among the nations, even from Babylon, from the midst of wickedness, which is spiritual Babylon." (D&C 133:14; see also DCE, 32–33.)

48:14 (1 Nephi 20:14). *"Chaldeans."* Chaldea was the area of Babylonia which lay south and east of the capital city, Babylon. The name *Chaldeans* was used to describe both a race associated with the Assyrians and a learned class in Babylon who specialized in astrology. (LDSBD, 632.)

Isaiah 48:16–19 and 1 Nephi 20:16–19

The Lord has not spoken in secret. From the beginning He has clearly declared His works and His will, which was in full accord with that of His Father. Verse 16 is a foreshadowing of the Savior's later declaration during His mortal ministry: "My meat is to do the will of him that sent me, and to finish his work." (John 4:34.)

The Lord's counsel and commandments are always for the blessing (profit) of the obedient, while they who reject His words sow the seeds of sorrow and disappointment. Truly, as verse 22 later declares, "There is no peace . . . unto the wicked," for "there is peace [only] in righteous doing." ("Choose the Right," *Hymns,* no. 239.)

16 Come ye near unto me, hear ye this; I have not spoken in secret from the beginning; from the time that it was, there am I: and now the Lord God, and his Spirit, hath sent me.

17 Thus saith the Lord, thy Redeemer, the Holy One of Israel; I am the Lord thy God which teacheth thee to profit, which leadeth thee by the way that thou *shouldest* go.

18 O that thou hadst hearkened to my commandments! then had thy peace been as a river, and thy righteousness as the waves of the sea:

19 Thy seed also had been as the sand, and the offspring of thy bowels like the gravel thereof; his name should not have been cut off nor destroyed from before me.

16 Come ye near unto me; I have not spoken in secret; from the beginning, from the time that it was declared have I spoken; and the Lord God, and his Spirit, hath sent me.

17 And thus saith the Lord, thy Redeemer, the Holy One of Israel; I have sent him, the Lord thy God who teacheth thee to profit, who leadeth thee by the way thou *shouldst* go, hath done it.

18 O that thou hadst hearkened to my commandments—then had thy peace been as a river, and thy righteousness as the waves of the sea.

19 Thy seed also had been as the sand; the offspring of thy bowels like the gravel thereof; his name should not have been cut off nor destroyed from before me.

48:18 (1 Nephi 20:18). "*Thy peace . . . as a river . . . thy righteousness as the waves of the sea.*" Those who observe God's commandments experience a peace of conscience that flows continually, even as a river does. Their righteousness will have a rippling and far-flung effect, just as the waves of the sea are set in motion by the forces of nature.

48:19 (1 Nephi 20:19). "*Thy seed also had been as the sand.*" Had Israel been obedient, she would have reaped the blessings of the Abrahamic promise of a posterity as countless as the sands of the sea or the gravel of the oceans. (Genesis 22:17.) Now, upon condition of repentance, she must await the future fulfillment of that promise.

Isaiah 48:20–22 and 1 Nephi 20:20–22

The Lord now pleads with Israel to repent and flee Babylon and Chaldea (the ways of the world). This same plea has been uttered in these latter-days: "Go ye out from Babylon . . . , from the midst of wickedness, which is spiritual Babylon." (D&C 133:5, 7, 14.)

Sidney Sperry suggests these verses foreshadow the Babylonian captivity, and Israel is urged to depart while singing praises to the Lord, who will redeem them. (BMC, 131–32.)

20 Go ye forth of Babylon, flee ye from the Chaldeans, with a voice of singing declare ye, tell this, utter <u>it</u> <u>even</u> to the end of the earth; say ye, The Lord hath redeemed his servant Jacob.	20 Go ye forth of Babylon, flee ye from the Chaldeans, with a voice of singing declare ye, tell this, utter to the end of the earth; say ye: The Lord hath redeemed his servant Jacob.
21 And they thirsted not <u>when</u> he led them through the deserts: he caused the waters to flow out of the rock for them: he clave the rock also, and the waters gushed out.	21 And they thirsted not; he led them through the deserts; he caused the waters to flow out of the rock for them; he clave the rock also and the waters gushed out.

| 22 There is no peace, saith the Lord, unto the wicked. | 22 And notwithstanding he hath done all this, and greater also, there is no peace, saith the Lord, unto the wicked. |

48:21 (1 Nephi 20:21). *"And they thirsted not."* This verse is a reminder of some of the miracles performed in Israel's behalf during the great exodus from Egypt. (Exodus 17:1–6.) Perhaps the Lord is reassuring them that He will take care of them during any future exodus from physical or spiritual captivity.

48:22 (1 Nephi 20:22). *"There is no peace . . . unto the wicked."* Perhaps this is another way of saying "wickedness never was happiness." (Alma 41:10.) Christ has given us "the gospel of peace" (Ephesians 6:15), "and the fruit of righteousness is sown in peace" (James 3:18).

CHAPTER 17

Isaiah 49 and 1 Nephi 21, 2 Nephi 6

OVERVIEW

One of the primary focuses of Isaiah 49 is the servant called from his mother's womb. As noted in the previous chapter, Nephi's avowed purpose in quoting chapters 48 and 49 of Isaiah was "that I might more fully persuade [all] to believe in the Lord their Redeemer." (1 Nephi 19:23.) For this reason, I believe that the servant Isaiah speaks of is none other than the Messiah or Savior, He who will be a "light to the Gentiles." Indeed, He will be the means of "salvation unto the ends of the earth."

Other commentaries have suggested that the servant could be Israel, Isaiah, or the prophet of the Restoration—Joseph Smith. (See IPSP, 408–10; GAWI, 173–75; DCBM 1:157–58.) Each such conclusion has logical support. Undoubtedly, as is often the case in prophecy, there are multiple applications or fulfillments of the great promises in this chapter. The case for Joseph Smith as the promised servant is particularly strong. However, as the commentary in this chapter will reflect, I believe the major focus of *the Servant* should be our Lord and Redeemer, Jesus Christ.

Spiritual darkness will be dispelled by this Servant-Messiah, and prisoners (on both sides of the veil) will be freed from the bondage of sin through their repentance.

The long dispersion of Israel will be ended as her children are gathered with power in the last days. The children of the covenant will far outnumber those of previous days, and the gathering places will seem far too narrow to hold her bulging numbers.

The powerful heads of state will become "nursing fathers and . . . nursing mothers" in restoring scattered Israel to the lands of her inheritance. No longer will despots and tyrants hold the Lord's people captive.

Such is the promise to covenant Israel of the last days!

President Wilford Woodruff, the fourth prophet of this dispensation, declared: "The revelations that are in the Bible, the predictions of the patriarchs and prophets who saw by vision and revelation the last dispensation and fulness of times plainly tell us what is to come to pass. The 49th chapter of Isaiah is having its fulfillment." (SOT, 112.)

Following Nephi's reading of these writings, his brothers wanted to know how they were to be understood. Were they to be understood in a spiritual or temporal context? A portion of Nephi's response follows:

"Wherefore, the things of which I have read are things pertaining to things both temporal and spiritual; for it appears that the house of Israel, sooner or later, will be scattered upon all the face of the earth, and also among all nations.

"And behold, there are many who are already lost from the knowledge of those who are at Jerusalem. Yea, the more part of all the tribes have been led away; and they are scattered to and fro upon the isles of the sea; and whither they are none of us knoweth, save that we know that they have been led away.

"And since they have been led away, these things have been prophesied concerning them, and also concerning all those who shall hereafter be scattered and be confounded, because of the Holy One of Israel; for against him will they harden their hearts; wherefore, they shall be scattered among all nations and shall be hated of all men."

He then speaks of the gentiles assisting in the restoration of scattered Israel and of a "mighty nation" being raised up in the land of America. He tells of a "marvelous work . . . of great worth" that will be especially beneficial to the seed of father Lehi (the Lamanites). "It shall also be of worth unto the Gentiles; and not only unto the Gentiles but unto all the house of Israel, unto the making known of the covenants of the Father of heaven unto Abraham, saying: In thy seed shall all the kindreds of the earth be blessed." (1 Nephi 22:1–9.)

COMMENTARY

Isaiah 49:1–8 and 1 Nephi 21:1–8

The Nephite text restores an important introduction to the chapter. (See comparative text.) The wicked pastors of the people of Israel are identified as the cause of Israel's being scattered. (See also Jeremiah 23:1–2.) While past efforts to gather Israel have proven fruitless for the most part, the time has now arrived when she will respond to the Lord's pleadings for her return.

The Holy One will not only be Israel's Redeemer but will also be a "light to the Gentiles" and bring the repentant among them into His covenant.

Isaiah 49	1 Nephi 21
1 Listen, O isles, unto me; and hearken, ye people, from far; The Lord hath called me from the womb; from the bowels of my mother hath he made mention of my name.	1 And again: Hearken, O ye house of Israel, all ye that are broken off and are driven out because of the wicked-ness of the pastors of my people; yea, all ye that are broken off, that are scattered abroad, who are of my people, O house of Israel. Listen, O isles, unto me, and hearken ye people from far; the Lord hath called me from the womb; from the bowels of my mother hath he made mention of my name.
2 And he hath made my mouth like a sharp sword; in the shadow of his hand hath he hid me, and made me a polished shaft; in his quiver hath he hid me;	2 And hath made my mouth like a sharp sword; in the shadow of his hand hath he hid me, and made me a polished shaft; in his quiver hath he hid me;

188

3 And said unto me, Thou
art my servant, O Israel, in
whom I will be glorified.

4 Then I said, I have
laboured in vain, I have spent
my strength for *nought*, and
in vain: yet surely my
judgment is with the Lord,
and my work with my God.

5 And now, saith the Lord
that formed me from the
womb to be his servant, to
bring Jacob again to him,
Though Israel be not
gathered, yet shall I be
glorious in the eyes of the
Lord, and my God shall be
my strength.

6 And he said, It is a light
thing that thou *shouldest* be
my servant to raise up the
tribes of Jacob, and to
restore the preserved of
Israel: I will also give thee
for a light to the Gentiles,
that thou mayest be my
salvation unto the end of the
earth.

7 Thus saith the Lord, the
Redeemer of Israel, and his
Holy One, to him whom
man despiseth, to him whom
the nation abhorreth, to a
servant of rulers, Kings shall
see and arise, princes also
shall worship, because of the
Lord that is faithful, and the
Holy One of Israel, and he
shall choose thee.

3 And said unto me: Thou
art my servant, O Israel, in
whom I will be glorified.

4 Then I said, I have *labored*
in vain, I have spent my
strength for *naught* and in
vain; surely my judgment is
with the Lord, and my work
with my God.

5 And now, saith the Lord—
that formed me from the
womb that I should be his
servant, to bring Jacob again
to him—though Israel be
not gathered, yet shall I be
glorious in the eyes of the
Lord, and my God shall be
my strength.

6 And he said: It is a light
thing that thou *shouldst* be
my servant to raise up the
tribes of Jacob, and to
restore the preserved of
Israel. I will also give thee
for a light to the Gentiles,
that thou mayest be my
salvation unto the ends of
the earth.

7 Thus saith the Lord, the
Redeemer of Israel, his Holy
One, to him whom man
despiseth, to him whom the
nations abhorreth, to servant
of rulers: Kings shall see and
arise, princes also shall
worship, because of the Lord
that is faithful.

8 Thus saith the Lord, In an acceptable time have I heard thee, and in a day of salvation have I helped thee: and I will preserve thee, and give thee for a covenant of the people, to establish the earth, to cause to inherit the desolate heritages;

8 Thus saith the Lord: In an acceptable time have I heard thee, O isles of the sea, and in a day of salvation have I helped thee; and I will preserve thee, and give thee my servant for a covenant of the people, to establish the earth, to cause to inherit the desolate heritages;

49:1 (1 Nephi 21:1). *"Listen, O isles . . . and hearken, ye people, from far."* Scattered Israel can be found throughout the earth. An isle of the sea could be any place reachable over water. For example, the family of Lehi and Sariah was led to the ancient Americas, which they considered to be "an isle of the sea." (2 Nephi 10:20.)

49:1, 5 (1 Nephi 21:1, 5). *"The Lord hath called me (formed me) from the womb."* Jesus Christ "was foreordained before the foundation of the world" to be our Savior. (1 Peter 1:20; see also Revelation 13:8; Ether 3:14.)

49:2 (1 Nephi 21:2). *"He hath made my mouth like a sharp sword."* In our dispensation the Lord declared: "Behold, I am God; give heed unto my word, which is quick and powerful, sharper than a two-edged sword." (D&C 6:2.) "A two-edged sword is one which has been sharpened on both sides to make it twice as effective. God's word and the still small voice of the Spirit are even sharper than this, for they are capable of piercing the most pernicious armament and of penetrating to the inner most depths of one's soul (D&C 85:6)." (DCE, 514–15.) When the Lord, or His servants, speak with the sharpness of the sword of their mouths, "the guilty taketh the truth to be hard, for it cutteth them to the very center." (1 Nephi 16:2.)

49:2 (1 Nephi 21:2). *"In the shadow of his hand hath he hid me."* "An 1832 revelation spoke of the faithful as being 'hid from the world with Christ in God' (D&C 86:9). The apostle Paul used this same phrase in writing to the early Saints in Colosse (Col. 3:3). The Prophet Joseph Smith gave an interpretation to this phrase. Placing his hands upon one of the faithful members of the Church, he said: 'Your life is hid with Christ in God, and so are many others. Nothing but the unpardonable sin can prevent you from inheriting eternal life for you are sealed up by the power of the priesthood unto eternal life, having taken the step necessary for that purpose.' (HC 5:391.) Thus, to be hid from the world is to be assured of eternal life or to have one's calling and election made sure." (DCE, 241–42.)

49:2 (1 Nephi 21:2). *"Made me a polished shaft; in his quiver."* An arrow whose shaft has been polished is true to its target. It flies fast and straight, never varying. The promised Servant (Christ) was absolutely true and never varied from His appointed target or work. He was surely polished in the furnace of affliction. It should be noted that Joseph Smith did refer to himself as "a smooth and polished shaft in the quiver of the Almighty." (TPJS, 304.) Certainly he too was true to his assigned mission.

49:3 (1 Nephi 21:3). *"Thou art my servant . . . in whom I will be glorified."* God is glorified through the gathering of His children and bringing about their immortality and eternal life. That *is* His work and His glory. (Moses 1:39.) Thus, whether gathered directly by the Servant-Savior or one of His disciples, it matters not. In either case, both He and His Father are glorified. (John 15:8.)

49:4 (1 Nephi 21:4). *"I have laboured in vain."* The statements of discouragement found in this verse sound similar to those made by the Lord of the vineyard when He saw the lack of good fruit coming forth in spite of His best efforts: "It profiteth me nothing, notwithstanding all our labor." (Jacob 5:32.)

49:4 (1 Nephi 21:4). "*Yet surely my judgment is with the Lord.*" In spite of discouraging setbacks, the Lord and His undershepherds continue to pursue the work of God. Their wages are guaranteed.

49:5 (1 Nephi 21:5). "*Though Israel be not gathered, yet shall I be glorious.*" Although Israel was not gathered during the mortal ministry of the Savior, yet the promise is sure, and her wandering flocks shall yet return to the fold of the Good Shepherd. In His postmortal ministry, He visited the "other sheep" in the Americas as promised (John 10:16; 3 Nephi 15:21) and still "other sheep" who were "not of [that] land, neither of the land of Jerusalem" (3 Nephi 16:1). His visit in 1820 to the young Prophet Joseph Smith commenced in earnest the work of the gathering, which shall continue in intensity until His glorious second coming. (See BICQ, 107–14.)

49:6 (1 Nephi 21:6). "*A light to the Gentiles.*" The aged seer Simeon, who was promised he would not die before seeing the Messiah, saw the baby Jesus in the temple where Mary and Joseph had gone to make an offering. Simeon declared, "Mine eyes have seen thy salvation. . . . A light to lighten the Gentiles." (Luke 2:25–32.)

Isaiah had also previously referred to the Savior in these terms. (Isaiah 42:6.) He who declared *Himself* to be the "life and the light of the world" (D&C 11:28) also called Joseph Smith "a light unto the Gentiles." (D&C 86:11.) Nevertheless, the Lord commanded all members of His church to "Arise and shine forth, that thy light may be a standard for the nations." (D&C 115:5.)

49:7 (1 Nephi 21:7). "*Him whom man despiseth.*" Christ was "despised and rejected of men" (Isaiah 53:3) and "set at nought" (Mark 9:12). Once again, Joseph Smith could also fit this description, for the prophecy has come true that his "name should be had for good and evil among all nations, kindreds, and tongues." (JS–H 1:33.)

49:7 (1 Nephi 21:7). "*Kings shall see and arise, princes also shall worship.*" The day will come when earthly royalty will declare their allegiance to the one Sovereign King, the Holy One of Israel; for "Christ will reign personally upon the earth." (A of F 1:10.)

49:8 (1 Nephi 21:8). "*In an acceptable time have I heard thee.*" In a time of favor, predetermined by the Lord, he has answered us. The Book of Mormon text adds the words, "O isles of the sea." The Lord will answer the prayers of Israel, though she is scattered to the "isles of the sea" (continents far beyond Asia). Remember that even the Americas were considered by their ancient inhabitants to be an "isle of the sea." (2 Nephi 10:20.) In His designated time, the Lord will gather His children. (See DCE, 5.)

49:8 (1 Nephi 21:8). "*Day of salvation.*" Virtually every time one makes a commitment to follow Christ, including accepting the saving covenants and ordinances of His gospel, it becomes a day of salvation. The Prophet Joseph Smith declared: "We believe that through the Atonement of Christ, all mankind may be saved, by obedience to the laws and ordinances of the Gospel." (A of F 1:3.)

49:8 (1 Nephi 21:8). "*I will preserve thee, and give thee my servant for a covenant of the people.*" Isaiah used similar wording in an earlier reference to the promised Messiah. (Isaiah 42:6.) The addition of the words "my servant" in the Nephite text is significant. Who is the Servant who has been given as a covenant? None other than Jesus Christ! We take upon us the name of Jesus Christ in the waters of baptism and regularly renew that covenant when partaking of the emblems of the sacrament. (D&C 20:37, 75–79.) The fulness of the gospel of Jesus Christ is the "new and everlasting covenant." (D&C 22:1; DCE, 381–82.)

49:8 (1 Nephi 21:8). "*Inherit the desolate heritages.*" In considering these words, one would naturally think of the great promises made to Israel that she will inhabit and restore once-fruitful lands that have long lain desolate. (Isaiah 61:4.) There may, however, be a far more significant meaning attached to this phrase. During their long years of apostasy, have not the children of Israel been deprived of the heritage that might have been theirs had they been worthy? Thus, when they repent and return, will they not then inherit the heritage that has long been desolate?

Isaiah 49:9–13 and 1 Nephi 21:9–13

The promise of redemption continues in these verses. It extends to both sides of the veil: Whether in the spirit prison, where the gospel message is taken to the disembodied spirits, or in mortality, spiritual darkness will be dispersed. In addition to spiritual redemption, the physical gathering of Israel will proceed. Those returning shall come from afar. The inhabitants in heaven and on earth will break forth in joyous singing because Israel "shall be smitten no more."

9 That thou mayest say to the prisoners, Go forth; to them that are in darkness, Shew yourselves. They shall feed in the ways, and their pastures shall be in all high places.	9 That thou mayest say to the prisoners: Go forth; to them that sit in darkness: Show yourselves. They shall feed in the ways, and their pastures shall be in all high places.
10 They shall not hunger nor thirst; neither shall the heat nor sun smite them: for he that hath mercy on them shall lead them, even by the springs of water shall he guide them.	10 They shall not hunger nor thirst, neither shall the heat nor the sun smite them; for he that hath mercy on them shall lead them, even by the springs of water shall he guide them.
11 And I will make all my mountains a way, and my highways shall be exalted.	11 And I will make all my mountains a way, and my highways shall be exalted.

12 Behold, these shall come from far: and, lo, these from the north and from the west; and these from the land of Sinim.	12 And then, O house of Israel, behold, these shall come from far; and lo, these from the north and from the west; and these from the land of Sinim.
13 Sing, O heavens; and be joyful, O earth; and break forth into singing, O mountains: for the Lord hath comforted his people, and will have mercy upon his afflicted.	13 Sing, O heavens; and be joyful, O earth; for the feet of those who are in the east shall be established; and break forth into singing, O mountains; for they shall be smitten no more; for the Lord hath comforted his people, and will have mercy upon his afflicted.

49:9 (1 Nephi 21:9). "*Say to the prisoners, Go forth.*" The footnote references imply that the prisoners spoken of are those who are presently confined to a spirit prison or "state of misery." These are they who "chose evil works rather than good" during their earthly sojourn. (Alma 40:13–14.) Following His death on Calvary, the disembodied Christ went to the spirit world where He organized His righteous followers into a missionary task force to take the gospel to those in the spirit prison. (D&C 138:18–21, 28–30.) As these confined spirits accept the gospel, and as saving ordinances are performed in their behalf in holy temples here on earth, the prisoners are set free.

This great work caused the Prophet Joseph to exclaim, "Let the dead speak forth anthems of eternal praise to the King Immanuel, who hath ordained, before the world was, that which would enable us to redeem them out of their prison; for the prisoners shall go free." (D&C 128:22.)

49:9 (1 Nephi 21:9). "*Them that sit in darkness.*" One of the scriptures of the Restoration states: "And when the times of the Gentiles is come in, a light shall break forth among them that sit in darkness, and it shall be the fulness of my gospel."

(D&C 45:28.) The ancient seer Joseph saw this dispersion of spiritual darkness when he prophesied "that the Messiah should be made manifest unto [the house of Israel] in the latter days, in the spirit of power, unto the bringing of them out of darkness unto light—yea, out of hidden darkness and out of captivity unto freedom." (2 Nephi 3:5.)

49:9 (1 Nephi 21:9). *"Their pastures shall be in all high places."* The spiritual pastures of the Lord's sheep—His redeemed—shall be in His holy temples. Here they shall be taught of His ways. "The mountain of the Lord's house" is the temple. (Isaiah 2:2; Micah 4:1; BICQ, 115–16.) Frequently, communications between heaven and mortals have been in "high places": Moses on Mount Horeb (Exodus 3) and Mount Sinai (Exodus 19); Nephi on "an exceedingly high mountain" (1 Nephi 11); and the brother of Jared "upon the top of the mount" (Ether 3).

Shortly before the organization (restoration) of The Church of Jesus Christ of Latter-day Saints, the Lord commanded His disciples to "declare glad tidings, yea, publish it upon the mountains, and upon every high place, and among every people that thou shalt be permitted to see." (D&C 19:29.)

49:10 (1 Nephi 21:10). *"They shall not hunger nor thirst; neither shall the heat nor sun smite them."* At first glance, this may appear to be a promise of swift travel made to those returning to possess their lands of inheritance. However, placing this statement in the context of John's revelation, a new meaning is revealed. John saw in vision a future time when some "arrayed in white robes" would be serving God "day and night in his temple." Then follows a repetition of Isaiah 49:10, with this added verse: "For the Lamb which is in the midst of the throne shall feed them, and shall lead them unto living fountains of waters." (Revelation 7:13–17.) The sun won't smite (burn) them because they will be spending their time in the temple. (See Psalm 121:6.)

49:11 (1 Nephi 21:11). "*I will make all my mountains a way, and my highways shall be exalted.*" The Lord will facilitate transportation. Roads will appear in mountain passes, and highways will be raised up in valley areas. This may have more direct reference to the Savior's second coming when "every valley shall be exalted and every mountain and hill shall be made low." (Isaiah 40:4; see also BICQ, 217–18.)

49:12 (1 Nephi 21:12). "*These shall come from far . . . and these from the land of Sinim.*" Israel will be gathered from the ends or four corners of the earth. Many scholars interpret "Sinim" to be China, while others identify it with a place near Aswan, Egypt. However, more broadly interpreted, it "stands for distant lands generally." (TOVBC, 445.)

49:13 (1 Nephi 21:13). "*<u>Those who are in the east</u> . . . O mountains.*" Monte Nyman described "those who are in the east" as the residents of "Jerusalem, while the 'mountains' appears to be a reference to Zion or America. Thus the Lord is declaring that the two capitals of Israel shall be established and smitten no more." (GAWI, 180.)

Isaiah 49:14–21 and 1 Nephi 21:14–21

Because of her long dispersion, and in an attitude of not accepting personal responsibility for her distressed condition, Israel or Zion will lament that the Lord has forgotten her. Yet, as the Nephite text shows, in her heart she knows her Redeemer "will show that he hath not." His memory of and feelings for her are even stronger than those of a mother for the child she has borne. The image of Israel is ever before the Lord.

Jehovah reiterates His promises that the children of Israel shall return from captivity. He swears with a divine oath ("as I live") that His word will be kept. Israel will be utterly amazed at her numbers and will plead for more space to hold her burgeoning population.

14 But Zion said, The Lord hath forsaken me, and my Lord hath forgotten me.

15 Can a woman forget her sucking child, that she should not have compassion on the son of her womb? yea, they may forget, yet will I not forget thee.

16 Behold, I have graven thee upon the palms of my hands; thy walls are continually before me.

17 Thy children shall make haste; thy destroyers and they that made thee waste shall go forth of thee.

18 Lift up thine eyes round about, and behold: all these gather themselves together, and come to thee. As I live, saith the Lord, thou shalt surely clothe thee with them all, as with an ornament, and bind them on thee, as a bride doeth.

19 For thy waste and thy desolate places, and the land of thy destruction, shall even now be too narrow by reason of the inhabitants, and they that swallowed thee up shall be far away.

14 But, behold, Zion hath said: The Lord hath forsaken me, and my Lord hath forgotten me—but he will show that he hath not.

15 For can a woman forget her sucking child, that she should not have compassion on the son of her womb? Yea, they may forget, yet will I not forget thee, O house of Israel.

16 Behold, I have graven thee upon the palms of my hands; thy walls are continually before me.

17 Thy children shall make haste against thy destroyers; and they that made thee waste shall go forth of thee.

18 Lift up thine eyes round about and behold; all these gather themselves together, and they shall come to thee. And as I live, saith the Lord, thou shalt surely clothe thee with them all, as with an ornament, and bind them on even as a bride.

19 For thy waste and thy desolate places, and the land of thy destruction, shall even now be too narrow by reason of the inhabitants; and they that swallowed thee up shall be far away.

20 The children <u>which</u> thou shalt have, after thou hast lost the <u>other</u>, shall *say again in thine ears*, The place is too strait for me<u>:</u> give place to me that I may dwell.

21 Then shalt thou say in thine heart, Who hath begotten me these, seeing I have lost my children, and am desolate, a captive, and removing to and fro? <u>and</u> who hath brought up these? Behold, I was left alone; these, where <u>had</u> they been?

20 The children <u>whom</u> thou shalt have, after thou hast lost the <u>first</u>, shall *again in thine ears say<u>:</u>* The place is too strait for me<u>;</u> give place to me that I may dwell.

21 Then shalt thou say in thine heart<u>:</u> Who hath begotten me these, seeing I have lost my children, and am desolate, a captive, and removing to and fro? <u>And</u> who hath brought up these? Behold, I was left alone; these, where <u>have</u> they been?

49:16 (1 Nephi 21:16). "*I have graven thee upon the palms of my hands.*" The marks of the crucifying nails in His palms could be a messianic meaning of this phrase. (Zechariah 13:6; 3 Nephi 11:14.) This could also have reference to the ancient custom of tattooing sacred images or symbols on one's palms as a constant reminder of that to which one was devoted. In Isaiah's imagery, the Lord could not use His hands without being reminded of Israel.

49:16 (1 Nephi 21:16). "*Thy walls are continually before me.*" This could suggest that the walls (plans) of the city of Zion are continually before the Lord's eyes. This is His constant vision or hope for Israel.

49:17 (1 Nephi 21:17). "*Thy children shall make haste against thy destroyers.*" Israel is to quickly leave those who have oppressed her, and the Lord promises that her destroyers (oppressors) will depart from her.

49:18 (1 Nephi 21:18). "*Thou shalt surely clothe thee with them all, as with an ornament, and bind them on thee, as a bride doeth.*" The returning children of Israel will be as clothing and jewelry adorning a new bride. In speaking of some of modern-day Israel who had been "cast out from the land of their inheritance," the Lord declared: "Yet I will own them, and they shall be mine in that day when I shall come to make up my jewels." (D&C 101:1–3.)

49:19 (1 Nephi 21:19). *"The land of thy destruction, shall even now be too narrow."* The lands to which Israel returns— her previously wasted and destroyed lands—will, in their rejuvenated condition, become overcrowded, scarcely able to contain the inhabitants.

49:19 (1 Nephi 21:19). *"They that swallowed thee up shall be far away."* Israel's former persecutors will be far removed from her.

49:20 (1 Nephi 21:20). *"The children which thou shalt have, after thou hast lost the other (first)."* Sidney Sperry indicates this "seems to mean that Zion's later children shall complain that they have too little room in which to dwell; hence, they plead for more." (BMC, 137.)

49:21 (1 Nephi 21:21). *"Who hath begotten me these, seeing I have lost my children."* Once again mother Israel expresses her amazement at the numbers of her posterity in the last days, knowing that her former children are gone. "Where did they all come from?" she exclaims.

Isaiah 49:22–26 and 1 Nephi 21:22–26; 2 Nephi 6:6–7, 13, 17–18

The prophet concludes this chapter with a reiteration of the Lord's promise to redeem His people. In fact, the gentiles and the mighty of the earth will assist in the process of restoring the dispersed to the lands of their inheritance. Nevertheless, it is by the power of the mighty God that His covenant people will be delivered.

22 Thus saith the Lord God, Behold, I will lift up mine hand to the Gentiles, and set up my standard to the people: and they shall bring thy sons in their arms, and thy daughters shall be carried upon their shoulders.

23 And kings shall be thy nursing fathers, and their queens thy nursing mothers: they shall bow down to thee with their face toward the earth, and lick up the dust of thy feet; and thou shalt know that I am the Lord: for they shall not be ashamed that wait for me.

24 Shall the prey be taken from the mighty, or the lawful captive delivered?

25 But thus saith the Lord, Even the captives of the mighty shall be taken away, and the prey of the terrible shall be delivered: for I will contend with him that contendeth with thee, and I will save thy children.

22 Thus saith the Lord God: Behold, I will lift up mine hand to the Gentiles, and set up my standard to the people; and they shall bring thy sons in their arms, and thy daughters shall be carried upon their shoulders. (See also 2 Nephi 6:6.)

23 And kings shall be thy nursing fathers, and their queens thy nursing mothers; they shall bow down to thee with their face towards the earth, and lick up the dust of thy feet; and thou shalt know that I am the Lord; for they shall not be ashamed that wait for me. (See also 2 Nephi 6:7, 13.)

24 For shall the prey be taken from the mighty, or the lawful captives delivered? (See also 2 Nephi 6:16.)

25 But thus saith the Lord, even the captives of the mighty shall be taken away, and the prey of the terrible shall be delivered; for I will contend with him that contendeth with thee, and I will save thy children.

2 Nephi 6:17. But thus saith the Lord: Even the captives of the mighty shall be taken away, and the prey of the terrible shall be delivered; for the Mighty God shall deliver his covenant people. For thus saith the Lord: I will contend with them that contendeth with thee—

26 And I will feed them that oppress thee with their own flesh; and they shall be drunken with their own blood, as with sweet wine: and all flesh shall know that I the Lord am thy *Saviour* and thy Redeemer, the mighty One of Jacob.

26 And I will feed them that oppress thee with their own flesh; they shall be drunken with their own blood as with sweet wine; and all flesh shall know that I, the Lord, am thy *Savior* and thy Redeemer, the Mighty One of Jacob. (See also 2 Nephi 6:18.)

49:22 (1 Nephi 21:22; 2 Nephi 6:6). "*I will lift up mine hand to the Gentiles, and set up my standard to the people.*" The covenant children of Israel will come from all the gentile nations of the earth. The Lord extends His hand to all to partake of the saving covenants and ordinances of His gospel. The Church of Jesus Christ of Latter-day Saints is the standard to which these converts will gather in order to make their covenants with Christ and receive their saving ordinances. (See DCE, 559–60.) Within the Church is found the fulness of the gospel or the new and everlasting covenant. (See DCE, 381–82.) The Lord declared: "And even so I have sent mine everlasting covenant into the world, to be a light to the world, and to be a standard for my people, and for the Gentiles to seek to it." (D&C 45:9.) The Book of Mormon, one of the "standard works" of the Church, has also been identified by the Lord as "a standard unto my people, which are of the house of Israel." (2 Nephi 29:2.)

It is of interest to note that Nephi states that "after they [scattered Israel] shall be nursed by the Gentiles, and the Lord has lifted up his hand upon the Gentiles and *set them up for a standard*, . . . the Lord God will raise up a mighty nation among the Gentiles." (1 Nephi 22:6–7; italics added.) Has not the land of America, the birth place of the Restoration and home of the headquarters of the restored Church, stood out as a standard (rallying point) for the freedom-loving and God-fearing people of the earth? Consider the words of Joseph Smith: "The Constitution of the United States is a glorious standard. . . . It is a heavenly banner. . . . It is like a great tree under whose branches men from every clime can be shielded from the burning rays of the sun." (TPJS, 147.)

49:22 (1 Nephi 21:22; 2 Nephi 6:6). *"They shall bring thy sons in their arms, and thy daughters shall be carried upon their shoulders."* Nephi gives commentary on this in 1 Nephi 22:6–12. In essence, the gentiles of the earth will assist in gathering scattered Israel in the last days. (See also commentary on 49:23.)

49:23 (1 Nephi 21:23; 2 Nephi 6:7; 10:9). *"Kings shall be thy nursing fathers, and their queens thy nursing mothers."* The mighty of the earth—royalty, presidents, government ministers—shall assist in the process of gathering the house of Israel. This could be through financial assistance to enable them to return to their homelands, such as the Jews to the Holy Land, or it could be in removing legal barriers that heretofore have prevented the preaching and establishment of the restored gospel in their lands. (See BICQ, 129–30.)

49:23 (1 Nephi 21:23; 2 Nephi 6:7, 13). *"They shall bow down to thee . . . and lick up the dust of thy feet."* Those who formerly despised and oppressed the Jews and the rest of the house of Israel—"the covenant people of the Lord" (2 Nephi 6:13)—will reverse their roles. "The sons also of them that afflicted thee shall come bending unto thee; and all they that despised thee shall bow themselves down at the soles of thy feet." (Isaiah 60:14.)

49:23 (1 Nephi 21:23; 2 Nephi 6:7). *"They shall not be ashamed that wait for me."* The apostle John wrote, "Abide in him [Christ]; that, when he shall appear, we may *have confidence, and not be ashamed* before him at his coming." (1 John 2:28; italics added.) The word *wait* in Hebrew means hope for or anticipate. Nephi tells us that "the people of the Lord are they who wait [hope] for him." (2 Nephi 6:13.) Thus, one who waits upon the Lord places his trust in Him and lives in accordance with His will as he or she anticipates His coming.

203

Such persons will have their "confidence wax strong in the presence of God" (D&C 121:45), for they will have no unresolved sins to cause them to be ashamed.

49:24 (1 Nephi 21:24; 2 Nephi 6:16). *"Lawful captive."* The covenant people of the Lord. (1 Nephi 21:24, footnote *a*.)

49:25 (1 Nephi 21:25; 2 Nephi 6:17). *"The captives of the mighty . . . and the prey of the terrible shall be delivered."* The "Mighty God shall deliver his covenant people" (2 Nephi 6:17; JST Isaiah 49:25) from the clutches of the "mighty" (rulers) and the "terrible" (wicked oppressors) of the earth. (See 1 Nephi 22:11–12.)

49:25 (1 Nephi 21:25; 2 Nephi 6:17). *"I will contend with him that contendeth with thee."* "For behold, I do not require at their hands to fight the battles of Zion; for, as I said in a former commandment, even so will I fulfil—I will fight your battles." (D&C 105:14.)

49:26 (1 Nephi 21:26; 2 Nephi 6:18). *"I will feed them that oppress thee with their own flesh; and they shall be drunken with their own blood."* Consider Nephi's later commentary: "And every nation which shall war against thee, O house of Israel, shall be turned one against another. . . . And all that fight against Zion shall be destroyed." Furthermore, "they shall be drunken with their own blood." (1 Nephi 22:13–14.)

Perhaps the depraved condition of the ancient Nephites is descriptive of those wicked ones of the future who will "be drunken with their own blood": "They have lost their love, one towards another; and they thirst after blood and revenge continually." (Moroni 9:5.) The carnage among the wicked may be such that they resort to cannibalism both to satisfy their physical hunger and to demonstrate their depravity. Once again we look to the past for a prototype of this abominable behavior: "They did murder them in a most cruel manner . . . and after they have done this, they devour their flesh like unto wild beasts, because of the hardness of their hearts; and they do it for a token of bravery." (Moroni 9:10.)

49:26 (1 Nephi 21:26; 2 Nephi 6:18). "*All flesh shall know that I the Lord am thy Saviour and thy Redeemer, the Mighty One of Jacob.*" There will be no equivocating at His coming; both the wicked and the righteous shall acknowledge Him as the God of Israel and the One who wrought the atonement. (See BICQ, 188–93.)

CHAPTER 18

Isaiah 50 and 2 Nephi 7

OVERVIEW

This short chapter begins with the Lord questioning Israel about her status as His wife. He reminds her that she sold herself for her iniquities and that He was not the one who put her away. Then follows a series of messianic statements foreshadowing events in the Savior's life. The people are admonished to put their trust in the Lord and are warned about the consequences accruing to those who walk by the light of their own reasoning.

COMMENTARY

Isaiah 50:1–3 and 2 Nephi 7:1–3

Monte Nyman suggests that Nephi's commentary on the quoted passages includes "three verses from 'the prophet,' obviously Isaiah. We do not have these verses in the present Bible text, but they fit very well into the context of Isaiah 49 and 50." (GAWI, 191.) These verses (1 Nephi 22:15–17) can be placed between Isaiah 49:26 and 50:1. The addition of these verses adds a valuable dimension of understanding to the biblical text.

The question posed to Israel about her divorced status is a metaphorical reference to the law of divorce given in Deuteronomy 24:1–4. Under this law, if a wife was found unfaithful (unclean) her husband could dissolve the marriage by giving her a "bill of divorcement." Even though Israel had been unfaithful to her husband—the Lord—He had never given her such a document; she was never officially divorced.

The Lord further states that neither has Israel been sold into bondage to relieve a debt, for He has no creditors. (At that time, one in debt could sell his children into servitude to pay the debt. See Exodus 21:7; Nehemiah 5:1–5.)

The Lord reminds the people of His power to redeem them. Nothing can stay His will and stated objectives.

Verses 2–3 and the last portion of verse 11 of the Isaiah text is repeated, with slight modifications, in Doctrine and Covenants 133:65–70.

Isaiah 50	2 Nephi 7
1 Thus saith the Lord, Where is the bill of your mother's divorcement, whom *I have* put away? or which of my creditors is it to whom *I have* sold you? Behold, for your iniquities have ye sold yourselves, and for your transgressions is your mother put away.	1 Yea, for thus saith the Lord: Have I put thee away, or have I cast thee off forever? For thus saith the Lord: Where is the bill of your mother's divorcement? To whom *have I* put thee away, or to which of my creditors have I sold you? Yea, to whom *have I* sold you? Behold, for your iniquities have ye sold yourselves, and for your transgressions is your mother put away.
2 Wherefore, when I came, *was there* no man? when I called, *was there* none to answer? Is my hand shortened at all, that it cannot redeem? or have I no power to deliver? behold, at my rebuke I dry up the sea, I make the rivers a wilderness: their fish *stinketh,* because there is no water, and *dieth* for thirst.	2 Wherefore, when I came, *there was* no man; when I called, yea, *there was* none to answer. O house of Israel, is my hand shortened at all that it cannot redeem, or have I no power to deliver? Behold, at my rebuke I dry up the sea, I make their rivers a wilderness and their fish to *stink* because the waters are dried up, and they *die* because of thirst.

3 I clothe the heavens with
blackness, and I make
sackcloth their covering.

3 I clothe the heavens with
blackness, and I make
sackcloth their covering.

50:1 (2 Nephi 7:1). "*For your transgressions is your mother put away.*" In speaking to latter-day Israel, who is to be redeemed, reference is made to her "mother" who was "put away" (separated) because of her "transgressions." Some have suggested this implies ancient Israel (the mother) was divorced (put away) but that the bill of divorcement does not apply to modern Israel. However, it appears that ancient "mother Israel" left her Husband (put herself away).

50:2 (2 Nephi 7:2). "*When I came [and] called there was none to answer.*" Latter-day revelation renders this a little differently: "In that day when I came unto mine own, no man among you received me, and you were driven out.

"When I called *again* there was none of you to answer; yet my arm was not shortened at all that I could not redeem, neither my power to deliver." (D&C 133:66–67; italics added.) The Lord was ever ready to redeem His people, but they did not respond.

50:2 (2 Nephi 7:2). "*Is my hand shortened?*" The Doctrine and Covenants uses the word "arm" in place of "hand." The Lord's ability to extend His saving hands or arms is not limited. He can reach out and encompass all, without restriction. "His grasp is galactic," noted Elder Neal A. Maxwell. (CR, April 1976, p. 39; see also D&C 35:8.)

50:2 (2 Nephi 7:2). "*At my rebuke I dry up the sea.*" The Lord makes reference to the manifestations of His power in behalf of Israel during her struggle to leave Egyptian bondage. (Exodus 7:14–21; 14:23–31.)

50:3 (2 Nephi 7:3). "*Clothe the heavens with blackness, and I make sackcloth their covering.*" One of the plagues the Lord inflicted on Pharaoh's Egypt was to cover the land with darkness. (Exodus 10:21–23.) Footnote references in the Book of

Mormon text identify Revelation 6:12 as a possible future fulfillment of this prophecy, when "the sun [shall become] black as sackcloth." (See also Matthew 24:29; D&C 45:42; BICQ, 183–85.) Sackcloth is a coarse fabric of a dark color and was used in making the garments worn by mourners.

Isaiah 50:4–9 and 2 Nephi 7:4–9

These verses are known among biblical scholars as a "servant's song." This is a major poetic passage wherein a servant of the Lord is described, although not specifically identified. (See IPSP, 358–60.) There are differences of opinion among commentaries regarding the identity of this Servant. While there may be dual meaning to these verses, the author believes the song in Isaiah 50 refers primarily to the Messiah. He will be treated despicably, but the power of God will be manifest in Him. Those who oppose Him will be destroyed.

4 The Lord God hath given me the tongue of the learned, that I should know how to speak a word in season *to* him that is weary: he *wakeneth* morning by morning, he *wakeneth* mine ear to hear as the learned.	4 The Lord God hath given me the tongue of the learned, that I should know how to speak a word in season *unto* thee, O house of Israel. When ye are weary he *waketh* morning by morning. He *waketh* mine ear to hear as the learned.
5 The Lord God hath opened mine ear, and I was not rebellious, neither turned away back.	5 The Lord God hath opened mine ear, and I was not rebellious, neither turned away back.
6 I gave my back to the smiters, and my cheeks to them that plucked off the hair: I hid not my face from shame and spitting.	6 I gave my back to the smiter, and my cheeks to them that plucked off the hair. I hid not my face from shame and spitting.

7 For the Lord God will help me; therefore shall I not be confounded: therefore have I set my face like a flint, and I know that I shall not be ashamed.

8 He is near that justifieth me; who will contend with me? let us stand together: who is mine adversary? let him come near to me.

9 Behold, the Lord God will help me; who is he that shall condemn me? lo, *they all* shall wax old as a garment; the moth shall eat them up.

7 For the Lord God will help me, therefore shall I not be confounded. Therefore have I set my face like a flint, and I know that I shall not be ashamed.

8 And the Lord is near, and he justifieth me. Who will contend with me? Let us stand together. Who is mine adversary? Let him come near me, and I will smite him with the strength of my mouth.

9 For the Lord God will help me. And all they who shall condemn me, behold, *all they* shall wax old as a garment, and the moth shall eat them up.

50:4 (2 Nephi 7:4). "*The tongue of the learned.*" God gives the Servant the power of the learned: He is knowledgeable and fluent in expression, and He shall not be confounded. Perhaps more importantly, He knows how to speak to Israel, whether to comfort her or to appropriately rebuke her. A similar promise is given by Jesus to His disciples. (Luke 21:12–15.) Monte Nyman suggests that "verse 4 also fits the calling and mission of Joseph Smith and the elders of restored Israel, who were to cause the wisdom of the wise men to perish (see Isaiah 29:14)." (GAWI, 192.) Victor Ludlow cautions, "we should not limit these references to the life of Christ, but should try to apply them to many of God's chosen servants." (IPSP, 422.)

50:4 (2 Nephi 7:4). "*A word in season.*" A word spoken at the appropriate time. (See Proverbs 25:11; DCE, 499–500.)

50:5 (2 Nephi 7:5). *"The Lord God hath opened mine ear."* Because of the Servant's willingness to listen, God spoke to Him. He was spiritually receptive to God's voice. Where there is no ear, so to speak, there is no voice. Joseph Smith later changed this verse to read: "The Lord God hath appointed mine ears." (JST Isaiah 50:5.)

50:6 (2 Nephi 7:6). *"I gave my back to the smiter."* The scourging of Christ by order of Pilate was clearly a fulfillment of this messianic statement. (Matthew 27:26.)

50:6 (2 Nephi 7:6). *"I gave . . . my cheeks to them that plucked off the hair."* Plucking the hair of a man's face or beard was looked upon as a shameful way of degrading him. (See 2 Samuel 10:1–4.) While our present New Testament makes no specific mention of this occurring to Christ, it is descriptive of the rude way in which He was treated by the Jews and the Romans during His final hours.

50:6 (2 Nephi 7:6). *"I hid not my face from shame and spitting."* Spittle from vile mouths was spewed upon the sinless Son of God by His tormentors. Yet He stood in regal silence as these fiends condemned themselves through their filthy actions. (Matthew 26:67.)

50:7 (2 Nephi 7:7). *"I set my face like a flint."* Flint is a very hard rock and is descriptive of something extremely hard and firm. One who sets his "face like flint" has determined a firm course to follow. He is not persuaded to turn aside from or abandon the set course.

50:8 (2 Nephi 7:8). *"He . . . justifieth me."* He is pronounced guiltless. No false accusations will succeed against the Servant of the Lord or His people.

50:8 (2 Nephi 7:8). *"Let us stand together."* This admonition is sandwiched between two rhetorical questions ("Who will contend with me?" and "Who is mine enemy?"). The apostle

Paul provides this insightful commentary: "If God be for us, who can *prevail* against us?" (JST Romans 8:31; italics added.)

50:8 (2 Nephi 7:8). "*I will smite him with the strength of my mouth.*" This added text from the Book of Mormon emphasizes the power of the Lord's word. Those who choose to oppose the work of the Lord shall be smitten (cursed) by His power. He has declared, "My words are sure and shall not fail." (D&C 64:31.)

50:9 (2 Nephi 7:9). "*They shall wax old as a garment.*" To wax is to increase in intensity. Thus those who condemn or fight against the Lord, His work, or His servants, will become as an old garment, useless and cast aside. The Savior admonished all to seek after things "which wax not old." (Luke 12:33; see also DCE, 627.)

50:9 (2 Nephi 7:9). "*The moth shall eat them up.*" The moth was frequently used as a symbol of destruction. (See Job 13:28; Isaiah 51:8; Matthew 6:19.) Those who oppose the Lord's work shall be destroyed.

Isaiah 50:10–11 and 2 Nephi 7:10–11

Once again, Isaiah poses a rhetorical question, the answer to which is obvious: Those who place their trust in the Lord will be protected. Assuredly all who follow the Lord and His chosen servants will not walk in darkness or have reason to fear. Yet those who walk by their own light, relying on their own limited reasoning, will be sorrowful, for they will be "cut off from among [His] people." (D&C 1:14.)

10 Who is among you that feareth the Lord, that obeyeth the voice of his servant, that walketh in darkness, and hath no light? <u>let him trust in the name of the Lord, and stay upon his God.</u>	10 Who is among you that feareth the Lord, that obeyeth the voice of his servant, that walketh in darkness and hath no light?

11 Behold, all ye that kindle a fire, that compass yourselves about with sparks: walk in the light of your fire, and in the sparks <u>that</u> ye have kindled. This shall ye have of mine hand; ye shall lie down in sorrow.

11 Behold all ye that kindle fire, that compass yourselves about with sparks, walk in the light of your fire and in the sparks <u>which</u> ye have kindled. This shall ye have of mine hand—ye shall lie down in sorrow.

50:10. "*Stay upon his God.*" Be supported by or rely upon your God.

50:11 (2 Nephi 7:11). "*All ye that kindle fire.*" Sidney Sperry provided the following insight: "Those who kindle fires and gird themselves with firebrands—that is, those who conspire evil and plan the destruction of the faithful or who walk by their own lights—shall be trapped by their own snares. They shall come to a sorrowful end." (BMC, 158; see also D&C 133:64–74.)

CHAPTER 19

Isaiah 51 and 2 Nephi 8

OVERVIEW

The chapter begins with an appeal to the children of Israel to remember their heritage and to follow the righteous example of their progenitors, Abraham and Sarah. The promises God made to these grand heads of Israel's people are still in force. While the heavens and the earth may pass away, the Lord's promises and covenants will abide forever. But the people must qualify for the promised blessings through their obedience and righteousness.

Because of her long dispersion and persecution, Israel calls upon the Lord to intervene in her behalf and use the power He used anciently in defeating Rahab and the dragon. The Lord responds by reminding Israel that He will protect and comfort her and she need not fear any man. "Thou art my people," He declares.

Two great prophets are promised specifically to the house of Judah in the last days. They shall prophesy and protect the people for a season (three and one-half years) before their ministry is complete and their enemies slay them. Nevertheless, in the end, God's purposes will be fulfilled and His people will be redeemed.

COMMENTARY

Isaiah 51:1–8 and 2 Nephi 8:1–8

As noted above, there is an initial appeal for the posterity of Abraham and Sarah to follow their ancestors' righteous examples. There follows the Lord's promise to comfort His people and to redeem her waste places. Israel is admonished to listen to the Lord and to follow His teachings. While the heavens and the earth, as we know them today, will ultimately vanish, the salvation of the Lord is everlasting. Those whose heart is set upon righteousness need not fear what mortal man can do.

Isaiah 51	2 Nephi 8
1 Hearken *to* me, ye that follow after righteousness, ye that seek the Lord: look unto the rock whence ye are hewn, and to the hole of the pit whence ye are digged.	1 Hearken *unto* me, ye that follow after righteousness. Look unto the rock from whence ye are hewn, and to the hole of the pit from whence ye are digged.
2 Look unto Abraham your father, and unto Sarah that bare you: for I called him alone, and blessed him, and increased him.	2 Look unto Abraham, your father, and unto Sarah, she that bare you; for I called him alone, and blessed him.
3 For the Lord shall comfort Zion: he will comfort all her waste places; and he will make her wilderness like Eden, and her desert like the garden of the Lord; joy and gladness shall be found therein, thanksgiving, and the voice of melody.	3 For the Lord shall comfort Zion, he will comfort all her waste places; and he will make her wilderness like Eden, and her desert like the garden of the Lord. Joy and gladness shall be found therein, thanksgiving and the voice of melody.
4 Hearken unto me, my people; and give ear unto me, O my nation: for a law shall proceed from me, and I will make my judgment to rest for a light of the people.	4 Hearken unto me, my people; and give ear unto me, O my nation; for a law shall proceed from me, and I will make my judgment to rest for a light for the people.
5 My righteousness is near; my salvation is gone forth, and mine arms shall judge the people; the isles shall wait upon me, and on mine arm shall they trust.	5 My righteousness is near; my salvation is gone forth, and mine arm shall judge the people. The isles shall wait upon me, and on mine arm shall they trust.

6 Lift up your eyes to the
heavens, and look upon the
earth beneath: for the
heavens shall vanish away like
smoke, and the earth shall
wax old like a garment, and
they that dwell therein shall
die in like manner: but my
salvation shall be *for ever*,
and my righteousness shall
not be abolished.

6 Lift up your eyes to the
heavens, and look upon the
earth beneath; for the
heavens shall vanish away like
smoke, and the earth shall
wax old like a garment; and
they that dwell therein shall
die in like manner. But my
salvation shall be *forever*, and
my righteousness shall not
be abolished.

7 Hearken unto me, ye that
know righteousness, the
people in whose heart is my
law; fear ye not the reproach
of men, neither be ye afraid
of their revilings.

7 Hearken unto me, ye that
know righteousness, the
people in whose heart I have
written my law, fear ye not
the reproach of men, neither
be ye afraid of their revilings.

8 For the moth shall eat
them up like a garment, and
the worm shall eat them like
wool: but my righteousness
shall be *for ever*, and my
salvation from generation to
generation.

8 For the moth shall eat
them up like a garment, and
the worm shall eat them like
wool. But my righteousness
shall be *forever*, and my
salvation from generation to
generation.

51:1 (2 Nephi 8:1). "*Look unto the rock from whence ye are hewn, and to the hole of the pit from whence ye are digged.*" The children of Israel are admonished to remember the works of their illustrious ancestors, Abraham ("the rock") and Sarah ("the hole of the pit" or rock quarry). It should be remembered that the God of Abraham, Isaac, and Jacob is the very One who was born in the lineage of Abraham and Sarah and who Himself is the Stone of Israel. (Genesis 49:24; Psalm 118:22; Matthew 21:42; D&C 50:44; DCE, 566.)

51:2 (2 Nephi 8:2). "*I called him alone, and blessed him, and increased him.*" Because of his great righteousness, the Lord promised Abraham that He would bless him and his posterity, making of them "a great nation." (Genesis 12:1–3.) "In thy seed," he was told, "shall all the kindreds of the earth be blessed." (3 Nephi 20:27; see also Galatians 3:8.) Through the ministry of Abraham the Lord's name would "be known in the earth forever." (Abraham 1:19.) Indeed, all who accept the gospel of Jesus Christ will be accounted as "Abraham's seed" (Galatians 3:26–29), which would be as numerous as the stars (Genesis 15:5).

51:3 (2 Nephi 8:3). "*The Lord shall comfort Zion: he will comfort all her waste places.*" In a later prophecy, another Old Testament prophet declared, "And the Lord shall yet comfort Zion, and shall yet choose Jerusalem." (Zechariah 1:17.) After the Latter-day Saints had traveled the plains as pioneers in going to the western United States, they frequently referred to their new-found home in the Rocky Mountains as "Zion." In fact, the rallying cry for emigrants was "Let us go up to Zion!" Certainly the faith, prayers, and labor of these early pioneers and those who have followed them have transformed "waste places, wilderness, and desert" into gardens and productive land.

The words in a Latter-day Saint hymn are reflective of the message found in this verse of Isaiah:

> "*For the wilderness has blossomed,*
> *blossomed like a rose;*
> *and the barren desert is a fruitful field;*
> *joy and gladness now are found therein,*
> *thanksgiving and the voice of melody.*"

("Let the Mountains Shout for Joy,"
by Evan Stephens; see also Isaiah 35:1.)

In a broader sense, the prophecy of Isaiah could also apply to the reclaiming of the land of Palestine by the returning Jews. The reference to the wilderness becoming "like Eden" has implications for the Millennium, when "the earth will be renewed and receive its paradisiacal glory." (A of F 1:10; see also DCE, 411; BICQ, 216–18.) Yet another commentary has suggested that "the Lord promised that through the restoration of the gospel in the latter days, his children—trusting in the immutable word of God—would become as a watered garden, the truths of the gospel becoming to them as the riches and comforts of Eden." (DCBM 1: 232.)

51:4 (2 Nephi 8:4). *"A law shall proceed from me."* This law is a teaching or doctrine. Monte Nyman opined that the "law" here spoken of "is undoubtedly the Book of Mormon. This law is associated with judgment in both verses 4 and 5, and it will come forth from the 'isles.' The Book of Mormon is to judge the nations as well as individuals (see 2 Nephi 25:22; D&C 20:13–15.)" (GAWI, 195.)

51:4 (2 Nephi 8:4). *"I will make my judgment to rest for a light of the people."* The Lord's justice will be established as a light for the people.

51:5 (2 Nephi 8:5). *"My salvation is gone forth."* Jesus Christ is "the messenger of salvation." (D&C 93:8.) His gospel is "the gospel of salvation." (D&C 93:51.) Since its restoration through the Prophet Joseph Smith, it has continuously gone forth to the inhabitants of the earth.

51:5 (2 Nephi 8:5). *"Mine arms shall judge the people."* The Lord's arms are symbolic of the power with which He administers divine justice, as well as a representation of His authority. All will be judged by the power of Jesus Christ, who is the Eternal Judge.

51:5 (2 Nephi 8:5). *"The isles shall wait upon me."* Isles represent far distant places. In 1831, the Lord told the leaders of His fledgling latter-day Church to "send forth the elders of my church unto the nations which are afar off; unto the islands of the sea; send forth unto foreign lands; call upon all nations." (D&C 133:8.) The inhabitants of these far distant places wait for the message of salvation.

51:6 (2 Nephi 8:6). *"The heavens shall vanish away like smoke, and the earth shall wax old like a garment."* The heavens will vanish (be dispersed) and the earth wax old (decay). This has reference to "the day of the Lord" or second coming. (2 Peter 3:10.) Many signs and wonders will occur in the heavens at that time, which may include those seen by the prophet Joel: "And I will shew wonders in the heavens and in the earth, blood, and fire, and pillars of smoke. The sun shall be turned into darkness, and the moon into blood, before the great and the terrible day of the Lord come." (Joel 2:30–31; see also JS–H 1:41; BICQ, 183–87.) The earth will undergo a baptism of fire, which will cleanse it of wickedness for the millennial reign of Christ. This cleansing will also prepare it for its final transformation following the last judgment, at which time "the earth will die; it will be dissolved, pass away, and then it will be renewed, or raised with a resurrection. It will receive its resurrection to become a celestial body," said President Joseph Fielding Smith. (See BICQ, 195–96, 235.) At both the beginning and the end of the Millennium there will be a "new heaven and new earth." (See BICQ, 219–20.)

51:7 (2 Nephi 8:7). "*The people in whose heart I have written my law.*" The righteous are those who have the Lord's words and commandments engraved on their hearts. These are the meek or teachable of the earth who open their hearts to the penetrating power of the Spirit. President Joseph Fielding Smith said: "The Spirit of God speaking to the spirit of man has power to impart truth with greater effect and understanding than the truth can be imparted by personal contact even with heavenly beings. Through the Holy Ghost the truth is woven into the very fibre and sinews of the body so that it cannot be forgotten." (DS 1:47–48.)

51:7 (2 Nephi 8:7). "*Fear ye not the reproach of men.*" In our day the Lord counseled those involved in His work: "And your whole labor shall be in Zion, with all your soul, from henceforth; yea, you shall ever open your mouth in my cause, not fearing what man can do, for I am with you. Amen." (D&C 30:11.) Proverbs sums it up with these words: "The fear of man bringeth a snare: but whoso putteth his trust in the Lord shall be safe." (Proverbs 29:25.)

51:8 (2 Nephi 8:8). *"The moth shall eat them up."* The moth was frequently used as a symbol of destruction. (See commentary on Isaiah 50:9.) Those who ridicule the Lord's people shall ultimately be destroyed in the flesh, but His righteousness and salvation will be never ending. This utterance of Isaiah is reminiscent of a statement by President George Albert Smith, seventh prophet in these latter days: "There have been some who have belittled [Joseph Smith], but I would like to say that those who have done so will be forgotten and their remains will go back to mother earth, . . . and the odor of their infamy will never die, while the glory and honor and majesty and courage and fidelity manifested by the Prophet Joseph Smith will attach to his name forever." (MOK, 80–81.)

Isaiah 51:9–11 and 2 Nephi 8:9–11

Israel has now awakened to her plight and pleads with the Lord to reach out and protect her as He did anciently. Some of His past victories are cited as reminders. As an almost immediate reply to these pleadings, Isaiah tells of the future occasion when the Lord will gather the ransomed and redeemed.

9 Awake, awake, put on strength, O arm of the Lord; awake, as in the ancient days, in the generations of old. Art thou not it that hath cut Rahab, and wounded the dragon?	9 Awake, awake! Put on strength, O arm of the Lord; awake as in the ancient days. Art thou not he that hath cut Rahab, and wounded the dragon?
10 Art thou not it which hath dried the sea, the waters of the great deep; that hath made the depths of the sea a way for the ransomed to pass over?	10 Art thou not he who hath dried the sea, the waters of the great deep; that hath made the depths of the sea a way for the ransomed to pass over?

11 Therefore the redeemed of the Lord shall return, and come with singing unto Zion; and everlasting joy shall be upon their head: they shall obtain gladness and joy; and sorrow and mourning shall flee away.

11 Therefore, the redeemed of the Lord shall return, and come with singing unto Zion; and everlasting joy and holiness shall be upon their heads; and they shall obtain gladness and joy; sorrow and mourning shall flee away.

51:9 (2 Nephi 8:9). *"Put on strength, O arm of the Lord."* Israel pleads for the Lord to display or use His power.

51:9 (2 Nephi 8:9). *"Art thou not he that hath cut Rahab, and wounded the dragon?"* In desperation, but almost rhetorically, Israel asks the Lord if He is not the same who previously defeated Rahab and the dragon. The psalmist also mentioned the utter defeat of Rahab. (Psalm 89:10.) The "dragon" is easily identified as Satan. (Revelation 12:7–9; 20:2.) The identity of "Rahab" is a little more difficult. Some scholars suggest Rahab represents Egypt while others say it is a sea monster representing Satan. Footnote reference *"c"* in the Book of Mormon text cites Isaiah 27:1 as a cross-reference, which speaks of "leviathan that crooked serpent." The footnote identifies "leviathan" as "a legendary sea-monster representing the forces of chaos that opposed the Creator." (LDSKJ, Isaiah 27:1, footnote *c*.)

51:10 (2 Nephi 8:10). *"Art thou not he who hath dried the sea [and] made the depths of the sea a way for the ransomed to pass over?"* This reference is to the miracle the Lord performed in parting the waters of the Red Sea to enable the "ransomed" children of Israel to safely pass through, while the pursuing Egyptians were destroyed. (Exodus 14:21–31.) In verse 15, the Lord affirmatively responds to the question raised in this verse.

51:11 (2 Nephi 8:11). *"The redeemed of the Lord shall return, and come with singing unto Zion."* Perhaps reflecting on the highway of safety mentioned in the previous verse, Isaiah now speaks of yet another highway of safety, one to be created by the Lord for His redeemed at some point in the future. This will be called "The way of holiness" and "the unclean shall not pass over it. . . .

"And the ransomed of the Lord shall return, and come to Zion with songs and everlasting joy upon their heads: they shall obtain joy and gladness, and sorrow and sighing shall flee away." (Isaiah 35:8–10.) This particular passage in Isaiah is cross-referenced with D&C 45:66–71, which speaks of the New Jerusalem.

Isaiah 51:12–17 and 2 Nephi 8:12–17

The Lord reminds the people of His power to comfort and again admonishes the people not to fear mortals. The God of Israel is the One who made this very earth. He is the One of everlasting power, to whom the people should give their attention and allegiance. Israel is admonished to open her eyes, to awaken from her stupor, and to recognize her role as the Lord's people.

12 I, even I, am he that comforteth you: who art thou, that thou *shouldest* be afraid of a man that shall die, and of the son of man which shall be made as grass;	12 I am he; yea, I am he that comforteth you. Behold, who art thou, that thou *shouldst* be afraid of man, who shall die, and of the son of man, who shall be made like unto grass?
13 And forgettest the Lord thy maker, that hath stretched forth the heavens, and laid the foundations of the earth; and hast feared continually every day because of the fury of the oppressor, as if he were ready to destroy? and where is the fury of the oppressor?	13 And forgettest the Lord thy maker, that hath stretched forth the heavens, and laid the foundations of the earth, and hast feared continually every day, because of the fury of the oppressor, as if he were ready to destroy? And where is the fury of the oppressor?

14 The captive exile hasteneth that he may be loosed, and that he should not die in the pit, nor that his bread should fail.

14 The captive exile hasteneth, that he may be loosed, and that he should not die in the pit, nor that his bread should fail.

15 But I am the Lord thy God, that divided the sea, whose waves roared: The Lord of hosts is his name.

15 But I am the Lord thy God, whose waves roared; the Lord of Hosts is my name.

16 And I have put my words in thy mouth, and I have covered thee in the shadow of mine hand, that I may plant the heavens, and lay the foundations of the earth, and say unto Zion, Thou art my people.

16 And I have put my words in thy mouth, and have covered thee in the shadow of mine hand, that I may plant the heavens and lay the foundations of the earth, and say unto Zion: Behold, thou art my people.

17 Awake, awake, stand up, O Jerusalem, which hast drunk at the hand of the Lord the cup of his fury; thou hast drunken the dregs of the cup of trembling, and wrung them out.

17 Awake, awake, stand up, O Jerusalem, which hast drunk at the hand of the Lord the cup of his fury— thou hast drunken the dregs of the cup of trembling wrung out—

51:12 (2 Nephi 8:12). "*The son of man who shall be made like unto grass.*" Why should one fear mortal man who is no more enduring than grass? Isaiah previously proclaimed, "All flesh is grass." (Isaiah 40:6.) In a latter-day revelation the Lord admonished his people not to fear those in positions of worldly power, "for they are as grass, and all their glory as the flower thereof which soon falleth." (D&C 124:7.) Place your confidence in the Lord, whose power is everlasting. The psalmist declared, "In God I have put my trust; I will not fear what flesh can do unto me." (Psalm 56:4.) Note that the expression "son of man" here is presented in lowercase letters—referring to mortals. This should not be confused with "Son of Man," who is Jesus Christ.

51:13 (2 Nephi 8:13). *"Hast feared continually every day, because of the fury of the oppressor."* In this verse the people are asked why they have forgotten the Creator and lived in constant fear of their oppressors. The oppressors are "Israel's captors, typifying evil rulers who oppress the righteous." (2 Nephi 8:13, footnote *c*.)

51:14 (2 Nephi 8:14). *"The captive exile hasteneth that he may be loosed, and . . . not die in the pit."* The dispersed of Israel, held captive by oppressors, will soon be set free. They will "not die in the pit" (go down to the grave) nor be deprived of food.

51:16 (2 Nephi 8:16). *"I have covered thee in the shadow of mine hand."* The Lord's protecting hand is extended over His people. (See commentary on Isaiah 49:2 and 1 Nephi 21:2.)

51:17 (2 Nephi 8:17). *"The cup of his fury . . . the dregs of the cup of trembling."* To drink of such a cup is to taste the bitterness eventually experienced by the wicked and unrepentant. Dregs are the last remaining and least desirable sediments that settle to the bottom of a cup of liquid. The great Nephite prophet-king Mosiah taught that those who drink of such a cup do so because their works are evil and mercy has lost her claim on them. (Mosiah 3:24–27; see also DCE, 116.)

Isaiah 51:18–20 and 2 Nephi 8:18–20

Isaiah laments the lack of leadership among the sons of Judah, but then speaks prophetically of "two sons" who will be raised up to assist the nation. Fortunately, latter-day revelation provides inspired commentary on the identity of these two. They are great prophets raised up to prophesy and protect the Jewish people during a critical period just prior to the Second Coming.

18 <u>There is</u> none to guide her among all the sons <u>whom</u> she hath brought forth; neither <u>is there any</u> that taketh her by the hand of all the sons <u>that</u> she hath brought up.

18 <u>And</u> none to guide her among all the sons she hath brought forth; neither that taketh her by the hand, of all the sons she hath brought up.

19 These two <u>things</u> are come unto thee; who shall be sorry for thee? desolation, and destruction, and the famine, and the sword: by whom shall I comfort thee?

19 These two <u>sons</u> are come unto thee, who shall be sorry for thee—<u>thy</u> desolation and destruction, and the famine and the sword—<u>and</u> by whom shall I comfort thee?

20 Thy sons have fainted, they lie at the head of all the streets, as a wild bull in a net: they are full of the fury of the Lord, the rebuke of thy God.

20 Thy sons have fainted, <u>save these two;</u> they lie at the head of all the streets; as a wild bull in a net, they are full of the fury of the Lord, the rebuke of thy God.

51:18 (2 Nephi 8:18). "*There is none to guide her.*" This may not only be indicative of a lack of leadership among the children of Judah, but also a reference to the absence of priesthood leadership.

51:19–20 (2 Nephi 8:19–20). "*These two <u>sons</u> are come unto thee . . . they lie at the head of all the streets.*" These two prophets were also spoken of by John the Revelator (Revelation 11:1–14), Zechariah (Zechariah 4:11–14), and Joseph Smith (D&C 77:15). The two will "have power to shut heaven, that it rain not in the days of their prophecy: and have power over waters to turn them to blood, and to smite the earth with all plagues, as often as they will." (Revelation 11:6.)

"The specified time of their ministry is 'a thousand two hundred and threescore days,' or three and one-half years. This is the same time as the Savior's mortal ministry. However, it would be wise not to be too confined in placing parameters on this period. Elder [Bruce R.] McConkie noted 'the detailed application of the 42 months to this period is yet to be revealed.'" (BICQ, 101.) Elder McConkie also suggested that these two will be members of the Council of the Twelve or of the First Presidency of The Church of Jesus Christ of Latter-day Saints.

At the end of their designated ministry, the two prophets will be slain. Their dead bodies will lie in the streets of Jerusalem for three and one-half days while the wicked of the world rejoice. However, their victory will be short-lived, for the two martyrs will arise as resurrected beings. A great earthquake, of a magnitude never before known, will follow and the Savior will shortly appear. The wicked will be destroyed and the earth prepared for the millennial reign. (BICQ, 100–104.)

Isaiah 51:21–23; 52:1–2; and 2 Nephi 8:21–25

The chapter concludes with the Lord's appeal to the people to repent and hearken to His words. If they do, He will be their Advocate with Heavenly Father. (See D&C 29:5.) In their sanctified state, they will no longer have to suffer the consequences of sin or drink the dregs from the Lord's cup of fury or justice. The last two verses of 2 Nephi 8 are the first two verses of Isaiah 52. These verses are interpreted in latter-day revelation as a call to the Lord's people to return to the Lord and put on the power and authority of the priesthood. (D&C 113:7–8.)

21 Therefore hear now this, thou afflicted, and drunken, but not with wine:	21 Therefore hear now this, thou afflicted, and drunken, and not with wine:
22 Thus saith thy Lord the Lord, and thy God that pleadeth the cause of his people, Behold, I have taken out of thine hand the cup of trembling, even the dregs of the cup of my fury; thou shalt no more drink it again:	22 Thus saith thy Lord, the Lord and thy God pleadeth the cause of his people; behold, I have taken out of thine hand the cup of trembling, the dregs of the cup of my fury; thou shalt no more drink it again.

23 But I will put it into the hand of them that afflict thee; <u>which</u> have said to thy soul, Bow down, that we may go over: and thou hast laid thy body as the ground, and as the street, to them that went over.

23 But I will put it into the hand of them that afflict thee; <u>who</u> have said to thy soul: Bow down, that we may go over—and thou hast laid thy body as the ground and as the street to them that went over.

Isaiah 52:1. Awake, awake; put on thy strength, O Zion; put on thy beautiful garments, O Jerusalem, the holy city: for henceforth there shall no more come into thee the uncircumcised and the unclean.

24 Awake, awake, put on thy strength, O Zion; put on thy beautiful garments, O Jerusalem, the holy city; for henceforth there shall no more come into thee the uncircumcised and the unclean.

2 Shake thyself from the dust; arise, <u>and</u> sit down, O Jerusalem: loose thyself from the bands of thy neck, O captive daughter of Zion.

25 Shake thyself from the dust; arise, sit down, O Jerusalem; loose thyself from the bands of thy neck, O captive daughter of Zion.

51:21 (2 Nephi 8:21). "*Afflicted, and drunken, but not with wine.*" Just as those whose physical, spiritual, and intellectual senses are dimmed by alcohol or drugs, those who immerse themselves in wickedness are afflicted with a loss of self-control and sound judgment. (See commentary on Isaiah 29:9 and 2 Nephi 27:4.)

51:22 (2 Nephi 8:22). "*Thy Lord the Lord, and thy God that pleadeth the cause of his people.*" The Lord God Jehovah, even Jesus Christ the Advocate, pleads the cause of His repentant people. "Wherefore he is able also to save them to the uttermost that come unto God by him, seeing he ever liveth to make intercession for them." (Hebrews 7:25; see also Jeremiah 50:34.)

51:22 (2 Nephi 8:22). "*The cup of trembling, even the dregs of the cup of my fury.*" The repentant will no longer have to taste such bitterness. (See commentary for Isaiah 51:17 and 2 Nephi 8:17.)

51:23 (2 Nephi 8:23). *"I will put it into the hand of them that afflict thee."* Those who have oppressed God's children will now be the ones to drink the dregs of His cup of wrath.

51:23 (2 Nephi 8:23). *"Bow down, that we may go over."* This refers to the practice of making conquered people lie on the ground while the victors walked over their bodies.

52:1 (2 Nephi 8:24). *"Put on thy strength, O Zion."* This is a plea to "those whom God should call in the last days, who should hold the power of priesthood to bring again Zion, and the redemption of Israel; and to put on her strength is to put on the authority of the priesthood, which she, Zion, has a right to by lineage; also to return to that power which she had lost." (D&C 113:7–8.)

52:1 (2 Nephi 8:24). *"Put on thy beautiful garments, O Jerusalem, the holy city."* "What comes about as a result of exercising the Priesthood is equivalent to putting on 'her beautiful garments,'" said Elder Hyrum M. Smith. (DCE, 40.) Perhaps this also implies the privilege of receiving sacred clothing in holy places.

52:1 (2 Nephi 8:24). *"There shall no more come into thee the uncircumcised and the unclean."* Circumcision was a token of the covenant people of Israel. Isaiah uses this description to emphasize that in the day when the earth is cleansed of the ungodly, none but the covenant people of Christ will enter into holy places. (See Joel 3:17; Zechariah 14:20–21.)

52:2 (2 Nephi 8:25). *"Shake thyself from the dust."* This is a reference to Israel's former position of lying prone on the ground while her captors walked over her.

52:2 (2 Nephi 8:25). *"Loose thyself from the bands of thy neck."* "The scattered remnants are exhorted to return to the Lord from whence they have fallen; which if they do, the promise of the Lord is that He will speak to them, or give them revelation. [See Isaiah 52:6–8.] The bands of her neck are the curses of God upon her, or the remnants of Israel in their scattered condition among the Gentiles." (BMC, 168; see also D&C 113:9–10.)

CHAPTER 20

Isaiah 52 and 3 Nephi 20
(with Miscellaneous Other Citations)

OVERVIEW

Isaiah's writings in chapter 52 are referenced by the apostles John and Paul in the New Testament (Revelation 18:4; 2 Corinthians 6:17); quoted by such Book of Mormon prophets as Nephi (1 Nephi 22:10–11), Jacob (2 Nephi 8:24–25), Abinadi (Mosiah 12:21–24; 15:29–31), and Moroni (Moroni 10:31); taught by the resurrected Lord in the ancient Americas (3 Nephi 16, 20, 21); and found sprinkled throughout the Doctrine and Covenants (e.g., D&C 38:42; 82:14; 84:98–99).

This is a chapter of hope, focusing on the house of Israel in the last days. Verses 8–10 of the Isaiah text are obviously significant, for they are quoted four times in the Book of Mormon, twice by Jesus Himself. He first recited these verses at the conclusion of His teachings as recorded in 3 Nephi 16, which included prophecies about the last days. He introduced the Old Testament seer's words by saying, "And then the words of the prophet Isaiah shall be fulfilled." (3 Nephi 16:17.) The people were then told to go to their homes to ponder and pray about His teachings and to prepare their minds for subsequent teachings the following day. (3 Nephi 17:3.)

The next day the Savior quoted Isaiah 54 in its entirety, slightly reordering the verses and omitting only verses 4 and 5. These verses may have been left out because they touched on Assyrian oppression during Isaiah's day—a circumstance which had no direct application to the Nephites or to the message of the last days which Jesus was teaching at that moment.

His message was that the gospel was to be taken throughout the earth in the last days by His chosen messengers and that Israel was to be gathered from the many nations of the world. To get a full appreciation of Isaiah's words, they should be read in the context of the Lord's teachings to the ancient Nephites in 3 Nephi.

COMMENTARY

Isaiah 52:1–2 and 3 Nephi 20:36–37; 2 Nephi 8:24–25; Moroni 10:31.

Verses 1 and 2 of the Isaiah text are found three times in the Book of Mormon. Jacob quotes them along with the entire text of Isaiah 51, which focuses on the gathering of Israel or Zion in the last days. As noted above, Jesus quotes these verses in the context of prophecies of the last days. Finally, Moroni cites them in the closing words of the Book of Mormon, where he is admonishing future readers of his text to "come unto Christ." (Moroni 10:27–34.) He adds some significant words to Isaiah's text, declaring that Zion's purpose in doing as commanded is that "the covenants which the Eternal Father . . . hath made unto thee, O house of Israel, may be fulfilled." (See text comparison.)

Because of their righteousness and acceptance of the gospel of Jesus Christ in its fulness, the Lord's people (both in Zion and Jerusalem) will be restored to power (priesthood power and authority) in the last days.

Isaiah 52	3 Nephi 20
1 Awake, awake; put on thy strength, O Zion; put on thy beautiful garments, O Jerusalem, the holy city: for henceforth there shall no more come into thee the uncircumcised and the unclean.	36 <u>And then shall be brought to pass that which is written:</u> Awake, awake <u>again, and</u> put on thy strength, O Zion; put on thy beautiful garments, O Jerusalem, the holy city, for henceforth there shall no more come into thee the uncircumcised and the unclean.

2 Nephi 8:24. Awake, awake, put on thy strength, O Zion; put on thy beautiful garments, O Jerusalem, the holy city; for henceforth there shall no more come into thee the uncircumcised and the unclean.

Moroni 10:31. And awake, and arise from the dust, O Jerusalem; yea, and put on thy beautiful garments, O daughter of Zion; and strengthen thy stakes and enlarge thy borders forever, that thou mayest no more be confounded, that the covenants of the Eternal Father which he hath made unto thee, O house of Israel, may be fulfilled.

2 Shake thyself from the dust; arise, and sit down, O Jerusalem: loose thyself from the bands of thy neck, O captive daughter of Zion.

37 Shake thyself from the dust; arise, sit down, O Jerusalem; loose thyself from the bands of thy neck, O captive daughter of Zion.

2 Nephi 8:25. Shake thyself from the dust; arise, sit down, O Jerusalem; loose thyself from the bands of thy neck, O captive daughter of Zion.

52:1 (3 Nephi 20:36). "*Awake, awake again.*" This is a command for the Lord's people to cease their spiritual slumbering, to shake off their apathy. In describing the spiritual awakening that had come to some converts to Christ, Alma said they were "awakened . . . out of a deep sleep, and they awoke unto God." (Alma 5:7.) Jacob had earlier admonished some who were spiritually asleep to "arouse the faculties of your souls; shake yourselves that ye may awake from the slumber of death." (Jacob 3:11.)

The prophetic plea is to "awake before it is too late!" We remember the fate of the young man named Eutychus, who fell asleep during the apostle Paul's sermon: he fell to his death. (Acts 20:9.) Surely we should be more concerned about the risks of falling to our spiritual death.

The Book of Mormon text adds the word "again" to the imperative to awake. "This was probably because Zion, or America, was 'awakening' at the time of the Savior's visit and 'putting on her strength,' but the Savior knew that within 400 years the Nephites would lose that strength and fall again into a spiritual sleep. The use of the word 'again' indicates a dual interpretation of the Isaiah text in this instance, and supports the idea that there are other dual interpretations through Isaiah." (GAWI, 197.)

52:1 (2 Nephi 8:24; 3 Nephi 20:36). *"Put on thy strength, O Zion."* On one occasion, Joseph Smith was asked to explain the meaning of this verse and to identify the people to whom it referred. The Prophet said it "had reference to those whom God should call in the last days, who should hold the power of priesthood to bring again Zion, and the redemption of Israel; and to put on her strength is to put on the authority of the priesthood, which she, Zion, has a right to by lineage; also to return to that power which she had lost." (D&C 113:7–8.)

52:1 (2 Nephi 8:24; 3 Nephi 20:36; Moroni 10:31). *"Beautiful garments."* In an 1832 revelation the Lord declared, "Zion must increase in beauty, and in holiness; . . . Zion must arise and put on her beautiful garments." As noted above, Zion puts on her strength through the authority of the priesthood. When that priesthood is exercised in righteousness, Zion puts on or displays "her beautiful garments." (See DCE, 40.) This verse may also be a reference to sacred garments that are provided in holy places; perhaps when we put on our "beautiful garments" we remember sacred covenants and the need to keep ourselves worthy to enter into the presence of God.

52:1 (2 Nephi 8:24; 3 Nephi 20:36). *"The uncircumcised and the unclean."* Circumcision of every male child was the outward sign of a special covenant between God and the great patriarch Abraham. (JST Genesis 17:8–20.) Accordingly, those who were uncircumcised were said to be "unclean," or "without the sign of the covenant." Isaiah used this imagery to indicate that only the *covenant people* will be allowed to partake of the blessings of Zion. It should be noted that since the days of the mortal ministry of Him who made the covenant with Abraham—even Jehovah or Jesus Christ—circumcision has not been required. (See D&C 74; DCE, 315–16.)

52:2 (2 Nephi 8:25; 3 Nephi 20:37; Moroni 10:31). *"Shake thyself [arise] from the dust."* The footnote reference suggests that this means to "arise from the dust and sit down in dignity, being redeemed at last." (LDSKJ, Isaiah 52:2, footnote *b*.) The dirt that has been kicked upon you in the past need no longer remain. You will no longer be oppressed and maligned!

52:2 (2 Nephi 8:25; 3 Nephi 20:37). *"Loose thyself from the bands of thy neck."* The interpretation is provided by the Prophet Joseph Smith: "We are to understand that the scattered remnants are exhorted to return to the Lord from whence they have fallen; which if they do, the promise of the Lord is that he will speak to them, or give them revelation. See the 6th, 7th, and 8th verses. The bands of her neck are the curse of God upon her, or the remnants of Israel in their scattered condition among the Gentiles." (D&C 113:10.)

Isaiah 52:3, 6 and 3 Nephi 20:38–39

The Lord reminds Israel of her apostasy ("ye sold yourself for nought"), but He will redeem her. In the day of her return, the people will know that He is the Lord God and their Savior. As noted above, verses 4 and 5 are not found in the Nephite text.

3 For thus saith the Lord, Ye have sold yourselves for *nought*; and ye shall be redeemed without money.	38 For thus saith the Lord: Ye have sold yourselves for *naught*, and ye shall be redeemed without money.
6 Therefore my people shall know my name: therefore *they shall know in that day* that I am he that doth speak: behold, it is I.	39 Verily, verily, I say unto you, that my people shall know my name; yea, *in that day they shall know* that I am he that doth speak.

52:3 (3 Nephi 20:38). "*Redeemed without money.*" The apostle Peter probably provided the best commentary on this verse: "Ye were not redeemed with corruptible things, as silver and gold . . . [b]ut with the precious blood of Christ, as of a lamb without blemish and without spot." (1 Peter 1:18–19.)

Isaiah 52:7–10 and 3 Nephi 20:40, 32, 34–35; Mosiah 12:21–24; 15:29–31; 3 Nephi 16:18–20; 1 Nephi 22:11

The Lord will send forth messengers throughout the earth to preach (and publish) the good tidings of the gospel. His people will be redeemed through His power, and He will establish the standard of Zion in preparing the people for the Millennium.

7 How beautiful upon the mountains are the feet of him that bringeth good tidings, that publisheth peace; that bringeth good tidings of good, that publisheth salvation; that saith unto Zion, Thy God reigneth!	40 And then shall they say: How beautiful upon the mountains are the feet of him that bringeth good tidings unto them, that publisheth peace; that bringeth good tidings unto them of good, that publisheth salvation; that saith unto Zion: Thy God reigneth!

Mosiah 12:21. How beautiful
upon the mountains are the
feet of him that bringeth
good tidings; that publisheth
peace; that bringeth good
tidings of good; that
publisheth salvation; that
saith unto Zion, Thy God
reigneth;

8 <u>Thy</u> *watchmen shall* lift up
<u>the</u> voice; with the voice
together shall they sing: for
they shall see eye to eye,
<u>when the Lord shall bring
again Zion.</u>

32 <u>Then</u> *shall* <u>their</u>
watchmen lift up <u>their</u> voice,
<u>and</u> with the voice together
shall they sing; for they shall
see eye to eye.

Mosiah 12:22. Thy watchmen
shall lift up the voice; with
the voice together shall they
sing; for they shall see eye to
eye when the Lord shall
bring again Zion;

Mosiah 15:29. <u>Yea, Lord,</u> thy
watchmen shall lift up <u>their</u>
voice; with the voice
together shall they sing; for
they shall see eye to eye,
when the Lord shall bring
again Zion.

3 Nephi 16:18. Thy
watchmen shall lift up the
voice; with the voice
together shall they sing, for
they shall see eye to eye
when the Lord shall bring
again Zion.

9 Break forth into joy, sing together, ye waste places of Jerusalem: for the Lord hath comforted his people, he hath redeemed Jerusalem.

34 Then shall they break forth into joy—Sing together, ye waste places of Jerusalem; for the Father hath comforted his people, he hath redeemed Jerusalem.

Mosiah 12:23. Break forth into joy; sing together ye waste places of Jerusalem; for the Lord hath comforted his people, he hath redeemed Jerusalem;

Mosiah 15:30. Break forth into joy, sing together, ye waste places of Jerusalem; for the Lord hath comforted his people, he hath redeemed Jerusalem.

3 Nephi 16:19. Break forth into joy, sing together, ye waste places of Jerusalem; for the Lord hath comforted his people, he hath redeemed Jerusalem.

10 The Lord hath made bare his holy arm in the eyes of all the nations; and all the ends of the earth shall see the salvation of our God.

35 The Father hath made bare his holy arm in the eyes of all the nations; and all the ends of the earth shall see the salvation of the Father; and the Father and I are one.

1 Nephi 22:11. Wherefore, the Lord God will proceed to make bare his arm in the eyes of all the nations, in bringing about his covenants and his gospel unto those who are of the house of Israel.

Mosiah 12:24. The Lord hath made bare his holy arm in the eyes of all the nations, and all the ends of the earth shall see the salvation of our God?

Mosiah 15:31. The Lord hath made bare his holy arm in the eyes of all the nations; and all the ends of the earth shall see the salvation of our God.

3 Nephi 16:20. The Lord hath made bare his holy arm in the eyes of all the nations; and all the ends of the earth shall see the salvation of God.

52:7 (Mosiah 12:21; 3 Nephi 20:40). "*How beautiful upon the mountains are the feet.*" When asked a question regarding the meaning of this and other verses in Isaiah 52 (Mosiah 12:20–24), the prophet Abinadi responded with a lengthy explanation of this phrase. He first reprimanded his questioners for their lack of spiritual understanding, reviewed basic commandments, cited messianic prophecies, and bore personal witness of the coming of the Son of God. (Mosiah 12:25–15:9.) He then identified the prophets as having published the good tidings of the gospel. He spoke of them in the past, present, and future tense. (Mosiah 15:10–17.) The Lord Himself is identified as "the founder of peace" (Mosiah 15:18), whose message (gospel) of peace is preached and published by the prophets. In an extended sense, all missionaries and teachers of the gospel are included among those whose beautiful feet tread the earth, or stand in front of a classroom, in proclaiming the Lord's gospel. (See D&C 19:29; 31:3.)

52:8 (Mosiah 12:22; 15:29; 3 Nephi 16:18; 20:32). "*Thy watchmen shall lift up the voice.*" There are minor differences in these texts, the most notable being the Savior's use of *"their watchmen"* in His second recitation of the verse. In this instance He was referring to the watchmen of Jerusalem rather than those in Zion. Watchmen are charged with the responsibility of safeguarding the people of the Lord and of keeping the doctrines of His gospel pure. Speaking for himself and others called to serve in the governing councils of The Church of Jesus Christ of Latter-day Saints, President Spencer W. Kimball declared, "We continue to warn the people and plead with them, for we are watchmen upon the towers, and in our hands we have a trumpet which we must blow loudly and sound the alarm." (DCE, 626.)

At the great day of the Millennium, the watchmen will no longer need to be on the lookout for iniquity; they will lift up their united voices in song and worshipful praise rather than in crying repentance.

52:8 (Mosiah 12:22; 15:29; 3 Nephi 16:18; 20:32). *"With the voice together shall they sing."* When the day comes that "all shall know [the Lord]" (the Millennium), they shall sing a "new song," the words of which are found in modern revelation. (D&C 84:98–102.)

52:8 (Mosiah 12:22; 15:29; 3 Nephi 16:18; 20:32). *"They shall see eye to eye."* Some commentaries suggest this means to look into the eyes of a friend. However, another meaning could be that these watchmen speak with a unified voice (they lift up the voice *together*). Latter-day revelation declares: "And every decision made by [these presiding] quorums [of watchmen] must be by the unanimous voice of the same; that is, every member in each quorum must be agreed to its decisions." (D&C 107:27.)

52:8 (Mosiah 12:22; 15:29; 3 Nephi 16:18). *"When the Lord shall bring again Zion."* When the Lord "returns to Zion, or restores Zion." (LDSKJ, Isaiah 52:8, footnote *c*.) The restoration of this Zion will occur with the building of the New Jerusalem, the site of which the Lord has designated as Independence, Jackson County, Missouri. (D&C 57:1–3.) The Prophet Joseph placed the building of this holy city in the context of Isaiah 52:8. (TPJS, 79–80.)

52:9 (Mosiah 12:23; 15:30; 3 Nephi 16:19; 20:34). *"Waste places of Jerusalem."* Ruins of Jerusalem. The people will sing with great joy because the city is to be rebuilt and reinhabited (redeemed for the habitation of the people of the Lord).

52:10 (1 Nephi 22:11; Mosiah 12:24; 15:31; 3 Nephi 16:20; 20:35). *"The Lord hath made bare his holy arm."* The Lord will show forth His power, specifically in leading people to salvation. Nephi states that "the kindreds of the earth cannot be blessed unless [God] shall make bare his arm." How will they be blessed? According to Nephi, "The Lord God will proceed to make bare his arm in the eyes of all the nations, *in bringing about his covenants and his gospel unto those who are of the house of Israel.*" He goes on to state that the people will be brought "out of captivity" as well as "out of obscurity and out of darkness; and they shall know that the Lord is their Savior and their Redeemer, the Mighty One of Israel." (1 Nephi 22:10–11; italics added.)

In His second recitation of this verse, the resurrected Savior substituted the word *"Father"* for "Lord." He then emphasized that "the Father and I are one." Whatever Jesus does, it is what the Father would do and has His full approval.

52:10 (Mosiah 12:24; 15:31; 3 Nephi 16:20; 20:35). *"All the ends of the earth shall see the salvation of our God."* Just as the aged Simeon declared, upon viewing the Christ child in the temple at Jerusalem, "mine eyes have seen thy salvation" (Luke 2:30), so shall *all*—to the furthermost regions of the earth—have an opportunity to see the salvation of their God. Ultimately, "at the name of Jesus every knee [shall] bow." (Philippians 2:10; see also Isaiah 45:23; Mosiah 27:31; D&C 88:104.)

Isaiah 52:11–12 and 3 Nephi 20:41–42; 21:29

This passage is a command for the people of the Lord to be clean, to eschew anything that would disqualify them from effectively serving Him or from entering into His holy presence. A similar command was repeated in 1831, when the Saints were told to go out "from the midst of wickedness, which is spiritual Babylon." They were then admonished that their flight should not be ill-planned, nor should they look back. (D&C 133:14–15.)

11 Depart ye, depart ye, go ye out from thence, touch <u>no</u> unclean <u>thing</u>; go ye out of the midst of her; be ye clean, that bear the vessels of the Lord.

41 <u>And then shall a cry go forth:</u> Depart ye, depart ye, go ye out from thence, touch <u>not that which is</u> unclean; go ye out of the midst of her; be ye clean that bear the vessels of the Lord.

12 For ye shall not go out with haste, nor go by flight: for the Lord will go before you; and the God of Israel <u>will</u> be your *rereward*.

42 For ye shall not go out with haste nor go by flight; for the Lord will go before you, and the God of Israel <u>shall</u> be your *rearward*.

3 Nephi 21:29. <u>And they shall go out from all nations; and they</u> shall not go out <u>in</u> haste, nor go by flight, for <u>I</u> will go before <u>them, saith the Father, and I</u> will be <u>their</u> *rearward*.

52:11 (3 Nephi 20:41). *"Touch no unclean thing."* The hands of the Saints of God should be without defilement of any kind. In a day when the world is awash in the filth of pornography, and immoral conduct is openly promoted and publicly condoned, this imperative of God extends to one's eyes, ears, and lips as well as to one's hands—all should be pure before God. The covenant people of the Lord should maintain the purity that qualifies them to enter His holy house and His presence. (D&C 97:15–17.)

52:11 (3 Nephi 20:41). "*Go ye out of the midst of her.*" As noted above, "her" refers to "wickedness or spiritual Babylon." In another Latter-day revelation the Lord admonished, "And go ye out from among the *wicked*. Save yourselves. Be ye clean that bear the vessels of the Lord." (D&C 38:42; italics added.)

52:11 (3 Nephi 20:41). "*The vessels of the Lord.*" Anciently, the priests who were authorized to work in holy places brought back to the temple those sacred utensils (carried in vessels) that had been stolen by the Babylonians. In our day, the "vessels of the Lord" are those individuals who have taken upon themselves the name of the Lord through sacred covenants. They are the vessels or receptacles who have "taken the Holy Spirit for their guide" (D&C 45:57), knowing that through transgression they "withdraw [themselves] from the Spirit of the Lord, that it [has] no place in [them]" (Mosiah 2:36; see also DCE, 620).

52:12 (3 Nephi 20:42; 21:29). "*Not go out with haste.*" Perhaps this has reference to the hasty exodus the children of Israel made from Egypt, where only the manna provided by the Lord for forty years kept them from succumbing to starvation. (Exodus 12:39; 16:1–36.) The flight from Babylon must be final; there should be no lusting after the former "flesh pots of Egypt" (Exodus 16:3) nor looking back on the sinful ways of Sodom (Genesis 19:15–26). There must be a deliberate and careful plan to leave behind the ways of the world and to be irrevocably committed to the God of Israel, even Jesus Christ.

52:12 (3 Nephi 20:42; 21:29). "*Rereward*" or "*rearward.*" Rearguard. (See DCE, 453.)

Isaiah 52:13–15 and 3 Nephi 20:43–45; 21:8

A special servant of the Lord is described in these verses. However, it should be noted that there may be at least a dual fulfillment of this prophecy; there may be more than one servant to whom the prophecy applies. The message of this servant shall be brought forth in a day when the mighty of the earth shall consider that which they had previously not heard. According to Monte Nyman, such a condition is "a sign of the Restoration [which] would be a day when kings would no longer hold absolute power but would be figureheads, with parliaments controlling the governments." (GAWI, 205.)

13 Behold, my servant shall deal prudently, he shall be exalted and extolled, and be very high.

43 Behold, my servant shall deal prudently; he shall be exalted and extolled and be very high.

14 As many were *astonied* at thee; his visage was so marred more than any man, and his form more than the sons of men:

44 As many were *astonished* at thee—his visage was so marred, more than any man, and his form more than the sons of men—

15 So shall he sprinkle many nations; the kings shall shut their mouths at him: for that which had not been told them shall they see; and that which they had not heard shall they consider.

45 So shall he sprinkle many nations; the kings shall shut their mouths at him, for that which had not been told them shall they see; and that which they had not heard shall they consider.

3 Nephi 21:8. And when that day shall come, it shall come to pass that kings shall shut their mouths; for that which had not been told them shall they see; and that which they had not heard shall they consider.

52:13 (3 Nephi 20:43). "*My servant.*" Victor Ludlow suggests at least four possibilities for the identity of this servant.

1. It could "refer to Israel as a whole."

2. It could be "the same servant described throughout Isaiah 53. If so, these verses describe Christ, his great works, and the persecutions and suffering he endured."

3. It could refer to Joseph Smith, the prophet of the restoration: "As the Savior comments upon these verses later in 3 Nephi 21:7–11, it appears obvious that he is not talking about himself, but about his servant."

4. It could have reference to "another modern prophet." Dr. Ludlow makes a strong case for President Spencer W. Kimball, who was the prophet when the commentary was written. However, he concludes by stating: "Isaiah could be describing any or all of these people. If this prophecy deals with one particular person, the servant might not yet have fulfilled his role. Some future prophet might be the servant who will perform this great work." (IPSP, 438–41.)

Most commentaries identify the servant in this verse as Christ. Certainly none were more "prudent" (sound in judgment and circumspect in conduct) than was the Perfect One. Following His atonement, He was exalted to His place alongside the Eternal Father.

52:14 (3 Nephi 20:44). "*His visage was so marred.*" His appearance was injured or disfigured. The qualifying phrase "more than any man" appears to make this applicable to the suffering Savior—He who experienced more torment and sorrow in Gethsemane, and perhaps again on Calvary, than any mortal man or woman will ever know.

Yet these words may have a dual application, and they may have meaning to Joseph Smith as well. Monte Nyman explains: "After the Savior quoted these verses to the Nephites, he gave a sign to them to show when these things were to take place. Since he had already been persecuted, crucified and resurrected, his quoting these verses shows that they had not yet been completely fulfilled. He said the prophecy would begin to be fulfilled when the works of the Nephites (the Book of Mormon) would come forth among the Gentiles (see 3 Nephi 21:2–9). He also said that when the Lamanites began to know of the Book of Mormon, the fulfilling of the prophecy would already have commenced. That the prophecy speaks of another servant besides Christ is clear from the Savior's explanation in 3 Nephi 21:10–11, which fairly well limits its fulfillment to the time of Joseph Smith." (GAWI, 204.)

In support of Dr. Nyman's conclusion, consider the Savior's words that "the life of my servant shall be in my hand; therefore they shall not hurt him, although he shall be marred because of them." (3 Nephi 21:10.) True it is that Joseph Smith and his brother Hyrum were martyred. Yet consider their ultimate condition in these comforting words heard by their grieving mother as she gazed upon the lifeless bodies of her slain sons: "Mother, weep not for us, we have overcome the world by love; we carried to them the gospel, that their souls might be saved; they slew us for our testimony, and thus *placed us beyond their power;* their ascendency is for a moment, *ours is an eternal triumph.*" (MOK, 78–79; italics added; see also D&C 136:39.)

52:15 (3 Nephi 20:45). "*So shall he sprinkle many nations.*" In a later correction of this verse, the Prophet Joseph rendered the word *sprinkle* as *gather.* (JST Isaiah 52:15.)

52:15 (3 Nephi 20:45; 21:8). "*That which had not been told them.*" According to the apostle Paul, this verse had application in his day. Paul deliberately sought to fulfill Isaiah's prophecy by teaching people who had not previously heard of Christ. (Romans 15:19–21.) (Also see the commentary at the beginning of this section.)

CHAPTER 21

Isaiah 53 and Mosiah 14, 15

OVERVIEW

Seven hundred years before the birth of the Messiah, the prophet Isaiah saw in vision the rejection and sorrow that would be suffered by the Son of God during His mortal sojourn. He witnessed the events of those final earthly moments when Jesus Christ would personally pay the price for all mankind's sins and would then give His life as part of the ransom to be paid for the redemption of all.

About five hundred and fifty years after Isaiah recorded this great prophecy, another prophet, by the name of Abinadi, quoted it to a people who were steeped in wickedness. Speaking with great "power and authority from God," Abinadi boldly called them to repentance. He recited the Ten Commandments and proclaimed that "salvation doth not come by the law alone" but requires the intervention (atone-ment) of God (Jehovah or Jesus Christ) Himself. He reminded the people that since the beginning of time on this earth, all the prophets have testified of the mission of this Messiah. (Mosiah 13.) Abinadi then quoted the fifty-third chapter of Isaiah in its entirety, in what is now Mosiah 14. During the rest of his sermon, he then provided some com-mentary.

President Joseph Fielding Smith observed: "Now *Bible* commentators will tell you that this [Isaiah 53] has nothing to do with the life of Jesus Christ. To them this story is one concerning suffering Israel. I want to tell you that it is a story, a synopsis of the life of our Redeemer, revealed to Isaiah 700 years before the Lord was born." (DS 1:23.)

COMMENTARY

Isaiah 53:1–3 and Mosiah 14:1–3

Speaking for himself and other prophets who have testified of the coming of the Messiah, Isaiah introduces this chapter with a rhetorical question: "Who hath believed [given credence to] our report (words or testimony)?"

The prophet then proceeds to describe the early mortal life of this promised Messiah, including a description of how He would be looked upon and treated by others.

Isaiah 53	Mosiah 14
1 Who hath believed our report? and to whom is the arm of the Lord revealed?	1 <u>Yea, even doth not Isaiah say:</u> Who hath believed our report, and to whom is the arm of the Lord revealed?
2 For he shall grow up before him as a tender plant, and as a root out of <u>a</u> dry ground: he hath no form nor comeliness; and when we shall see him, there is no beauty that we should desire him.	2 For he shall grow up before him as a tender plant, and as a root out of dry ground; he hath no form nor comeliness; and when we shall see him there is no beauty that we should desire him.
3 He is despised and rejected of men; a man of sorrows, and acquainted with grief: and we hid as it were our faces from him; he was despised, and we esteemed him not.	3 He is despised and rejected of men; a man of sorrows, and acquainted with grief; and we hid as it were our faces from him; he was despised, and we esteemed him not.

53:1 (Mosiah 14:1). *"Who hath believed our report?"* It is of interest to note how the apostle John later used these words of Isaiah to illustrate the lack of belief on the part of the people in his days: "But though he [Jesus] had done so many miracles before them, yet they believed not on him:

"That the saying of Esaias [the Greek form of Isaiah] the prophet might be fulfilled, which he spake, Lord, who hath believed our report? and to whom hath the arm of the Lord been revealed?" (John 12:37–38.)

53:1 (Mosiah 14:1). "*Arm of the Lord.*" The Lord's holy arm is symbolic of the authority of His position and "the power with which he administers divine justice. . . . Thus, his arm may prove to be a blessing or a curse depending upon one's desire for and state of righteousness." (DCE, 26.) As applied to chapter 53 of Isaiah, the arm of the Lord is revealed in the Being of the mortal Messiah.

53:2 (Mosiah 14:2). "*He shall grow up before him as a tender plant, and as a root out of a dry ground.*" The Christ child will grow up as any child of tender years, dependent upon the care of others. As a plant or root growing in arid ground, He will need the nurturing of others to survive. In addition to the conditions of the physical ground, the young Seedling—who would later declare Himself to be the "root . . . of David" (Revelation 22:16)—will also find Himself being raised in the spiritually dry and barren conditions of an apostate people.

53:2 (Mosiah 14:2). "*He hath no form nor comeliness; . . . there is no beauty that we should desire him.*" "There was nothing about him to cause people to single him out," noted President Joseph Fielding Smith. "In appearance he was like men; and so it is expressed here by the prophet that he had no form or comeliness, that is, he was not so distinctive, so different from others that people would recognize him as the Son of God. He appeared as a mortal man." (DS 1:23.)

53:3 (Mosiah 14:3). "*He is despised and rejected of men; a man of sorrows, and acquainted with grief . . . ; he was despised, and we esteemed him not.*" Some understanding of how He was despised and rejected can be gleaned from the incident of His return "into his own country" following the commencement of His ministry. His powerful teachings were greeted with such comments as "From whence hath this man these things? and what wisdom is this which is given unto him? . . .

Is not this the carpenter, the son of Mary? . . . And they were offended at him." Furthermore, because of their unbelief, "he could there do no mighty work." (Mark 6:1–6.)

Certainly He experienced sorrow at the rebelliousness of the people He was trying to teach and save. Undoubtedly there are tears still shed by this holiest of Men, whom we worship as a God, as He views the stiffneckedness and wickedness of our day. Surely those who treat lightly their covenants with Him, or who are disobedient to His commandments, could be counted among those who "esteem him not."

Throughout His mortal ministry there were those who "esteemed him not." Some accused Him of bearing false witness (John 8:12–20) or of being possessed of a devil (John 10:19–20). Others vainly sought to tempt Him to misuse His powers (Luke 11:16), and there were those who challenged His authority to minister and teach (Matthew 21:23). Some sought to twist His words "that they might accuse him." (JST Luke 11:53–54.) His life was sought on occasion (Luke 4:16–30; John 5:1–23), but such efforts failed, for His mission was not yet completed. Finally, He was betrayed by a trusted associate (Matthew 26:14–16), mockingly interrogated (John 18:14, 28–32; Matthew 26:63–64) and sentenced to a flogging and to death by crucifixion (Matthew 27:22–26). (For a more complete review of His trials and persecutions, see *Martyrs of the Kingdom,* pp. 28–46.)

Isaiah 53:4–6 and Mosiah 14:4–6

These verses give a brief synopsis of the suffering Christ bore in our behalf during His gift of the atonement in Gethsemane and on Calvary.

4 Surely he *hath* borne our griefs, and carried our sorrows: yet we did esteem him stricken, smitten of God, and afflicted.	4 Surely he *has* borne our griefs, and carried our sorrows; yet we did esteem him stricken, smitten of God, and afflicted.

5 But he was wounded for
our transgressions, he was
bruised for our iniquities: the
chastisement of our peace
was upon him; and with his
stripes we are healed.

6 All we like sheep have
gone astray; we have turned
every one to his own way;
and the Lord hath laid on
him the iniquity of us all.

5 But he was wounded for
our transgressions, he was
bruised for our iniquities; the
chastisement of our peace
was upon him; and with his
stripes we are healed.

6 All we, like sheep, have
gone astray; we have turned
every one to his own way;
and the Lord hath laid on
him the iniquities of us all.

53:4 (Mosiah 14:4). *"He hath borne our griefs, and carried our sorrows."* President Howard W. Hunter, fourteenth prophet of our dispensation, provided this commentary on the Savior's sorrows: "When his body was taken from the cross and hastily placed in a borrowed tomb, he, the sinless Son of God, had already taken upon him not only the sins and temptations of every human soul who will repent, but all of our sickness and grief and pain of every kind. He suffered these afflictions as we suffer them, according to the flesh. He suffered them all. He did this to perfect his mercy and his ability to lift us above every earthly trial." (*Ensign*, May 1988, pp. 16–17; see also 2 Nephi 9:21; Alma 7:11–12.)

His suffering sacrifice for our sins, offered in Gethsemane, is beyond mortal man's ability to comprehend. It was so intense that He bled at every pore of His sinless body. (D&C 19:16–19; Mosiah 3:7; Luke 22:44; DCE, 49.) One of His latter-day apostles, Elder James E. Talmage, penned this description of our suffering Savior:

"Christ's agony in the garden is unfathomable by the finite mind, both as to intensity and cause. . . . He struggled and groaned under a burden such as no other being who has lived on earth might even conceive as possible. It was not physical pain, nor mental anguish alone, that caused Him to suffer such torture as to produce an extrusion of blood from every pore; but a spiritual agony of soul such as only God was capable of experiencing." (Talmage, 613.)

One Latter-day Saint biblical scholar, Dr. Victor Ludlow,

provides some interesting insights into how Jesus bore our sins. He noted, "The word *forgive* does not appear in this chapter of Isaiah, though the Hebrew root *nasa*, from which the word *forgive* is usually translated, does appear twice, as 'borne' in verse 4, and 'bare' in verse 12. (See Isa. 2:9; 33:24.) Christ 'bore' or carried our sins so that we do not have to carry their burden. (John 1:29; see 1 Pet. 1:18–20.) Or, as we say, 'He has *forgiven* us,' meaning he 'gave' the price 'before.' Indeed, almost two thousand years before our time, he gave the necessary payment in the Garden of Gethsemane. As we take advantage of his suffering, we can find the joy God wants all men to experience as they are cleansed and worthy to live in his presence. (2 Ne. 2:25; 9:21.)" (IPSP, 452.)

53:4 (Mosiah 14:4). "*We did esteem him stricken, smitten of God, and afflicted.*" Little did we realize in premortal councils how much Jesus was offering when He volunteered to be our Savior. No wonder a modern-day apostle, Elder Neal A. Maxwell, has observed: "Never has anyone offered so much to so many in so few words as did Jesus when He said, 'Here am I, send me.' [Abraham 3:27.]" (EAIA, 115.)

We loved and esteemed Him for His selfless sacrifice, knowing He was the key to our eternal salvation. For without His freewill and sinless offering, we would never break the bonds that would hold us captive to death and hell. (2 Nephi 9.) No wonder we "shouted for joy" (Job 38:4–7) when the plan of God was announced and Jesus was foreordained to be our Redeemer. (Moses 4:1–4; Abraham 3:22–28.) Yet, as He suffered through those torturous hours in Gethsemane, how all heaven must have wept in knowing of His agony.

Was He "smitten of God"? Not in the sense that His Father was meting out some kind of punishment. Yet the great Elohim knew the agony to which His Only Begotten would be subjected as He fulfilled His foreordained assignment. Of necessity, the Father of us all had to deny or to turn a deaf ear to the agonizing plea, "O my Father, if it be possible, let this cup pass from me." According to President Brigham Young, the total withdrawal of the Father's spirit in Gethsemane pre-cipitated the sweating of blood. (JD 3:206.)

Some commentaries have suggested that the reference to Christ's being smitten of God could apply to His seemingly forsaken condition on the cross. However, the author believes the above explanation to be more plausible.

53:5 (Mosiah 14:5). "*He was wounded for our transgressions, he was bruised for our iniquities.*" See commentary on 53:4.

53:5 (Mosiah 14:5). "*The chastisement of our peace was upon him.*" The peace of mind (forgiveness and a clear conscience) available to all upon conditions of true repentance—which includes submitting to the saving ordinances of the gospel—was made possible only through the "chastisement" (suffer-ing) the Savior experienced in our behalf.

53:5 (Mosiah 14:5). "*With his stripes we are healed.*" With or because of His wounds, bruises, and contusions we are healed. A stripe is the welt or discoloration on the flesh made by a lash or rod. The apostle Peter used similar language when he spoke of Christ having borne our sins and healing us with His stripes. (1 Peter 2:24.)

53:6 (Mosiah 14:6). "*All we like sheep have gone astray.*" Like sheep without a shepherd, all have wandered into forbidden paths and pastures of sin. Each must be reclaimed (redeemed) by the Good Shepherd, He who has given His life for the sheep. (John 10:11.) Peter noted that the Saints of his day had "returned unto the Shepherd and Bishop of [their] souls." (1 Peter 2:25.)

Isaiah 53:7–9 and Mosiah 14:7–9; 15:6, 10

Isaiah now speaks of the indignities to which the King of kings was subjected in courts of unworthy earthly rulers—Annas, Caiaphas, Herod, and Pilate. The Sinless One was first brought before the deposed high priest Annas, who one chronicler said "ranks with Judas among the abominable of the earth." (John 18:13; MM 4:143.) He was next paraded before Caiaphas, the incumbent high priest of the Sanhedrin, and others of that body. Here Jesus was spat upon, mocked, and buffeted. (Matthew 26:57–68.) Although next taken to Pilate, he was sent by this puppet Roman ruler to the adulterous and murderous Herod, who had jurisdiction over Galileans. "Herod with his men of war set him at nought, and mocked him" before returning Jesus to Pilate for further mockery, abuse, and final judgment. (Luke 23:11.)

Judged of wicked men, the Righteous One was sentenced to death, cutting Him off from family and posterity. He was crucified alongside criminals deserving of their conviction, if not their punishment. And, finally, the mortal remains of this sinless Son of God were laid temporarily in the tomb of a man of worldly means whose charity extended to Him who once poignantly declared, "The foxes have holes, and the birds of the air have nests; but the Son of man hath not where to lay his head." (Matthew 8:20.)

7 He was oppressed, and he was afflicted, yet he opened not his mouth: he is brought as a lamb to the slaughter, and as a sheep before her shearers is dumb, so he *openeth* not his mouth.

7 He was oppressed, and he was afflicted, yet he opened not his mouth; he is brought as a lamb to the slaughter, and as a sheep before her shearers is dumb so he *opened* not his mouth.

Mosiah 15:6. And after all this, after working many mighty miracles among the children of men, he shall be led, yea, even as Isaiah said, as a sheep before the shearer is dumb, so he *opened* not his mouth.

8 He was taken from prison and from judgment: and who shall declare his generation? for he was cut off out of the land of the living: for the transgression of my people was he stricken.

8 He was taken from prison and from judgment; and who shall declare his generation? For he was cut off out of the land of the living; for the transgressions of my people was he stricken.

Mosiah 15:10. And now I say unto you, who shall declare his generation? Behold, I say unto you, that when his soul has been made an offering for sin he shall see his seed. And now what say ye? And who shall be his seed?

9 And he made his grave with the wicked, and with the rich in his death; because he had done no violence, neither was any deceit in his mouth.

9 And he made his grave with the wicked, and with the rich in his death; because he had done no evil, neither was any deceit in his mouth.

53:7 (Mosiah 14:7; 15:6). *"Yet he opened not his mouth."* In the hearing before the Sanhedrin, which was the highest Jewish court in both civil and ecclesiastical matters, many false witnesses were brought forward to testify against Jesus. In regal dignity, the Prisoner refused to respond to their false accusations, "But he held his peace, and answered nothing." Only to the question, "Art thou the Christ, the Son of the Blessed?" did He give His straightforward response: "I am." (Mark 14:55–62.)

Further fulfillment of the prophesied silence of the Son of God when faced with his oppressors was in the presence of King Herod Antipas. Though this evil man questioned Jesus "in many words," the Savior "answered him nothing." (Luke 23:8–9.) Elder James E. Talmage observed that "Herod is the only character in history to whom Jesus is known to have applied a personal epithet of contempt ["that fox"]. . . . As far as we know, Herod is further distinguished as the only being who saw Christ face to face and spoke to Him, yet never heard His voice." (Talmage, 636.)

53:8 (Mosiah 14:8). "*He was taken from prison and from judgment.*" He was unjustly taken as a prisoner by the Jews and Romans and through their oppressive judgment He was taken away from this life.

53:8 (Mosiah 14:8; 15:10). "*Who shall declare his generation? for he was cut off out of the land of the living.*" In taking away His life, His persecutors also took away potential posterity—His seed. Nevertheless, the Book of Mormon prophet Abinadi provides an answer to Isaiah's query, "Who shall declare his generation?"

"Behold I say unto you, that whosoever has heard the words of the prophets, yea, all the holy prophets who have prophesied concerning the coming of the Lord—I say unto you, that all those who have hearkened unto their words, and believed that the Lord would redeem his people, and have looked forward to that day for a remission of their sins, I say unto you, that these are his seed, or they are the heirs of the kingdom of God. . . .

"Yea, and are not the prophets, every one that has opened his mouth to prophesy, that has not fallen into transgression, I mean all the holy prophets ever since the world began? I say unto you that they are his seed." (Mosiah 15:10–13.)

53:9 (Mosiah 14:9). "*He made his grave with the wicked.*" "And there were also two other, malefactors [criminals], led with him to be put to death." (Luke 23:32.)

53:9 (Mosiah 14:9). "*And with the rich in his death.*" Lying in the hill country northwest of Jerusalem was the community of Arimathaea, which was also called Ramah or Ramathaim. This was the home of a wealthy counselor and disciple of Jesus, named Joseph. Following the death of Christ, Joseph received permission from Pilate to take the body of Jesus for burial. Joseph wrapped it in clean linen cloth and then "laid it in his own new tomb, which he had hewn out in the rock" in a hillside just outside Jerusalem. (Matthew 27:57–60.)

53:9 (Mosiah 14:9). *"Because he had done no violence [evil], neither was any deceit in his mouth."* The word *because* should be rendered as *although*. Christ was put to death *although* He was guiltless of any evil. His chief apostle, Peter, said of Him, "Who did no sin, neither was guile found in his mouth." (1 Peter 2:22.)

Isaiah 53:10–12 and Mosiah 14:10–12; 15:10

Isaiah now shifts his focus from the past sorrows of the Savior to a more hopeful future. He identifies some of the triumphs Jesus will now enjoy because of His great sacrifice—the atonement.

10 Yet it pleased the Lord to bruise him; he hath put him to grief: when thou shalt make his soul an offering for sin, he shall see his seed, he shall prolong his days, and the pleasure of the Lord shall prosper in his hand.

10 Yet it pleased the Lord to bruise him; he hath put him to grief; when thou shalt make his soul an offering for sin he shall see his seed, he shall prolong his days, and the pleasure of the Lord shall prosper in his hand.

Mosiah 15:10. And now I say unto you, who shall declare his generation? Behold, I say unto you, that when his soul has been made an offering for sin he shall see his seed. And now what say ye? And who shall be his seed?

11 He shall see of the travail of his soul, and shall be satisfied: by his knowledge shall my righteous servant justify many; for he shall bear their iniquities.

11 He shall see the travail of his soul, and shall be satisfied; by his knowledge shall my righteous servant justify many; for he shall bear their iniquities.

12 Therefore will I divide him a portion with the great, and he shall divide the spoil with the strong; because he hath poured out his soul unto death: and he was numbered with the transgressors; and he *bare* the sin of many, and made intercession for the transgressors.	12 Therefore will I divide him a portion with the great, and he shall divide the spoil with the strong; because he hath poured out his soul unto death; and he was numbered with the transgressors; and he *bore* the sins of many, and made intercession for the transgressors.

53:10 (Mosiah 14:10). *"It pleased the Lord to bruise him."* Our Father in Heaven was not pleased with the treatment His Son received at the hands of wicked men, but He was pleased with His Son's willingness to obediently fulfill the great atoning sacrifice. (See "smitten of God" commentary on 53:4; see also John 3:16–17.)

As a side note, Sidney Sperry observed that there is some difficulty with a literal translation of this verse, as it appears both in the Bible and the Book of Mormon, because it implies that "it pleased Jehovah to bruise Jehovah." Dr. Sperry suggests that it is possible that the original text of Isaiah was improperly copied on the Brass Plates as well as in later texts from which the Bible was translated. In the original it should have read "it pleased Elohim (God) to bruise Jehovah (Lord)." In any event, the scriptures make clear that Jesus (Jehovah) acts with full authority for His Father and the two act in unity, in total accord. (BMC, 305–6.)

53:10 (Mosiah 14:10; 15:10). *"Make his soul an offering for sin."* In a mini-sermon on sacrifice and service delivered to His apostles, Jesus declared: "The Son of man came not to be ministered unto, but to minister, and to give his life a ransom for many." (Matthew 20:28.)(Also see commentary on 53:4.)

53:10 (Mosiah 14:10; 15:10). *"He shall see his seed."* Elder Bruce R. McConkie suggested that this prophecy also included all the righteous in the spirit world whom the disembodied Jesus visited during the three days in which His body lay in an earthly tomb. (PM, 361–62.) (Also see "Who shall declare his generation" commentary on 53:8.)

53:10 (Mosiah 14:10). *"He shall prolong his days, and the pleasure of the Lord shall prosper in his hand."* Elder McConkie provided the following commentary on this phrase: "If this prophecy was meant to be fulfilled during his mortal sojourn on earth, we would list it as having failed. He did not prolong his days; a voluntary death overtook him in the prime of life. Nor did the pleasure of the Lord find full fruition while he dwelt in a state where death lies in wait for the weary pilgrim. It is only in the resurrection that the pleasure of the Lord is perfected, for it is only when 'spirit and element' are 'inseparably connected' that either God or man can 'receive a fulness of joy.' (D&C 93:33.) Thus, having made his soul an offering for sin; having seen his seed—all the righteous dead from the days of Adam to that moment—as they assembled to greet and worship him in the paradise of their Lord; and having thereafter risen in glorious immortality to live and reign forever, our Messiah truly fulfilled the prophetic utterance, for then his days were prolonged forever and the pleasure in his hand was infinite." (PM, 362.)

53:11 (Mosiah 14:11). *"He shall see of the travail of his soul, and shall be satisfied."* Both the Father and the Son shall be satisfied with the results of the atonement. In bearing witness of Jesus' divine nature at the time of His baptism, and with a complete foreknowledge that His Son would not stumble in sin or turn aside from completing the atonement, God the Father declared: "This is my beloved Son, *in whom I am well pleased.*" (Matthew 3:17; italics added.)

53:11 (Mosiah 14:11). *"Justify many."* The doctrine of justification is really summarized in the third Article of Faith: "We believe that through the Atonement of Christ, all mankind may be saved, by obedience to the laws and ordinances of the Gospel." (A of F 1:3.) One who is justified is declared righteous (just) and pronounced innocent before God. This presupposes that the individual remains on the road of righteousness, doing all that is required for celestial salvation. (2 Nephi 31:19–20.) We are incapable of becoming justified through our own efforts alone. We must rely on the grace of Christ. (2 Nephi 25:23; Alma 22:14.)

53:12 (Mosiah 14:12). "*Therefore will I divide him a portion with the great.*" Jesus Christ "continued from grace to grace, until he received a fulness. . . . [H]e received all power, both in heaven and on earth, and the glory of the Father was with him, for he dwelt in him." (D&C 93:13–17.) Thus, He whose name was a key element in the original title of the Melchizedek Priesthood—even "*the Holy Priesthood, after the Order of the Son of God*" (D&C 107:3)—qualified first and foremost for the great promise given to those who honor that priesthood: to receive "all that [the] Father hath." (D&C 84:33–40.) In the words of the apostle Paul, He "thought it not robbery to be equal with God." (Philippians 2:6.)

53:12 (Mosiah 14:12). "*He hath poured out his soul unto death.*" Christ voluntarily gave His life that He might bring about the resurrection for all. "No man taketh it from me," He declared, "but I lay it down of myself. I have power to lay it down, and I have power to take it again." (John 10:18.)

53:12 (Mosiah 14:12). "*He was numbered with the transgressors.*" See "He made his grave with the wicked" commentary on 53:9.

53:12 (Mosiah 14:12). "*He bare the sin of many, and made intercession for the transgressors.*" See commentary on 53:4.

CHAPTER 22

Isaiah 54 and 3 Nephi 22

OVERVIEW

The resurrected Lord felt so keenly about Isaiah 54 that He quoted it in its entirety to the ancient inhabitants of the Americas—knowing it would be published as part of the Book of Mormon in the latter days. It is apparent that this is one of the most significant chapters in all scriptural literature. Certainly it warrants our fervent desire to understand it and to carefully consider its message.

Chapter 21 of 3 Nephi contains the Savior's teachings regarding the gathering of Israel at the time of the coming forth of the Book of Mormon. He taught that a great gentile nation would be established for a free people in the land of America. However, He stressed that those who refuse to believe the words of the prophet-servant (Joseph Smith) to be raised up would be "cut off from among my people who are of the covenant." (3 Nephi 21:11.) He also announced the future building of the New Jerusalem in America and the return of the lost tribes of Israel.

This is the setting into which Jesus Christ interspersed a recitation of Isaiah 54, commencing with the introductory phrase: "*And then shall that which is written come to pass.*" (Italics added.) Of this phrase, Sidney Sperry has written: "This is, of course, an indication given by our Lord that the prophet Isaiah saw the things of which He had been speaking (ch. 21) and wrote concerning them, or at least concerning what would happen when they were fulfilled.

"The fulfillment of this beautiful poem—Isaiah 54 is all poetry—is to be found in this dispensation. Part of it has probably already been fulfilled since the restoration of the gospel; the remainder will be in a time yet future." (BMC, 412.)

In this chapter of hope and encouragement, Isaiah speaks of the growth and gathering of Israel or Zion in the latter days. She is likened to a woman who has long been barren because of her separation from her husband, a separation brought about by her unfaithfulness. But now she has repented and returned to her forgiving husband (the Lord). As a result, the multitudes of her children have become so large in number that the stakes that hold her covering must constantly be spread out farther. Because of her faithfulness, her husband will never again forsake her. The chapter closes with the promise that "no weapon that is formed against thee [covenant Israel or the Lord's people, Zion] shall prosper."

COMMENTARY

Isaiah 54:1–3 and 3 Nephi 22:1–3

For years Israel, or Zion, has been as a barren woman, but now she is told to sing and rejoice, for her children are becoming so multitudinous that she will constantly need to enlarge the place of her tent or dwelling. She does this by moving the stakes outward from the center pole (center stake), thus providing a greater area of protection and shelter. She, who was separated from her husband, will be so amazed at the increase in the numbers of her children that she might be inclined to proclaim other prophetic words spoken by Isaiah: "Who hath begotten me these seeing I have lost my children, and am . . . a captive . . . ? and who hath brought up these? Behold, I was left alone; these, where had they been?" (Isaiah 49:21.)

Isaiah 54	3 Nephi 22
1 Sing, O barren, thou that didst not bear; break forth into singing, and cry aloud, thou that didst not travail with child: for more are the children of the desolate than the children of the married wife, saith the Lord.	1 And then shall that which is written come to pass: Sing, O barren, thou that didst not bear; break forth into singing, and cry aloud, thou that didst not travail with child; for more are the children of the desolate than the children of the married wife, saith the Lord.
2 Enlarge the place of thy tent, and let them stretch forth the curtains of *thine* habitations: spare not, lengthen thy cords, and strengthen thy stakes;	2 Enlarge the place of thy tent, and let them stretch forth the curtains of *thy* habitations; spare not, lengthen thy cords and strengthen thy stakes;
3 For thou shalt break forth on the right hand and on the left; and thy seed shall inherit the Gentiles, and make the desolate cities to be inhabited.	3 For thou shalt break forth on the right hand and on the left, and thy seed shall inherit the Gentiles and make the desolate cities to be inhabited.

54:1 (3 Nephi 22:1). "*Children of the desolate.*" There are several possible interpretations of this phrase, according to LDS scholars. Sidney Sperry suggested the phrase means "Zion in her desolate, barren state." (BMC, 413.) Monte Nyman opined that they "represent the large number of people from the tribes of Israel who will gather to Zion following the building of the New Jerusalem." (GAWI, 211.) A trio of commentators identify them as "scattered Israel, those who for generations have lived without the light of the gospel, who have not been fruitful in the faith of their fathers." (DCBM 4:155.) Victor Ludlow, following the text of modern Biblical translations, identified *desolate* as a modifier of *woman:* "many children have been born to the 'desolate' or forsaken woman." He then added this commentary:

"The desolate woman and her relationship to the [married] wife can be understood in two ways: (1) The desolate woman represents the Gentiles, and the wife Israel; thus the Gentiles will bring forth greater spiritual fruits than Israel has delivered; (2) the desolate woman is Israel in her scattered condition, while the wife is those people remaining in the Holy Land. Thus Israel will bring forth more children (both physically and spiritually) outside the land of her original inheritance than in it. (See Gal. 4:22–31; Rev. 12:1–6.) In either case, Isaiah uses these images to symbolize the relationship of the Lord to Israel; those who join with covenant Israel are the children of that relationship." (IPSP, 459.)

54:2 (3 Nephi 22:2). *"Enlarge the place of thy tent . . . strengthen thy stakes."* "The clarion call to 'enlarge' and 'strengthen' the stakes of Zion was given anciently to Isaiah (Isa. 54:2), repeated to the Nephites (3 Ne. 22:2), and reiterated in our day (D&C 109:59; 133:9). A stake is an ecclesiastical unit of The Church of Jesus Christ of Latter-day Saints and covers a specific geographical area. According to the Lord, stakes are 'curtains or the strength of Zion' (D&C 101:21). They are places where the Saints of God may be instructed more perfectly in the doctrines of salvation." (DCE, 559.) As the number of stakes increases, the influence of the protective tent expands to reach more of the earth's inhabitants. The ultimate goal is to stretch it over the entire earth, to gather all people under its protection.

54:3 (3 Nephi 22:3). *"Thy seed shall inherit the Gentiles, and make the desolate cities to be inhabited."* So great shall be the latter-day growth of redeemed Israel that her children will be found in the nations of the gentiles throughout the world. Her influence for good will be felt even in places considered to be spiritually or physically "desolate." As she gathers in strength, additional stakes will be established and the tent of Zion will further expand.

The plea of the Lord to His covenant people of the latter days is: "For Zion must increase in beauty, and in holiness; her borders must be enlarged; her stakes must be strengthened; yea, verily I say unto you, Zion must arise and put on her beautiful garments." (D&C 82:14.)

Isaiah recited a similar plea in verse 1 of chapter 52: "Awake, awake; put on thy strength, O Zion; put on thy beautiful garments." In response to the question of what Isaiah meant when he said "Put on thy strength, O Zion—and what people had Isaiah reference to?" the Prophet Joseph Smith declared: "He had reference to those whom God should call in the last days, who should hold the power of priesthood to bring again Zion, and the redemption of Israel; and to put on her strength is to put on the authority of the priesthood, which she, Zion, has a right to by lineage; also to return to that power which she had lost." (D&C 113:7–8.)

Isaiah 54:4–8 and 3 Nephi 22:4–8

The Lord reaffirms His role as the husband to covenant Israel. He has forgiven the wayward wife of her sinful earlier years and, upon her repentance, has reestablished their relationship.

4 Fear not; for thou shalt not be ashamed: neither be thou confounded; for thou shalt not be put to shame: for thou shalt forget the shame of thy youth, and shalt not remember the reproach of thy widowhood any more.

4 Fear not, for thou shalt not be ashamed; neither be thou confounded, for thou shalt not be put to shame; for thou shalt forget the shame of thy youth, and shalt not remember the reproach of thy youth, and shalt not remember the reproach of thy widowhood any more.

5 For thy Maker is *thine* husband; the Lord of hosts is his name; and thy Redeemer the Holy One of Israel; The God of the whole earth shall he be called.

5 For thy maker, *thy* husband, the Lord of Hosts is his name; and thy Redeemer, the Holy One of Israel—the God of the whole earth shall he be called.

6 For the Lord hath called thee as a woman forsaken and grieved in spirit, and a wife of youth, when thou wast refused, saith thy God.	6 For the Lord hath called thee as a woman forsaken and grieved in spirit, and a wife of youth, when thou wast refused, saith thy God.
7 For a small moment have I forsaken thee; but with great mercies will I gather thee.	7 For a small moment have I forsaken thee, but with great mercies will I gather thee.
8 In a little wrath I hid my face from thee for a moment; but with everlasting kindness will I have mercy on thee, saith the Lord thy Redeemer.	8 In a little wrath I hid my face from thee for a moment, but with everlasting kindness will I have mercy on thee, saith the Lord thy Redeemer.

54:4 (3 Nephi 22:4). "*Shame of thy youth.*" This refers to her unfaithfulness in her earlier years, when she sought after false gods rather than remaining true to her covenant Husband—the Lord God Jehovah. This was a time not only of shameful conduct, but also of spiritual sterility, when she was not blessed with increase. Some commentators have suggested this shame could mean her periods of captivity, such as the Egyptian bondage.

54:4 (3 Nephi 22:4). "*Reproach of thy widowhood.*" Israel's period of exile, when she was without her Protector, her Husband.

54:5 (3 Nephi 22:5). "*Thy Maker is thine husband.*" Five of the holy titles applied to Jehovah are mentioned in this verse. It is an emphatic emphasis that there is but *one* God of Israel, *one* Husband to whom she should be faithful.

54:6 (3 Nephi 22:6). "*A woman forsaken . . . and a wife of youth.*" Because of her unfaithfulness, Israel—a bride chosen in her early or youthful years—had become a forsaken wife. Be it remembered, however, that it was she who left the house of her Husband.

54:7 (3 Nephi 22:7). "*For a small moment have I forsaken thee.*" Israel's barren or forsaken years will seem but a "small moment" when she considers her bright future and the extent of eternity. One is reminded of similar language being applied to the seemingly forsaken prophet of God unjustly languishing in Liberty Jail in the winter of 1838–39: "My son," declared the voice of Israel's Husband, "peace be unto thy soul; thine adversity and thine afflictions shall be but a small moment."

The Lord then added this comforting promise, which could well apply to the repentant wife of whom Isaiah prophesied: "And then, if thou endure it well, God shall exalt thee on high; thou shalt triumph over all thy foes." (D&C 121:7–8.)

54:8 (3 Nephi 22:8). "*In a little wrath I hid my face from thee.*" While the rejected Husband had turned away from His unfaithful wife in a moment of righteous anger, He has now returned with everlasting love. Lest there be misunderstanding regarding the divine attributes of Deity, a brief explanation of God's wrath or anger is appropriate. Anger, as understood or displayed by mortals, is not a characteristic of God's conduct.

"A distinction should be made between the appropriate anger of God, which is a righteous application of the law of justice, and the unbridled anger of a fallible mortal. The Lord has consistently counseled his children against anger (Matt. 5:21–22; 3 Ne. 11:21–22); furthermore, we have been instructed that the devil 'is the father of contention, and he stirreth up the hearts of men to contend with anger, one with another' (3 Ne. 11:29). One who is angry loses the Spirit and his love of his fellowman (Moro. 9:3–5).

"In contrast, properly understood, God's anger is a divine display of his love. It is a manifestation of truth. (See 2 Ne. 1:24–27.)" (DCE, 18.)

Isaiah 54:9–10 and 3 Nephi 22:9–10

The Lord gives absolute assurance to His redeemed wife that she will never again be forsaken. Part of that assurance may well be His absolute knowledge of the future; He knows she will never again depart from her covenants.

9 For this <u>is as</u> the waters of Noah unto me<u>:</u> for as I have sworn that the waters of Noah should no more go over the earth<u>;</u> so have I sworn that I would not be wroth with thee<u>, nor rebuke thee.</u>	9 For this<u>,</u> the waters of Noah unto me<u>,</u> for as I have sworn that the waters of Noah should no more go over the earth<u>,</u> so have I sworn that I would not be wroth with thee<u>.</u>
10 For the mountains shall depart<u>,</u> and the hills be removed<u>;</u> but my kindness shall not depart from thee, neither shall the covenant of my peace be removed, saith the Lord that hath mercy on thee.	10 For the mountains shall depart and the hills be removed<u>,</u> but my kindness shall not depart from thee, neither shall the covenant of my peace be removed, saith the Lord that hath mercy on thee.

54:9 (3 Nephi 22:9). *"For this is as the waters of Noah unto me."* In yet another verification of the reality of the Flood, the Lord compares the oath He now makes to remain with Israel to that which He made when He swore to Noah that the great Flood would not be repeated. Zion, His covenant people, will never be cast off. Such a vow reminds us of the dream interpreted by the prophet Daniel, where he saw "the God of heaven set up a kingdom, which shall never be destroyed: and the kingdom shall not be left to other people, but it shall break in pieces and consume all these kingdoms, and it shall stand for ever." (Daniel 2:44; see also D&C 65:2–3; 104:86; 112:30.)

54:10 (3 Nephi 22:10). *"For the mountains shall depart, and the hills be removed."* The Lord's covenant with Israel will still be in place when mountains and hills that are now so prominent are gone; or, in other words, at the time the "earth [is] renewed and receive[s] its paradisiacal glory." (A of F 1:10.)

Of this time, President Joseph Fielding Smith has written: "The earth is to be *renewed* or *restored* to its primitive beauty and condition, and when that day comes the high mountains which are seen today will be *debased* and the valleys *exalted*." (DS 2:316.)

Isaiah 54:11–13 and 3 Nephi 22:11–13

Perhaps as a result of his allusion to paradisiacal conditions in the previous verse, Isaiah now appears to turn his attention to the City of Zion, the New Jerusalem. His description of this holy city is similar to that given by John the Revelator. (Revelation 21:18–21.) If verses eleven and twelve do not directly relate to that great city, it is possible that they provide symbolic descriptions of conditions prevalent in the societies or stakes of Zion established throughout the earth.

11 O thou afflicted, tossed with tempest, and not comforted, behold, I will lay thy stones with fair *colours*, and lay thy foundations with sapphires.

12 And I will make thy windows of agates, and thy gates of carbuncles, and all thy borders of pleasant stones.

13 And all thy children shall be taught of the Lord; and great shall be the peace of thy children.

11 O thou afflicted, tossed with tempest, and not comforted! Behold, I will lay thy stones with fair *colors*, and lay thy foundations with sapphires.

12 And I will make thy windows of agates, and thy gates of carbuncles, and all thy borders of pleasant stones.

13 And all thy children shall be taught of the Lord; and great shall be the peace of thy children.

54:11 (3 Nephi 22:11). "*I will lay thy stones with fair colours, and lay thy foundations with sapphires.*" Building stones will be set in hard mortar, and crystalline substances will be used to enhance their brilliancy. The building materials will be worthy of the finished product.

54:12 (3 Nephi 22:12). "*Windows of agates . . . gates of carbuncles . . . borders of pleasant stones.*" "Windows [pinnacles or turrets] of agates [rubies], gates of carbuncles [sparkling jewels], borders [walls] of pleasant [precious] stones." These could symbolize the beauty of the holy city, or dwelling place of the Saints of God, and the material blessings that will be poured out upon the righteous.

54:13 (3 Nephi 22:13). "*Great shall be the peace of thy children.*" This verse may have specific reference to millennial conditions, when "children shall grow up without sin unto salvation." (D&C 45:58.) It may also imply that there will be some direct teaching of these blessed children by the Lord Himself. However, there may be a more immediate application. This entire verse is used by the Primary of The Church of Jesus Christ of Latter-day Saints as its general theme. The goal of the Church and righteous parents everywhere is to teach the children about their Heavenly Father and their Lord and Savior, Jesus Christ, that the peace of righteousness might prevail in their lives.

In speaking of Isaiah's promise of peace to the children, President Spencer W. Kimball, twelfth prophet of the Lord in the latter days, said, "Surely every good parent would like this peace for his offspring. It comes from the simple life of the true Latter-day Saint as he makes his home and family supreme." (*Ensign*, July 1973, p. 16.)

The Savior's tender feelings for children were evident in His mortal ministry in the Holy Land (JST Matthew 19:13–15), as well as in His postmortal ministry in the Americas, where "he took their little children, one by one, and blessed them, and prayed unto the Father for them." (3 Nephi 17:21.) Furthermore, in a revelation given in 1831, He specifically charged parents with teaching their children "the doctrine of repentance, faith in Christ the Son of the living God, and of baptism and the gift of the Holy Ghost by the laying on of the hands." (D&C 68:25.)

Isaiah 54:14–17 and 3 Nephi 22:14–17

The promise of the Lord's protection is given to His righteous followers. They have no need to fear oppression or terror, for those who fight against the people of Zion shall fail.

As a side note, it should be observed that from the day that Cain conspired with the devil to take his brother Abel's life and possessions, the righteous have suffered at the hands of the wicked. For divine purposes that we will all some day understand and appreciate, the Lord has not always intervened to stop oppression of His Saints and other good people of the earth. Nevertheless, when considered in the context of eternity, as noted in the commentary on 54:7, suffering and sorrow are but "a small moment." Regardless of circumstances, the true Saint will always declare, "The Lord gave and the Lord hath taken away; blessed be the name of the Lord." (Job 1:21.)

14 In righteousness shalt thou be established: thou shalt be far from oppression; for thou shalt not fear: and from terror; for it shall not come near thee.

15 Behold, they shall surely gather together, but not by me: whosoever shall gather together against thee shall fall for thy sake.

16 Behold, I have created the smith that bloweth the coals in the fire, and that bringeth forth an instrument for his work; and I have created the waster to destroy.

14 In righteousness shalt thou be established; thou shalt be far from oppression for thou shalt not fear, and from terror for it shall not come near thee.

15 Behold, they shall surely gather together against thee, not by me; whosoever shall gather together against thee shall fall for thy sake.

16 Behold, I have created the smith that bloweth the coals in the fire, and that bringeth forth an instrument for his work; and I have created the waster to destroy.

17 No weapon that is formed against thee shall prosper; and every tongue that shall <u>rise</u> against thee in judgment thou shalt condemn. This is the heritage of the servants of the Lord, and their righteousness is of me, saith the Lord.	17 No weapon that is formed against thee shall prosper; and every tongue that shall <u>revile</u> against thee in judgment thou shalt condemn. This is the heritage of the servants of the Lord, and their righteousness is of me, saith the Lord.

54:14 (3 Nephi 22:14). "*Thou shalt be far from oppression; for thou shalt not fear.*" This appears to describe millennial conditions when righteousness will prevail upon the earth. In fact, all living creatures will live together in peace. (See BICQ, 215–16.)

54:15 (3 Nephi 22:15). "*They shall surely gather together . . . against thee.*" Because of the absence of malice and enmity in the Millennium, this verse must have fulfillment prior to that period of peace. Up until that time, the righteous will continue to be challenged by "the enemy in the secret chambers [who] seeketh [their] lives." (D&C 38:28; see also DCE, 503–4.) While there may be a few individual casualties—martyrs and even a few who succumb to apostasy—the designs of the wicked shall fail, for they will not prevail against the people of the Lord nor His Church.

54:15 (3 Nephi 22:15). "*Whosoever shall gather together against thee shall fall for thy sake.*" In his inspired dedicatory prayer of the Kirtland Temple, the Prophet Joseph declared: "We ask thee, Holy Father, to establish the people that shall worship, and honorably hold a name and standing in this thy house, to all generations and for eternity;

"That no weapon formed against them shall prosper; that he who diggeth a pit for them shall fall into the same himself." (D&C 109:24–25; see also 1 Nephi 14:3.) Whether in mortality or the hereafter, "all that fight against Zion shall be destroyed." (1 Nephi 22:14.) They shall be "cut off from among the people." (D&C 1:14.)

54:16 (3 Nephi 22:16). "*The smith that bloweth the coals in the fire.*" Just as the Lord created the blacksmith who may forge a weapon in his fire, the Lord can also create a "waster" to destroy any weapons created by man.

54:17 (3 Nephi 22:17). "*No weapon that is formed against thee shall prosper.*" As persecution against the Lord's people and His Church continues to increase in the last days, the promise of the Lord remains sure. No matter what the weapon—slander or violence—it will fail. Within a short time after the restoration of the priesthood and the establishment of The Church of Jesus Christ of Latter-day Saints, a revelation was received in response to the publication of newspaper articles critical of the Church. The Prophet Joseph Smith was admonished to "confound your enemies. . . . [L]et them bring forth their strong reasons against the Lord." Then came this promise:

"Verily, thus saith the Lord unto you—there is no weapon that is formed against you shall prosper;

"And if any man lift his voice against you he shall be confounded *in mine own due time.*" (D&C 71:7–10; italics added.)

Thus, while it may appear that the efforts of some enemies of the Lord are having some success, they arc ultimately doomed to fail "in [His] own due time." (Also see the commentary on 54:15 and 54:16.)

Perhaps these bold words of the Lord's prophet of the Restoration, even Joseph Smith, would serve as an appropriate conclusion to the commentary on this chapter:

"No unhallowed hand can stop the work from progressing; persecutions may rage, mobs may combine, armies may assemble, calumny may defame, but the truth of God will go forth boldly, nobly, and independent, till it has penetrated every clime, swept every country, and sounded in every ear, till the purposes of God shall be accomplished, and the Great Jehovah shall say the work is done." (HC 4:540.)

Index

Abinadi, 52, 238, 246, 255
Abrahamic covenant, 7, 183–84, 214–17
Ahaz, 62, 64–70
America as Zion, 11, 13, 195, 197, 202. *See also* Jackson County, Missouri
Ammon, 117–18
Amoz, 2
Angels, destroying, 124–26
Anger, understanding the Lord's, 46, 50, 265–66
Annas, 252–53
Anthon, Charles, 163–65
Apostasy, 7
Apostate teachings, Israel adopted, 15
Apparel of daughters of Zion, 29–32
Ariel, 152–53
Assyria: scatters Syria and Israel, 62, 66–68, 70, 77–78, 86–88; fails to invade Judah, 77–78, 105–6, 144–46; description of, 96; as God's chastiser of the wicked, 98; punished by the Lord, 99–102; destruction of, 106; conquers Philistia, 148–49
Atonement, 249–52, 256–59

Babylon: destroys Assyria, 102; destruction of, 123, 130–33, 136–40, 142–44; description of, 124; king of, 136–44

Babylon, spiritual, 182, 184–85, 241–42
Banner of the Lord, 125
Baptism, 177–78, 190, 193
Bashan, oaks of, 17, 19
Bees, 71–72
Black magic, 81–83
Bondage, spiritual, 44, 47–48
Book of Mormon: as most correct form of Isaiah's writings, 4–5; helps to understand Isaiah, 7; foreseen by Isaiah, 7, 151; as ensign, 115–16; coming forth of, 159–66, 170–72; as standard, 201–2; as law, 215, 218
Book, sealed, 160–66
Branch, symbolism of, 36–37
Brass plates, 4, 9, 176
Bribes, 45, 50
Burials, 142–43
Burning of wicked, 45, 50. *See also* Fire
Businesses of the proud, 17, 20
Butter, 70, 73

Caiaphas, 253
Calling and election made sure, 190–91
Canaan, 170–72
Cannibalism, 93–94, 204–5
Captive, lawful. *See* Israel (ancient)
Captives, shaved, 73
Captivity, 32–33